END
OF THE
ROAD

Brian Keene

Cemetery Dance Publications
❖ Baltimore ❖
2020

Cemetery Dance Publications
132B Industry Lane, Unit #7
Forest Hill, MD 21050
www.cemeterydance.com

ISBN: 978-1-58767-793-9

Cover Artwork and Design © 2020 by Desert Isle Design, LLC
Interior Design © 2020 by Desert Isle Design, LLC

This one is dedicated to:

Stephen King, who first invited me to the danse macabre, and thus, introduced me to all the fine people herein.

Jesus Gonzalez and Tom Piccirilli.
We'll danse again, brothers.
We'll danse again...

ACKNOWLEDGEMENTS:

Thanks to Richard Chizmar and Brian Freeman for sponsoring these original columns, and for publishing them in collected form.

Thanks to Blu Gilliand, who was in charge of wrangling me into meeting weekly deadlines while crisscrossing the country, and trying to make sense of the columns I sent him (which varied from Word documents to text messages to half-coherent missives scrawled on the back of a cocktail napkin).

Thanks to Gabino Iglesias, for the best Introduction ever.

Thanks to World Horror 2016 in Provo, UT, Bradley's Books in DuBois, PA, Quaker Steak in Youngstown, OH, Dark Delicacies in Burbank, CA, Mysterious Galaxy in San Diego, CA, Barnes and Noble in Tucson, AZ, The Poisoned Pen in Scottsdale, AZ, Bookworks in Albuquerque, NM, Long Pig Saloon in El Paso, TX, Borderlands Books in San Francisco, CA, The York Emporium in York, PA, Star Line Books in Chattanooga, TN, Tubby & Coo's Mid-City Book Shop in New Orleans, LA, Camelot Books in Land O' Lakes, FL, Mojo Books and Records in Tampa, FL, Barnes and Noble in Orlando, FL, The Book Tavern in Augusta, GA, Scares That

Care Weekend III in Williamsburg, VA, the Monongalia Arts Center in Morgantown, WV, BAM in Beckley, WV, Rickert & Beagle Books in Pittsburgh, PA, The Comic Store in Lancaster, PA, Books on the Square in Providence, RI, The Book Nook in Ludlow, VT, RiverRead Books in Binghamton, NY, Imaginarium 2016 in Lousiville, KY, the Haverhill Public Library in Haverhill, MA, the KGB Bar in New York, NY, BizarroCon 2016 in Troutdale, OR, the Frederick Community College in Frederick, MD, and New Year's Party Con 2016 in Allentown, PA.

Thanks to co-pilots Mary SanGiovanni, Stephen Kozeniewski, Jamie LaChance, Kasey Lansdale, Tod Clark, John Urbancik, Mike Lombardo, Dave Thomas, and David Keene.

Thanks to Ron Davis, Cathy and Hannah Gonzalez, Glenda and Chuy Gonzalez, Michelle Scalise-Piccirilli, Robert Swartwood, Deena Dib, Geoff Cooper, Mike Oliveri, Michael T. Huyck Jr., Gak, Regina Mitchell, Rain Graves, Ryan Harding, Jack Haringa, Weston Ochse, Yvonne Navarro, Mark Sylva, Sarah Pinborough, Tim Lebbon, Jeff Strand, Lynne Hansen, Kelly Laymon, Connor Rice, Dallas Mayr, Linda Addison, Michael Arnzen, Kevin J. Anderson, Michael Bailey, Bailey Hunter, Dave Butler, Josh Hutton, Richard Wolley, Bryan Killian, David Skal, Jonathan Maberry, Yvonne Navarro, Ben Coes, Chet Williamson, Kelli Owen, Lesley and Brian Conner, Rachel Autumn Deering, Jessica Deering, Robert Ford, Sara Tantlinger, Jenny, Lee Seymour, Gene O'Neill, Jason Pokopec, Michelle Garza, Melissa Lason, Laird Barron, Ronald Kelly, F Paul Wilson, Tom Monteleone, Hal Bodner, Laura Lee Bahr, John Skipp, David J. Schow, Kerry, Paul and Shannon Legerski, Dick Grunert, David Agranoff, Stephen Coonts, Paul Goblirsch, Joe Nassise, Suzin

Clark, Nick Mamatas, Wrath James White, Steven L. Shrewsbury, Nate Southard, Maurice Broaddus, Jude Terror, Cullen Bunn, Tim Seely, Seth Lindberg, Eddie Coulter, Gavin Dillinger, Mark Hickerson, Cherie Priest, Chris and Alicia Stamps, Paul Campion, Monica Kuebler, David Barnett, K. Trap Jones, Mery-et Lescher, Armand and Shelly Rosamilia, Bryan and Jennifer Smith, Matt and Melissa Hayward, Jonathan Yudkin, Joe and Karen Lansdale, Jonathan Janz, Ronald Malfi, Paul and Lisa Synuria, Brian Hatcher, Michael Knost, M Stephen Lukac, Asher Ellis, Kevin Lucia, Dan Padavona, Jerry Gordon, Jason Sizemore, Mehitobel Wilson, Deb Kuhn, Jim Moore, Rio Youers, Joe Hill, Paul Tremblay, Glenn Chadbourne, Adam Cesare, Christoph Paul, Leza Cantoral, Josh Malerman, Nick Cato, Errick Danger Nunnally, Carlton Mellick III, Rose O'Keefe, Jeremy Robert Johnson, Kevin L. Donihe, Jeff Burk, Mary Fan, and Augie.

FEAR AND LOATHING ON THE FAREWELL TOUR...AND BEYOND: AN INTRODUCTION

→ GABINO IGLESIAS

At the end of April 2011, I was a freelance journalist dreaming of being a writer. I'd been writing for a while, but I wanted to see my name on a cover. I wanted to be a published author, not just a journalist, which was something I'd become after reading Hunter S. Thompson and deciding to quit law school to pursue writing (please, keep your opinion regarding my life decisions to yourself). The wish to be an author was old by then. It had started in my early teens as I devoured Richard Laymon paperbacks in my tiny room. I wanted to make others feel what Laymon made me feel. In any case, I was going to cover the World Horror Convention, which was being held in Austin, Texas. Some of my favorite authors were going to be there and I planned on interviewing all of them, including Brian Keene. However, when I started telling people about my plans to interview the man who wrote one of the novels that pushed me to favor horror over other genres, *Darkness on the Edge of Town*, everyone told me to skip that interview because Brian Keene was an asshole.

The convention came and went. I hung out with Joe Lansdale, interviewed Jack Ketchum, shared some chicken nuggets with Peter Straub, and shook hands with Carlton Mellick III. What I didn't do was interview Brian Keene. Yeah, I was a bit intimidated. What if he was an asshole? At the time, not knowing was better than finding out everyone had been right about him, so I didn't talk to him at all.

Fast forward to November 2012. I was hanging out at BizarroCon in Portland, Oregon. My first book had just been published. I was, at long last, a published author...and I had a ton of questions. Also, Brian Keene was attending the convention. This time around, however, felt different. People liked Keene there. My friends said nice things about him and he was always cracking jokes. He actually seemed like a cool guy. At one point, I ran into Keene in a hallway of the oh-so-haunted Edgefield Hotel. Liquid courage was galloping through my veins like a horse escaping downhill, so my inhibitions were somewhere south of the soles of my shoes. Result: I approached Keene, introduced myself, and shook his hand. I told him I loved his work. Then I told him about not interviewing him at the WHC in Austin because everyone told me he was an asshole. He laughed and told me that wasn't the first time he'd heard something like that. We talked shop. Then we talked again the next day. Over the weekend, Keene gave me a course on being an author, developing a persona, keeping family life private, and making sure I always acted like a professional and got paid. Turns out everyone had been wrong about him.

In the years since, I have come to understand that Brian is sometimes obligated to be an asshole. Why? Because he made it. Sure, he's not swimming in money, but he's the most successful horror author of his generation. Comics, movies, novels, collections, nonfiction, hardcover releases, books that are certified cult classics, the respect of his peers, radio, critical acclaim, a plethora of awards: you name it, he's done it. And that leads to a lot of this: "Will you please read my novel, Mr. Keene?" "Would you give me a blurb, Mr. Keene?" "Can you get my book published, Mr. Keene?" "Will you hook me up with your agent, Mr. Keene?" "Can I be on your show, Mr. Keene?" "Would you help me get my book turned into a movie, Mr. Keene?" "Can you hook me up with someone in the comic business, Mr. Keene?" At the end of the day, you can only ask a man who's trying to put food on the table and meet his own deadlines so many favors before he starts saying no, and saying no makes him an asshole. So does being successful while many other careers get stuck in a perennial state of agitated stagnation. Perhaps Austrian writer Vicki Baum said it best: "Fame always brings loneliness. Success is as ice cold and lonely as the North Pole."

You see, the thing about writers is that they are out there, their words are out there, and that makes people feel like they know them. If I'm talking about books with someone and mention Brian Keene, whoever is chatting with me will think of him as an author and nothing more. That's wrong. Keene is an author, sure, but he's also a father, an ex-husband, a boyfriend, a friend, and a mentor. He has bills to pay and sickness to deal with while working a gig with no health insurance, and sons to turn into decent people, and relationships to maintain, and pain, and sadness, and good times, and demons pulling him from the keyboard, and memories, and hopes, and dreams, and nightmares, and...you get the point. He is that zombie guy, but he's also someone I call Batman because he's the first to destroy unscrupulous presses and editors, the first to defend new authors from established assholes, the first to fight for equality, for diversity, for justice. Ah, far from an asshole now, isn't he? Yeah, Keene is opinionated, doesn't put up with nonsense, and regularly uses his platform in ways that ruffle many feathers, but I dare you to find an instance in which he sided with the deceitful, the misogynists, the bigots.

I won't talk about who Keene really is any more, but I will say this: when someone reached out to option my novel *Zero Saints* for film, I didn't call my parents or my childhood friends or a lawyer; I called Brian. He replied immediately. After reading this book and knowing what Jack Ketchum did with Keene's first contract, you'll understand why that moment feels like a passing of the proverbial torch. And Brian has done the same thing, and much more, with a large number of authors in the new generation.

All of that brings us to the real purpose of this introduction: to talk about the book you're holding and what it means. This beautiful thing, which hopefully gets Brian the recognition he deserves as a rare talent whose nonfiction chops match his flare for fiction, is a rare, wonderful hybrid. This book chronicles horror's rise as a marketing category, discusses its peak, explores the way it collapsed in the mid-Nineties and how that collapse led to the growth of the small/indie presses, looks at the way the Internet changed the game and the relationship between authors and readers, talks about the return of horror novels to bookstore shelves, and, ultimately, explains the second collapse of our genre at the end of the millennium's first decade. Despite all that, this is far from being merely a history of horror told from the inside. What you're holding is also a love letter to the genre, a journal about being on the road, and a hilarious, touching, smart, oftentimes gloomy, and always brutally honest memoir about two decades spent at the center of horror fiction. As mentioned above, this is the life narrative of a man/writer/father/ex-husband/boyfriend/ mentor/friend to many wrapped in the story of one last time on the road. This is an entertaining look at how publishing works and at the way there are no guarantees in this gig, no days off, no insurance, no promise that it won't change tomorrow. This is a who's who of horror packed with entertaining stories, convention memories, friends new and old, and philosophical insights that range from stuff you'd hear at your local bar to things you'd expect to hear from Nietzsche. This is a collection of columns about the things Brian Keene has said, written, lived, and done, but also of the things he regrets, the things he has lost, and the way things left unsaid haunt him every damn day. Finally, this is a story about coping, about the way losing our best friends can alter our life in very significant ways and how Brian climbed out of the ashes of his pain to keep putting words on paper, which is the only true measure of a writer.

The short years I've spent in this business have taught me that you can judge someone accurately by the things they do and the company they keep. With that in mind, it becomes impossible to see Brian as an asshole...who stands up for the little guy and just happened to be best friends with folks like J.F. Gonzalez and Tom Piccirilli. Both of these amazing authors, lost too soon, wanted Brian to write what you now hold. Call me crazy, but without ever meeting those literary giants, I can easily picture Chuy and Pic smiling at Brian from behind the veil and saying, "We asked you to write this because we knew only you could, brother."

Now that this is here, it bridges the gap between a nervous Keene two decades ago and Brian Keene now, a man who many claim destroyed horror when he actually took it home and tucked it in bed to save its ass a few times. Oh, and for those of you who belong to my generation, sit down, shut up, and pay attention because what you're about to read is also a manual for young and new-ish writers that, besides telling us how to go about this, makes one thing very clear: this thing we're inheriting from Brian and his generation? Yeah, this thing is fucking sacred, and you're about to hear a hell of a sermon.

Gabino Iglesias
Austin, TX
May 2017

FOREWORD

In the Fall of 2015, I had several things going on, all of which led to this book.

First and foremost, I was still dealing with the deaths of three friends—a pal from my pre-writer days named Jason Parkin, and fellow authors J.F. Gonzalez (also known to friends and family as Jesus or "Chuy") and Tom Piccirilli (also known to friends and occasionally family as "Pic"). Of the three, I was especially struggling with Jesus's passing. I think that's because, with Pic, we (his friends) had advanced warning. We (and he) had a long time to prepare for it. Don't get me wrong. It fucking sucked when cancer finally robbed us of him, and it hurt—and indeed, it still hurts—but we knew it was going to happen. With Jesus, the cancer took him quick. There were no warning signs, other than in the weeks leading up to it, he'd mentioned that he felt like he had a lingering cold. So, there wasn't a lot of time to mentally prepare for what happened next.

Also, I was more intimately involved with the aftermath of Jesus's passing. Many years ago, Jesus and I had put each other in charge of our literary estates—not actually believing that either of us would ever grow old or die or need such legal agreements. We were angry young men, out to set the literary world on fire. We were following a trail blazed by authors we both idolized—Stephen King,

Jack Ketchum, the Splatterpunks, Alan Moore, Richard Laymon, Karl Edward Wagner, and so many others. We had all the time in the world to make our mark on the genre—and we did. We did. But growing older? Getting cancer? Needing to follow through on those literary estates? Those things seemed as vaguely impossible as a resumption of the Cold War or a reality television host becoming President of the United States of America. Sure, they could happen—but probably not, and if so, not for an impossibly long time.

Until they did.

It is April 29, 2017, as I write this Foreword, and the Cold War has resumed, and a reality television host is President of the United States of America, and I will turn fifty later this year, and my best friend is three years gone. He is dead, and I am still going through his literary estate: finishing his unfinished novels, finding homes for his unpublished work, and making sure his wife and daughter get their royalty checks on time and that publishers aren't taking advantage of them.

You want to hear a weird bit of synchronicity? You want an example of how the universe aligns? Quite literally, as I sat here writing the above paragraph, I got a text from author Paul Tremblay. He was reaching out to let me know he'd just listened to the latest episode of my weekly podcast, *The Horror Show with Brian Keene.* Writer Kelli Owen was our guest on that particular episode, and during her interview, we had a very frank discussion about how grief and depression impacts the creative process, and how it had changed Kelli. Paul texted to let me know that he'd seen a loved one go through something similar—and how they had changed. Not changed for the good or changed for the better, but just changed.

The same thing has happened to me. I've pretty much made it through the grieving process for Jason, Jesus, and Pic. These days, at least. Oh, I still have moments of sudden anger about how things turned out, but for the most part, I'm in a much better mental and emotional state than I was in the Fall of 2015.

This book is about how I came to terms with that grief and loss. It's also about the horror genre. For years, people have mentioned to me that I should write a book about modern horror—our generation's version of Stephen King's *Danse Macabre*. They've said I should write a book about the genre's history from the Nineties until now. I don't know why these people thought I should be the one to do this, but they were all people who were much smarter than me—friends like Bev Vincent and Christopher Golden, my girlfriend Mary SanGiovanni, my former editor Don D'Auria, and even Jesus and Pic (before they passed). In the Fall of 2015, I was considering writing such a book, and had begun to make notes toward it, chronicling horror's rise as a marketing category, its mid-Nineties collapse, the growth of the small press (such as Cemetery Dance, Subterranean Press, Necro Publications, and others), the resurgence during the Internet's infancy, the genre's return to bookstore shelves, and then the second collapse at the end of the millennium's first decade, which rocked both the mass-market and the small press simultaneously.

Portions of this book could be considered an expansion of those notes. It is not meant to be as thorough as *Danse Macabre*, but I'd like to think it is as useful and informative as some of Douglas Winter or Karl Edward Wagner's old columns were, in examining the genre's history.

The final thing I was dealing with in the Fall of 2015 was a return to the bookstore shelves—a place I hadn't been, for the most part, since 2010. I mentioned the second collapse above. I was impacted by that. I saw a good eighty percent of my annual income vanish overnight. And as a result, I was distrustful of any mass-market publisher, preferring instead to opt for a mix of self-publishing and working with small press publishers who had survived the collapse and whom I trusted. Eventually, however, I'd signed with Macmillan, who were going to release a trade hardcover of my novel *Pressure* in bookstores nationwide in 2016. In addition to that, I had a second novel, *The Complex*, coming out from small press publisher Deadite Press. With both books coming out around the same time, I needed to do some heavy promotion, so that one wouldn't dominate the other.

Early in my career, I often did lengthy, extensive book signing tours. I believe I owe a large part of my enduring popularity to those tours. However, I hadn't done one for nearly eight years—not since the birth of my second son. I decided that it might be time to go out on the road again. Ostensibly, it was to promote the books, but subconsciously, it was also to come to terms with all of the other things I've mentioned above.

Or perhaps to escape them.

I talked about it with both my sons, and with my youngest son's mother, and with Mary. All of them were understanding and supportive, and thus, I began planning a book signing tour—cheekily called the Farewell (But Not Really) Tour. A t-shirt company got onboard and made black tour shirts that looked just like the kind of tour shirt you'd buy at a Guns N' Roses concert. A plethora of bookstores and other venues reached out, interested in hosting me. And both Macmillan and Deadite Press got onboard, lending their marketing and promotional departments and a little bit of money. I financed some more of the costs myself, but I was still roughly $10,000 short of what I'd need to support such an endeavor.

That's where Richard Chizmar, Brian Freeman, and Cemetery Dance came in. I knew that they were looking for content for the Cemetery Dance website—regular material that would keep people clicking on a weekly basis. Rich called me, asking if he could come up to the house and go fishing. I said sure, and then I proposed writing an exclusive weekly column for them, chronicling the tour, in exchange for Cemetery Dance paying the rest of my expenses. Rich readily agreed (he's always been an ardent fan and supporter of my non-fiction). And thus, the tour was financed, and I hit the road.

This book is a collection of those columns, chronicling that journey, and everything that happened—but it is also a love letter to a genre that has given me so much enjoyment throughout my life, and equally a love letter to the dear friends I've made along the way—the literary heroes I looked up to, the brothers and sisters who fought in the trenches at my side, and the kids who came along after and now look up to us. It also includes material that did not appear in the weekly online columns—stuff that was either cut at the time or (as in the case of this Introduction) written specifically for this collection.

Okay. You ready? Got everything you need? It's a long trip. We'll be visiting big cities and small towns, seedy bars and posh restaurants, big chain bookstores and little independent shops, and we'll even get lost in the desert at one point. There will be laughter and tears, romance and thrills, altered states and even a few ghosts.

And eventually, we'll reach the end.

Brian Keene
Somewhere along the Susquehanna River
April 2017

The following is a true story...

 **CHAPTER ONE**

IN WHICH WE ANSWER WHO, WHAT, WHERE, AND WHY

My name is Brian Keene. I'm a writer by trade and a road warrior by heart. Neither of these things make for very wise career or life choices, but at the age of forty-eight, it's a little late for me to decide that I'd like to become an IT Specialist or an HVAC technician instead.

Both writing and the road got in my blood at an early age. My parents were transplants from West Virginia, which is like a ghetto with trees and mountains instead of pawn shops and tenement buildings. Seriously. All of the despair and poverty and crime that plague America's ghettos can also be found in rural West Virginia. But, just like the ghettos, you can also find hope and inspiration there (even today, when meth production has overtaken coal mining as the state's most popular employment opportunity). It was that hope and inspiration that motivated my parents to move north to Pennsylvania. Dad was just out of the army, after a year spent in Vietnam followed by a stint on riot duty in Washington, D.C., and Detroit. Mom was fresh out of college. And I was still sucking on pacifiers and learning how to crawl. The year was 1967.

At that point, the most successful person in our family was my grandfather—a straightforward, crafty, kind-hearted, slow-to-anger-but-capable-of-destroying-everything-when-pushed, con-artist and womanizer who made his living as a moonshiner. During Prohibition, he used to hide his shine in the basement of the county courthouse, because it was the last place the authorities would think to look. Many in our family say that I take after him.

Sometimes that makes me uncomfortable.

But I digress.

My parents wanted a better life for toddler Brian (and my little sister who would soon follow) so we moved to Pennsylvania, where Dad got a job in a paper mill. We didn't have a lot of money (especially when the union was on strike) but they always kept us fed and clothed, and more importantly (to six-year-old Brian) they always had money to buy me comic books. I've written at length for the *Stephen King Revisited* website about my early love of comic books and how, via their influence, I decided at the age of eight that I wanted to grow up to be a writer. But I've never written about how those comics—and my interest in writing—were tied to the road.

Until now.

Several times a year, we'd make a seven-hour drive back to West Virginia to visit family. For most children, seven hours spent in the backseat of a car is an interminable hell, but I never minded. Those seven hours blew past because I always had a stack of Marvel, DC, and Charlton comic books to read. And if I ran out of comic books, I'd stare out the window and make up stories about the places we passed and the towns we drove through. Water towers became Martian tripods striding out of H.G. Wells' *War of the Worlds* (a novel which I hadn't read at that age, but knew from the Marvel Comics adaptation). Mountaintops glimpsed from the backseat became volcanoes ready to blow, or landing sites for alien spacecraft. I made up stories back home, as well. I made up stories about everyone and everything in our neighborhood—the old church and cemetery next door, the spooky hollow where a witch was murdered in the 1930s, our neighbors, my friends. But those same locations got boring after a while, so I always looked forward to our family road trips because it gave me new places and people to make up stories about.

So, yeah, by age eight—years before I'd discover Kerouac or Hunter S. Thompson—I was already equating writing with the road.

And I guess I never stopped making the equation.

I sold my first bit of writing—an essay about Godzilla movies—in 1996. I did my first book signing tour—for a deservedly out-of-print and not-ready-for-prime-time short story collection called *No Rest for the Wicked*—in 2001. I've been doing both of those things ever since. That's twenty years. Twenty years of writing books, stories, comic books, and the occasional bit of journalism for money. Twenty years of going out on the road to promote the things I wrote. Twenty years of deadlines, both hit and missed. Twenty years of blowing through advances and chasing down royalty checks. Twenty years of drinking in convention bars and dirty biker bars and upscale yuppie bars and weird hipster bars. Twenty years of signing books for people everywhere from the Barnes and Noble on 5th Avenue in New York City to a Waldenbooks in a strip mall in a small Kentucky town.

At first, I did book signing tours to build an audience. And it worked. Later on, I did book signing tours to convince the bookstore chains to order more copies of my books. And that worked, too. These days, I'm a brand. The publishing business doesn't think of me as an author. They think of me as a brand.

I'm going to state a fact now, and I want to preface it with a note that it doesn't come from a place of arrogance or cockiness or braggadocio, but simply to illustrate my point. I am one of the most successful horror writers of my generation. That's a fact. I'm not wealthy, but I've managed to make a solid middle-class living crafting stories about zombies and giant worms and serial killers and a sentient darkness from outer space. I make my living writing rather than working in a factory. My books are in print in different countries, and they sell every month. I've got a shelf full of awards—so many damn awards that the shelf bows in the middle. A flag was flown in my honor over the American military base in Afghanistan. I've been the answer to a trivia question on a game show. My readers include well-known actors and musicians and stand-up comedians and even a few politicians from both sides of the aisle. I've had a pretty good run.

So, that's fact number one. Fact number two is that I owe at least half of my success to the extensive touring I did early in my career. (There are other factors that contributed to my success as well, but we'll get to those in later chapters.)

As I said, twenty years I've been doing this. But a lot has changed in twenty years. The truth is, authors don't need to do these extensive promotional book signing tours anymore. We can build an audience without ever leaving our homes. That audience can buy our books without ever leaving their homes, as well. And even if that wasn't the case—even if the old models of writing and publishing and bookselling still existed—I don't need to do an extensive promotional tour anymore because I'm a brand. I've already built an audience. My books already sell, and so do the books my friends write. And yet—me and my friends—we still do these tours. Joe Hill is out on the road this summer. Paul Tremblay is out on the road this summer.

Kevin J. Anderson is out on the road this summer. Jonathan Maberry is out on the road this summer. Stephen Graham Jones is out on the road this summer. And I'm out here, too.

If you're asking why, know that I've asked myself that same question. I have two sons. One of them is twenty-five years old. The other one is eight. They require two very different sets of parenting skills. My oldest son can fend for himself. But my eight-year-old—he's only going to be eight once. I've been there his whole life. I'm lucky enough to have a job that has *allowed* me to be there for his whole life. And yet now, I'm heading out on the road again. My tour runs from April through December. A significant portion of that involves crisscrossing the country during the summer, with wingmen and wingwomen such as country and blues singer Kasey Lansdale, author John Urbancik, and high-school football coach Tod Clark for part of the ride. I'm missing out on a summer with my child. Why?

Because I don't want to miss any more summers after this one.

And because all of my friends keep dying.

In the last three years, I've lost three of my best friends. On a warm August day in 2014, my girlfriend (author Mary SanGiovanni) and I were deep in the middle of the New Jersey Pine Barrens, exploring the region for some background research for a novel Mary was working on. When we got to an area with cell phone service, my phone rang. It was my second ex-wife—the mother of my eight-year-old—and she was distraught. I immediately thought something had happened to our son, but instead, was stunned to learn that a friend of ours, Jason, had died of a sudden brain aneurysm. Jason and I had been friends for years. We were friends long before I ever became a writer—but the last few of those years were turbulent. You see, Jason and I made up two corners of a lover's square. My second ex-wife and Mary made up the other two corners. Two guys, two women, and one big fucking mess. He and I stopped speaking altogether for a while, and when we did finally try to make peace with each other, it was forced and slow-going. We were still working our way through all of that when he died, and now I get to live with everything that was left unsaid, and unsettled.

I was still dealing with Jason's death when, that November, J.F. (Jesus) Gonzalez died. That happened quick, in retrospect. From his initial diagnosis ("Hey, Brian, you'll have to work on that new novel we're writing together by yourself today, because I need to go to the doctor for a check-up") to the moment his heart monitor went flat-line, it was just a little over one month. I watched that motherfucking cancer whittle him down to nothing. That was the scariest aspect, to be honest—the speed at which he deteriorated. He was one of my best friends. Just one of the best friends I've ever had. We wrote four published novels together, plus a collection and a screenplay, and a bunch of other stuff. Collaborating with him— one of us could end in the middle of a sentence and the other could pick up where we'd left off. Our voices meshed, our styles meshed, and our appreciation of the genre meshed. Our friendship was like that, too.

When it comes to politics, I'm a middle-of-the-road centrist. Jesus was a card-carrying liberal. Among the things he despised with a passion was FOX News. Now, I don't care for FOX News either (or CNN or MSNBC for that matter). But I don't actively loathe them the way Jesus did. The last practical joke I ever played on him (and we played jokes on each other all the time) was two days before he died. I'd gone to the hospital to visit him. He couldn't talk, because he had a breathing tube down his throat, but he could write (his wife, Cathy, had gotten him a dry erase board to use to communicate with everyone), and he was alert, and able to see the television. When it was time for me to leave, I squeezed his hand and told him that I loved him. He squeezed my hand back and his eyes said the same. Those eyes were droopy and heavy-lidded, I knew he'd probably be asleep before I even made it to the ground floor. As it turned out, it didn't even take that long. He was asleep before I'd left the room. Upon seeing this, I turned around, crept back inside, and turned his television to the FOX News Channel, so it would be on when he woke up. I remember grinning and giggling at this grand practical joke.

That was the last time I ever saw him.

After Jesus's death, I sort of lost my mind, and took a really self-destructive turn. Mary and I broke up for several months. I quit writing. Drank when I was alone. I managed to hold it together enough for my sons, but other than that, I pretty much became a hermit. Soon as I dropped my youngest son off with his mother, I'd come home and start drinking. Deadlines piled up—novels and comic scripts and stories that I'd promised to people long before my friends started dying. I couldn't write shit. (Well, okay, there are some critics who will tell you that all I've ever been capable of is writing shit, but fuck them.) I couldn't write. I'd sit down, turn on the computer, and just stare at the blank screen. That little blinking cursor seemed like it was laughing at me. I decided that I was done. That I had no more words to write. That happens sometimes. T.E.D. Klein delivered one hell of a seminal novel and four excellent novellas and then stopped. My friend Geoff "Coop" Cooper did the same. The mid-list horror paperbacks of the Eighties are littered with names we never heard from again. I figured it was my turn.

One day, about a month or so after Jesus's death, filmmaker Mike Lombardo and I were over at his house, helping Jesus's wife, Cathy, with some things. I had decided by then to quit writing and see if I could get my old foundry job back again, or maybe return to radio. I hadn't told anyone at that point, and decided Cathy and Mike would be the first to find out. However, before I could inform them of my decision, my phone began buzzing.

And buzzing.

And buzzing.

And buzzing.

Turned out Stephen King had just read *Darkness on the Edge of Town*, one of my relatively older novels, and was saying nice things about it on Twitter. Every single person in our industry who was in possession of my phone number had decided to simultaneously text me and tell me this was occurring.

I knew I wanted to be a writer when I was six years old. I knew I wanted to be a horror writer when I was around ten or eleven—after I read my first Stephen King book (and for the complete story on that, I'll refer you again to that aforementioned piece I wrote for the *Stephen King Revisited* website). So, Stephen King made me want to be a horror writer. And years later, he made me want to be a horror writer all over again just as I was about to quit. That simple act of kindness rejuvenated my creativity. And so, I put the whiskey bottle away and put my ass back in the chair and my fingers back on the keyboard.

Problem was, I had slowed down tremendously. I hadn't dealt with my grief in a healthy way, and the results showed in my work. I normally write six or seven hours a day. I can average several thousand words during that time—perhaps a complete short story or half a comic book script or a chapter or two of a novel. But now, thanks to depression, I was lucky if I did a thousand words in a day. But hey, at least I was writing again. Baby steps, and all that.

It took me a long time to work through the loss of Jason and Jesus, and I was just starting to come to grips with it all when Tom Piccirilli died.

Now, unlike Jesus, Pic was sick for a long time. He'd had brain cancer once before, and it had supposedly been terminal at that point, and all of us had gone to see him and tell him goodbye (that story is recounted in my book *Trigger Warnings*). But he kicked cancer's ass. We were overjoyed when Pic beat the cancer, and distraught when it returned. His death hit me hard, but it affected me in a much different way than Jason or Jesus's did, and I'm still not sure I understand why. I loved Pic. He really was like a big brother to me. And yet, I guess somewhere deep down inside, I suspected it would happen. I guess after Jason and Jesus, I assumed it would come. I cried when he was gone, but I didn't drink myself into oblivion and stop writing the way I'd done when Jesus passed.

Jason, Jesus, Pic—each of their deaths impacted me in a different way, and I dealt with and processed each of them in different ways. Something I did in all three cases was eventually write about them. And even when I wasn't consciously writing about them, they were lurking in the spaces between the words. Usually, that's all I need to do. I write things out of my system. That's where novels like *Dark Hollow* and *Ghoul* and *The Girl on the Glider* came from. I had something on my chest, something dark and tumorous squatting on my soul and taking a big shit on my spirit, and I wrote it out of my system. And for the most part, I've done that this time, as well.

But here's the thing. You can make peace with the loss of a person—or even three people—who are close to you. You can crawl back from the bottle, climb back from the brink. You can be there and be strong and be responsible for your sons and for your girlfriend and for everyone else in your life—but at the end of the day, there's still a little voice inside of your head that says, "You're next."

That voice is impossible to silence, and so you start listening to it. You make your literary estate and fill out your will and start thinking about all the novels and stories you'd hoped to write one day, and you rank them in order of, "Which ones do I absolutely need to finish first?" And then you figure you'd better say goodbye to everyone...just in case.

So...why go back out on the road at this point in my career?

I'm doing this so that I never have to do it again. I'm doing this because I miss you guys (my readers). You've grown in numbers, and it's hard to talk with all of you one-on-one these days. I'm doing this because it will be nice to see all of you one more time and have that one-on-one interaction. I owe you that much. In the words of Prince, "we could all die any day..." Now, I've no plans to die. There are some things I'd like to finish first. But when it seems like your friends keep dying, and your pop culture icons keep dying, and your own health problems are becoming more and more of a daily concern... you gotta suck it up and be a realist. To quote another of my favorite musicians, Waylon Jennings, "living legends are a dying breed, there ain't too many left. To tell the truth I ain't been feeling real hot lately my damn self..."

I'm hitting the road one last time so that when I reach the end of it, I can stay home with my son.

But there's more to it than that. As I said before, twenty years is a long time, and things have changed. Book tours have changed, publishing has changed, bookselling has changed, conventions have changed, travel has changed, horror fiction—and the horror genre— has changed. I've changed, too.

The only things that haven't changed are writing and the road. They stay the same, while everything changes around us. The words we type today are the past tomorrow. And yet, everything is connected. It's connected like the highways on a map are connected. This holds true for the history of our genre, as well.

A few months ago, I visited The York Emporium—a warehouse-sized used bookstore in my hometown—with Adam Cesare, Scott Cole, and Mike Lombardo in tow. Adam is a horror writer, Scott is a bizarro writer, and Mike, as I said above, is a horror filmmaker. All three are part of the Millennial generation. All three are going through the same struggles I went through nearly twenty years ago. While browsing through the shelves, I found three signed copies of John Skipp and Craig Spector's *The Light at the End*—one of the absolute classics of the splatterpunk sub-genre. I made sure Adam, Scott, and Mike each went home with one, and I felt a real sense of history as I handed those books to them—three generations of horror writers, one generation after the other, helping each other and all hoping for the same thing.

That same weekend, Mike and I finished a year-long task of moving all of Jesus Gonzalez's papers, books, and private effects. While going through boxes, Jesus's wife, Cathy, found a bunch of hand-written letters from Robert Bloch that he'd sent to Jesus, Mike Baker, and Mark Williams. None of those four authors are with us now, and my time is probably limited, but it pleased me that Mike understood the importance of those letters, and why they mattered, and why the people in them mattered, and the generational sense of history that was imbued in them.

I am heading out on the road, surrounded by a history that I've somehow become a part of. It is May 2016 as I write this. The tour ends in December 2016. Over the next nine months, I'm going to write about it weekly here at Cemetery Dance Online. I'm going to write about it from out there on the road. I'm going to examine that history, and what has changed, and what remains the same. In bookselling. In publishing. In touring. In our society. And especially in myself.

I will find all of those things out here at the end of the road.

My name is Brian Keene. I'm a writer by trade and a road warrior by heart. Neither of these things are wise career or life choices. The tolls add up.

I rode into town twenty years ago.

Now I'm riding out, again, and you're all coming with me...

→ **CHAPTER TWO**

HOW THE MID-LIST DIED

Stephen Graham Jones signed his new novel, *Mongrels*, at Bookworks in Albuquerque, New Mexico, this week. I'll be signing at that same store next month. There's a reason both of us—and many of our peers—chose that store. If you think of the retail bookselling market as a geographical location, it currently resembles the wasteland from a *Mad Max* movie. But Bookworks, and hundreds of other independent bookstores, are bright, colorful oases sprouting from that formerly toxic ground.

What happened? What caused the apocalypse? And what is allowing these indie bookstores to flourish? Two things: corporate stupidity and the changes in publishing.

Once upon a time, Dorchester Publishing was America's oldest mass-market paperback publisher. They published horror, romance, western, adventure, mystery, and other genres. When they imploded a few years ago, most of the mid-list collapsed with them.

What is the mid-list, you ask? Easy. Take yourself back in time ten or twenty years ago. Imagine walking into a Waldenbooks or

Borders bookstore. At the front of the store, you had big cardboard displays or "end-capped" shelves featuring the latest guaranteed bestsellers—fiction by folks like Stephen King, James Patterson, and Danielle Steel; non-fiction by Glenn Beck, John Stewart, and Rachel Ray; memoirs and advice books ghostwritten for reality television stars, athletes, and politicians. Walk past these, and you got to the shelves where you found perennial sellers—classics by Shakespeare, Dickens, Steinbeck, Hemingway, Thompson, Bukowski, and others. The mid-list existed in the middle of these two groups. It was primarily composed of paperback genre fiction with a smaller print run than the manufactured bestsellers—sold in bookstores and airports and newsstands, impulse buys with a maximum shelf life of one to three months, after which the unsold copies had their covers unceremoniously ripped off and sent back to the publishers for a full credit. That's right. Publishers spent money manufacturing and producing the books, sent them to bookstores, and the bookstores could then damage the product, rendering it unsaleable, and the publishers didn't see a dime from it. Hell of a way to run an operation, right?

That was the mid-list. It was where most of the authors you read lived. We could make a living working there. Not a great living, but a reliable middle-class wage. It was the land of Ed Gorman and Bill Pronzini, of Richard Laymon and Jack Ketchum, of Rick Hautala and Charles Grant, of William W. Johnstone and Ruby Jean Jenson, of Tom Piccirilli and J.F. Gonzalez and Bryan Smith and Mary SanGiovanni and myself and hundreds of others who you've read and enjoyed. And we never moved beyond it because the system was rigged.

The advance money an author got paid for a mid-list paperback was much lower than for that of a manufactured bestseller. That's because the majority of the money went to the publisher first, and the writers of those manufactured bestsellers second. And the paper mill. And the trucking company. There wasn't much left for the mid-list authors. Mid-list books were released with zero to little fanfare, marketing, or promotion for the same reasons. Your book had three months to find an audience—to find readers—before the remaining copies got yanked off the shelves to make room for the next batch of mid-list titles.

When Dorchester Publishing collapsed, it took a lot of the mid-list with it. That's because their Leisure Books imprint was a big producer of mid-list titles, particularly horror and romance.

The mid-list is dead now. It is never coming back.

Neither are Borders or Waldenbooks.

I have many friends who were booksellers or managers for Borders and Waldenbooks, and they repeat the same story. The demise of those chains was down to corporate stupidity—of executives trying to sell books the same way one sells soft drinks or cement blocks or blenders, of not understanding and anticipating their customer's needs, of turning their stores into libraries where the public could browse the merchandise and drip coffee all over it and then leave without making a purchase, of the books being pushed further and further to the back of the store to make way for toys and plants and all sorts of other non-book related ephemera that they thought they should sell instead. I don't know about you, but when I go to a bookstore, I don't want to buy plants or toys. If I want toys, I go to a fucking toy store. If I want plants, I go to a greenhouse. If I go to a bookstore, I'd like to buy books. So did a lot of other people. Eventually, Borders and Waldenbooks went the way of Dorchester.

I have friends who currently work as booksellers or managers for America's two surviving chain bookstores—Barnes and Noble and Books-a-Million, and they tell me confidentially that the situation is the same in their stores. I predict it's just a matter of time before the same rot that whittled Borders down to nothing does the same to them.

The mid-list is gone. Borders is gone. But that doesn't matter, because over the last twenty years, we've had a new thing come along—something called the Internet. With it came Amazon, and suddenly, mid-list writers didn't have to play a rigged game anymore. Our books had a shelf life beyond that one to three-month span. Readers could find us, discover us, and find our backlist. If your local chain bookstore didn't have our latest, you could buy it online.

Which brings us back to the start of this column. The number one question I am most often asked is, "Why can't I buy all of your books at Barnes and Noble?"

To understand why, you need to consider the changes that have taken place in publishing over the last twenty years, particularly those that took place after the demise of the mid-list and the closure of Borders. After those things occurred many mid-list, cult, or genre authors decided to take advantage of the advances in digital and print-on-demand publishing and do it for themselves. They cut out the publisher, cut out the chain stores, and marketed directly to the readers. For example, Bryan Smith, who was inarguably one of Dorchester's most popular horror writers, began self-publishing via Kindle and CreateSpace and has since made more money from that than he ever did through traditional publishers. Other authors, such as myself, decided to diversify their publication routes. Since Dorchester's fall, I've routinely divided my releases between self-publishing (via Amazon's CreateSpace and Kindle), the small press (via publishers such as Deadite Press and Apex Book Company), and mainstream publishing (via big publishing conglomerates such as Macmillan). I do this because I don't like having all my eggs in one basket. Your mileage may vary.

The problem is that big retail chain stores like Barnes and Noble and Books-a-Million won't carry my small press titles. The vast majority of my backlist is published by Deadite Press. Barnes and Noble and Books-a-Million will carry Deadite Press titles, but only if Deadite will allow them to strip the covers off the unsold copies after three months and return them. Deadite Press is having none of that. And why should they? Deadite Press is taking advantage of these new publishing and distribution models, and selling the books directly to readers, rather than via the bookstore middlemen. Deadite Press doesn't need Barnes and Noble. Why would they agree to a policy that is fundamentally flawed and unfair to them? Answer—they wouldn't.

And that's why you can't find my books (or books by many of your other favorite former mid-listers) at a retail giant near you. And I am totally okay with that, because you know where you can find my books? In independent bookstores. See, the indie stores that have sprung up in the wake of Borders don't subscribe to those same outdated distribution and sales models that the big chains cling to. Many of them are willing to—are you ready for this—order books and pay up front for those books and then sell those books to their customers, rather than moving them to the back of the store to make way for more *Pokémon* cards and calendars. That's why, if you look at the places I'm signing over the next nine months, the majority of them are independent bookstores—places like Dark Delicacies, The Poisoned Pen, Mysterious Galaxy, Borderlands Books, Tubby and Coo's, Star Line Books, and dozens more.

"But," one of you is saying right now, having checked my tour dates, "you're also signing at a few big retail chain stores."

Yes, Skippy, I am. And I'll explain why in the next column, when we delve into the economics of writing for a living in this brave new post-Borders, post-mid-list world.

CHAPTER THREE

MAKING A LIVING IN A POST MID-LIST WORLD WITHOUT BORDERS

So, we ended last week's column about the deaths of the mid-list and the Borders bookstore chain with the following question: "If self-publishing, independent presses, and independent bookstores are more preferable to former mid-list authors then why are you still selling books to mainstream publishers and signing in big chain bookstores, as well, Keene?" Is the answer:

A) Money.

B) People are stupid.

C) To have a stable, secure writing career in this post-mid-list world without Borders, full-time writers of genre fiction need to diversify.

D) All of the above.

The correct answer is D—all of the above. Let's examine why, and let's talk about how a former mid-lister makes a living as a writer in 2016. To clarify, I define making a living as a writer as: writing is my only vocation, I do it full-time, and am able to support myself off my writing income. Other people may define it differently, and that's fine. But for the interests of this article, that's how I personally define it.

(Twenty years ago, I wouldn't have had to type a caveat like that and derail the fucking point of the article, but this is 2016, and a lot of people on the Internet are part of answer B, above. Some of them may even be your friend on Facebook.)

But I digress.

Thirty years ago, a mid-list genre writer could make a decent living writing for one or two publishers, provided their books sold well. If you could bang out more than one title per year, and were selling enough copies to earn back your advance and make the publisher a profit, the publisher would treat you decently. No, they probably weren't going to treat you to lobster and high-class erotic dancers the way legend says Kirby McCauley did for his authors, (one of my favorite things to do is to go drinking with authors Tom Monteleone and F. Paul Wilson and get them to tell me Kirby McCauley stories), but your editor at Zebra or Dell Abyss would probably spring for a steak and a stripper.

Twenty years ago, when I started getting published, this adage still held true. Yes, mid-list authors—especially horror authors— were being paid less than they were a decade before (I remember a former titan of late-Eighties and early-Nineties horror fiction who had been away for a while and who, upon his return to publication, was shocked by the decrease in pay and told me with sincere regret what I would have been making per book had I just been born twenty years earlier). But despite that, if your books sold well, you could still make a decent living by staying with one or two main publishers. Maybe you wrote horror novels for one and westerns for another. Or maybe you wrote thrillers under one name and romance novels under a pseudonym. And even if your books weren't selling well enough for you to write full-time, you could at least make a decent secondary income writing for one or two publishers.

In hindsight, this was a stupid thing to do. And I include myself in that stupidity. I was a reader back when Zebra and Dell Abyss went under. As a reader, rather than a writer, it never occurred to me that those closures put some of my favorite authors in the unemployment line. All I knew was that I couldn't find any new Ronald Kelly or Brian Hodge books at Borders anymore.

Which is why I say that I was stupid twenty years ago, when the vast majority of my published works were brought out by two publishers. Dorchester/Leisure Books published me in mass-market paperback—books that were available at Borders, in airports, grocery stores, and pretty much anywhere else books were sold. Small press Delirium Books published signed, limited edition collectible hardcovers of those works, as well as other books that were considered unsaleable to the mass-market (short story collections, non-fiction collections, novellas, and novels that were considered too bizarre or unclassifiable for a mainstream audience). Occasionally, I would sell a one-off novel or novella to another publisher—mostly Cemetery Dance, Bloodletting Press, Necessary Evil, and other small presses. That was done because I was younger then, and able to write faster, and at an incredibly prolific point in my life, and I didn't want to bury Dorchester or Delirium in a deluge of stuff with my name on it. But for the most part, I was content to publish the majority of my work through those two outlets—one mainstream and the other small press.

Which is why I was fucked when, ten years later, due to changing marketplace conditions and a downturn in the global economy, one of those publishers changed their business model and the other went out of business, and I was suddenly broke. In the space of a few short months, both of my most reliable income streams had vanished, and I was fucked—all because I'd forgotten the lesson of what happened with Zebra and Dell Abyss twenty years before. The same thing happened to all the other mid-listers trying to make a living at that time. I guess we'd all forgotten that lesson. Thus, what you were left with was hundreds of mid-list authors, all scrambling to get a piece of an ever-shrinking, rapidly-changing pie.

Some, like Bryan Smith, Robert Swartwood, and Scott Nicholson, decided to do it themselves, taking full advantage of the vast changes in publishing, bookselling, and technology, and going into business for themselves, self-publishing their titles and marketing them directly to readers. Others, like Sarah Pinborough, James Moore, and Tim Lebbon, started writing more decidedly non-mid-list work that, while still dark in nature, tone, and theme, didn't necessarily have HORROR stamped on the spine, or feature a cover with a bunch of zombie hands reaching for the reader, and thus, had a better chance of selling to a mainstream audience. There is nothing wrong with either of these methods. Nobody can argue with Bryan, Robert, and Scott's success. Nobody can argue with Sarah, Jim, or Tim's success either. There are many paths to success as a writer, and the only thing those paths have in common is sitting your ass down in a chair and actually writing, rather than Tweeting about writing or Facebooking about writing or all the other things we do to distract us from actually writing.

Me? I follow a third path. I self-publish some of my work. I publish some of my work with small presses and independent publishers. And I publish some of my work via the mainstream publishing houses. This is the path I have chosen for myself simply because if there is one thing I've learned from working in this business for the last twenty years it's that everything—every fucking thing—can change in an instant. A mainstream publisher who appears outwardly solvent and rolling in cash can file bankruptcy the next quarter, or get bought out by a corporate conglomerate who decides they're only going to publish celebrity memoirs. Today's small press success story can be tomorrow's "Whatever happened to?" Our current self-publishing benefactor could change the terms of service next week, impeding how the authors using that platform earn a living. In my opinion, diversification of publishers and publishing methods is the most secure way to earn a living in a post-mid-list world without Borders. Your mileage may vary.

Speaking of earning a living, let's take a closer look at answer A—which was money. My main independent publisher, Deadite Press, pays me monthly royalties. What that means is that I get a check from them every single month. Let's say hypothetically, on average, that check is about $2,000 a month. That's $24,000 a year. If we add in other independent publishers I work with, Apex Book Company or Thunderstorm Books or Cemetery Dance, for example, we can hypothetically reach $34,000 a year. Add in what I make from self-publishing, and we round out with a hypothetical annual income of around $40,000.

Forty grand a year. Not bad, especially considering that I live in rural Pennsylvania. Author Chuck Wendig once described Pennsylvania as "Philadelphia and Pittsburgh with Kentucky in the middle" and for the most part, that's accurate. But one of the benefits of living in this region is that one can exist on $40,000 a year. You might not be comfortable, but you can live.

But what if I don't want to just get by? I've got a twenty-five-year-old and an eight-year-old and a girlfriend and two ex-wives and a host of bills to pay. I'm in a job with no health insurance and no

401K and no retirement plan. So, while I can live off forty grand a year, and keep a roof over our heads and keep everybody fed, it would be nice to start saving a little money for a rainy day. That's where the mainstream comes in. Let me be blunt—I'd be happy to continue working with Deadite, Thunderstorm, Cemetery Dance, Apex, and other independent presses until I die. But at the end of the day, those sales aren't going to boost me over the forty thousand hump. Enter mainstream publishing.

"Hi Brian," says a mainstream publisher. "We are interested in publishing more horror. We'll call it a thriller on the spine, but it will be horror. We already asked Joe Hill and Jonathan Maberry, and they said no, so now we're asking you."

Which is always nice to hear. It's always nice to hear that they asked your friends to the dance first, and your friends said no, so now they're asking you. No, I'm kidding. But not really. Make no mistake, I've had mainstream publishers approach me with that very query in the past, but for the record, my current mainstream publisher—Macmillan/Thomas Dunne—said no such thing. They are wonderful people. And I don't hold it against Joe or Jonathan, either. They are both dear friends and wonderful guys. Back in the day, if you wanted to publish a horror anthology, the publisher wouldn't look at it unless you had a story by Stephen King, Clive Barker, or Dean Koontz. These days, I'm told (by publishers) that Joe, Jonathan, and I are that trifecta. Which is simultaneously weird and cool.

But I digress again.

Let's say our hypothetical mainstream publisher offers you a $10,000 or $20,000 advance on a novel—something that small press publishers and independent publishers can't financially justify doing without filing for bankruptcy. When you get that offer, it pushes you over that magical forty-thousand-dollar annual income. Now you're at fifty or sixty thousand dollars. Now you can actually start saving money, and paying for things like that Xbox One your child has been asking for, or the new cornea the eye surgeon says you need, which you haven't been able to afford because you don't have health insurance.

And you can pay for those things for one year.

Because that's the problem with an advance. An advance is simply that. The publisher gives you X amount of money—an advance on future sales of your book. If the advance was $20,000, you don't get paid again until after you've sold enough books to earn $20,000 in royalties. So, sell $21,000-worth, and you'll start getting paid again.

Which brings me back to why I'm out here on the road for the next nine months, crisscrossing the country and signing in both independent bookstores and the remaining big chain stores.

Money.

Yes, I know what I said in our first installment. I know I said that my time is almost up, and I want to say goodbye to everyone before I leave this place and join my friends in that big horror convention hotel barroom in the sky. All of that is true. But it's also about the money. If I can get independent bookstores to order more copies of my new novel *The Complex* from Deadite Press, then those monthly royalty checks go up in size. And if I can get mainstream bookstores to order more copies of my other new novel *Pressure* from Macmillan/Thomas Dunne, then I earn out that advance and get another check. And if I get Cemetery Dance Online to pay me for a weekly column with the option to collect it in book form when these nine months are up, then I can use that money to finance the whole tour.

And then next year, I'm still above that forty-thousand mark.

It's a hell of a way to make a living, but it's the only way I know how in a post-mid-list world without Borders.

That would have been a great sentence to end this week's column on, but I just remembered that I forgot to talk about answer B—people are stupid.

The most frustrating thing for me as a writer and a public figure is that there still exists a portion of the public who are unfamiliar with Google and seemingly unaware that the Internet exists beyond Facebook. I can't tell you how many times I want to Tweet back to somebody, in my best Samuel L. Jackson voice, "Google, motherfucker! Do you use it?" or take them by their figurative little cyber hand and go up to their browser's address bar, and typing B-R-I-A-N-K-E-E-N-E-D-O-T-C-O-M for them. Of course, I never do because, despite what you may have heard about me, I'm not a complete asshole.

And they're not stupid. I said that for comedic effect and out of frustration. But they're not stupid. They're like me, younger Brian who, thirty years ago, didn't know about the collapse of Zebra or Dell Abyss and just wondered why he couldn't find a new Ronald Kelly or Brian Hodge or Skipp and Spector novel at his local bookstore.

Despite all of the changes in how books are published and how books are marketed and sold, and how people purchase them—despite all of this—there is still a portion of the reading public who only buy their books in retail chain stores. They don't own a Kindle or other e-book reader. They don't shop on Amazon or other online retailers. And they don't spend time going to authors' websites and reading inside-baseball accounts of what's happening in publishing. Their needs are simple. They want to buy a book, and then click "Like" on their sister's cat picture on Facebook, and maybe play a game on their phone or tablet. And there's nothing wrong with that.

But we need to reach them. I need to reach them. And this tour will do that, somewhat. No, it won't reach all of them, simply because not all of them are online enough or aware enough to even know that there is a book signing tour taking place. But for the ones who are, for the ones who see it scroll by in their Facebook feed, nestled between funny cat videos or various political screeds, or even for the ones who just happen to be in the bookstore that day—it's an opportunity to explain to them where the books have gone, and where they can go to buy them. It's a chance to educate them about the small press and the independent press, and independent bookstores.

So, there's that, too.

That's not as good of an ending as the one before, so I'm gonna re-type that previous portion.

It's a hell of a way to make a living, but it's the only way I know how in a post-mid-list world without Borders.

Next week, we travel to our first stop on the tour—the annual World Horror Convention, where we'll examine its history and how it has changed over the last twenty years, and whether or not it is still vital and needed within our industry.

CHAPTER FOUR

A BRIEF HISTORY OF THE WORLD HORROR CONVENTION

The World Horror Convention, more commonly known as WHC, is perhaps best described as an annual trade show for horror writers, publishers, artists, booksellers, agents, and others with an interest in the field. Fans of horror fiction are welcome to attend, too, and they do, but WHC is a professional gathering, and it's expensive, and you're not apt to see cosplayers or a guy in the dealer's room selling bootleg copies of *Manimal* on DVD like you would at a fan or media convention such as San Diego Comic Con or Dragon Con. The first WHC was held in Nashville, Tennessee, in 1991. There's been one every year ever since, usually in the United States or Canada, although the 2010 event was held in the United Kingdom, finally putting the *World* in the World Horror Convention.

I attended my first WHC in 1999. It was held in Atlanta. I was a complete newbie, having published a handful of stories and articles in a few amateur zines. It is fair to say that the World Horror

Convention changed my life. At the time, I was working for a radio station, doubling as a sales representative and an on-air personality. Writing for a living was something I aspired to do, but so was a trip to Mars. I didn't think either were attainable in any sort of real sense. Hell, I would have settled for just being professionally published, but that seemed like a pipe dream as well.

I arrived in Atlanta and hopped on a shuttle bus from the airport to the hotel and met the first member of our tribe that I had ever encountered.

WHC 1999 – Bottom Row: Brian Keene, Geoff Cooper, Michael T. Huyck, Mike Oliveri, and Polagaya Fine. Top Row: Jack Haringa, Rain Graves, Brett Savory, Ryan Harding, and Feo Amante. This is how friends used to gather before Facebook was invented. (Photo copyright James Futch 1999)

Well, okay. An aside. Before that, my interactions with authors had been conducted solely online, using Windows 3.0 and a very primitive chat room called *Horrornet* that took approximately twenty minutes to refresh every time you typed a response. I'd only physically encountered a real author once—when Joe R. Lansdale did a signing at my friend's comic book store. I managed to mumble something about how much I liked *The Drive-In* before shuffling away. I also once stood outside a club where John Skipp was playing music with his band, convinced that if I handed him my manuscript, he would help me get it published. Unfortunately, I didn't get to meet him that night.

And here we are now, years later, and I am lucky enough to call both Joe and Skipp friends.

And in a weird bit of synchronicity, Joe's daughter, Kasey Lansdale, and I did a signing at the same comic book store years later.

I should warn you now that the meat of this nine-month series of columns—of which this is column number four—is going to be built around the concept of Eternal Return. It's something I believe in very strongly, and I've based my entire fictional mythos around it and String Theory. Eternal Return proposes that the universe and all existence and energy has been recurring, and will continue to recur, in a self-similar form an infinite number of times across infinite time and space. Or, if you want to put it in horror terms, think Rust Cohle's "Time is a flat circle" speech from *True Detective*, or delve deep into the writings of Laird Barron or Alan Moore. We won't come back to this until much later in the year, but I'm throwing it out there now. Writers call that "foreshadowing."

But I digress.

Where were we? Oh, yes. On a shuttle bus in Atlanta in 1999 on our way to Brian's first WHC.

Before we even arrived at the hotel, I met a guy about the same age as me. I don't know how we recognized each other. I don't know what about us said, "I'm going to the World Horror Convention." Maybe it was a chemical thing. Maybe there was something in our eyes. We struck up a conversation and he introduced himself as Gak.

I recognized his name. We'd been appearing in the same fanzines together—he as an aspiring artist and me as an aspiring writer. Here we are, almost twenty years later, and Gak's artwork is now indelibly inked across much of my back in the form of a large tattoo.

Time is a flat circle, indeed.

When we got to the hotel, Gak disappeared. My room wasn't ready yet, and I found myself standing in the lobby, not sure what to do next. There was a guy dressed all in black sprawled across one of the sofas in the lobby. There was no one else around. And then the guy, somehow sensing that I'm there for the convention, calls me over to him. I approach him with caution, and then he reaches into his bag and shows me something he'd just bought in the dealer's room. To this day, I can't tell you what the item was, because it quickly dawned on me that the guy was author John Shirley. He's trying to show it to me and have an intelligent conversation with me about it, and meanwhile, I'm standing there with my mouth clamped shut because I know if I open it, I'm going to shout unhelpful things like, "You're John Shirley! You're John Shirley! You wrote *A Splendid Chaos*! You're John Shirley!"

And that was my first WHC. Over the course of that weekend, I discovered just how open and welcoming the horror professional community is. I was an absolute nobody, and yet I found myself having dinner with Brian Hodge and Yvonne Navarro, and partying on a hotel rooftop with Neil Gaiman and Ramsey Campbell. I also met most of the peers who I'd been talking with online in that archaic, Internet 1.0 chat room—folks like Tom Piccirilli, John Urbancik, Jack Haringa, Geoff Cooper, Mike Oliveri, Michael T. Huyck, Ryan Harding, Regina Mitchell, and so many more. In the almost twenty years that have followed, they remain some of the best friends I have ever had in life.

As I said earlier, before attending WHC, I'd approached writing as a pastime—a hobby. I'd write things occasionally and send them out to zines, and sometimes they'd get published but more often they got rejected. When WHC was over and I'd gone home again, that all changed. Suddenly, I was driven to write. It changed my entire outlook and approach to this vocation. I began writing every evening, no matter how tired I was. The publication versus rejection ratio changed. I became more involved with our community. I finally began to view myself as a writer, rather than as a guy who worked a succession of various jobs and wrote occasionally on weekends. I'd always dreamed of writing for a living. Attending that first WHC was what finally gave me the resolve to actually strive toward it.

At my second World Horror Convention, Richard Laymon—an author who was a huge influence on me, and whom I looked up to immensely—introduced me to his editor, Don D'Auria, and told him about a little zombie novel I was working on at the time (of which Laymon had read the first few chapters and offered some advice). Don asked me to send it to him, and I did.

At my third World Horror Convention, Jack Ketchum sat down with me at the hotel bar and went over the contract for that zombie novel with a red pen and taught me everything I'd ever need to know about negotiating a publishing contract. I still have that red-penned original at home, and I still have the receipt for the bottle of scotch I bought him in return. That novel was *The Rising*, and it launched my career and made me a full-time writer.

None of that would have been possible without WHC, and I've been attending WHC—whenever possible—ever since.

WHC 2014 Yvonne Navarro, Weston Ochse, Mary SanGiovanni, a much older Brian Keene, Carlton Mellick III, and Don D'Auria minutes before Brian's induction as a World Horror Grandmaster. (Photo copyright Kelli Owen 2014)

But I wondered, flying in to this year's WHC, if Millennials and younger horror writers saw it in the same light? Was it as useful to them as it had been to our generation and the generation before us—or, like seemingly everything else in our society, had its sense of community been replaced by online social networking? Was WHC still a vital thing? Was it still good? Or had time gnawed on its bones the way it seemed to be doing everything else in my life?

Here's the thing about WHC. It is only as good as the people who are hosting it. WHC is overseen by the World Horror Society. Each year, individuals can bid on the right to host WHC in their city. The World Horror Society Board of Directors then awards the bid to the group they think will do the best job. Most years, this works out just fine. There have been plenty of lovely World Horror Conventions. Some years, it works out phenomenally (Denver 2000, Seattle 2001, New York 2005, San Francisco 2006, Toronto 2007, Brighton 2010, and especially Austin 2011 are fondly remembered and praised as exceptional conventions). And occasionally, just occasionally, there are years that are remembered less-than-fondly (Kansas City 2003 and Portland 2014 immediately come to mind. Indeed, in that latter case, had it not been for the combined efforts of the HWA and Deadite Press's Rose O'Keefe and Jeff Burk, all three of whom stepped in at the last minute to save the day, I seriously doubt the Portland WHC would have happened at all).

But the important thing about WHC is that it doesn't matter who is hosting it from year to year. Their individual competence or incompetence doesn't matter. What matters is that when you come to WHC, you are among friends. You are among family. Horror writers have always been welcoming of anyone, regardless of race, creed, gender, or sexual orientation. Indeed, we've often been the first to do so. You will never find a more welcoming, friendly, and good-humored group than the people in this tribe.

As my plane landed in Utah, and I found my driver waiting to take me to this year's WHC, I wondered if that would still hold true.

→ **CHAPTER FIVE**

SPIRITS

The first time I ever went to Utah, it was to meet with some producers who wanted to option my novel *The Rising* for film. It didn't work out because we had conversations like this:

THEM: "We see *The Rising* as sort of a buddy road comedy starring Chris Tucker and Gary Sinise."

ME: "But it's a serious novel about a father looking for his son during the zombie apocalypse."

THEM: "Not if we option it."

ME: "I'm leaving now."

As if that wasn't bad enough, during that trip, I also got hit by a van while crossing the street, which seems to be a common malady among horror writers.

In hindsight, that wasn't a good weekend.

Brian and Modern Family's Nolan Gould prepare to pelt the paparazzi. (Photo copyright Mary SanGiovanni 2012)

The second time I visited Utah, it was to attend the Sundance Film Festival. Particularly, it was to attend the premiere of *Ghoul*, a movie based on one of my novels. The studio allowed me to bring some friends along: authors Mary SanGiovanni, Mike Oliveri, and Michael T. Huyck; my loyal pre-readers Mark Sylva and Tod Clark, and Tod's lovely wife Suzin. There was lots of laughter and smiles, and actor Nolan Gould and I got in trouble for throwing snowballs at the paparazzi trying to take his photograph.

That was a good weekend.

It occurred to me, sitting in the car on my way to WHC 2016, that my score with Utah was 1 and 1.

My status as a Guest of Honor at this year's World Horror Convention was purely accidental and pretty much last minute. Originally, I had planned on skipping this year's WHC because I'd be on the road for the rest of the year, but then, Sarah Pinborough—who was a Guest of Honor—asked me to come hang out with her at the convention for the weekend, and since I would pretty much do anything Sarah asked me to, up to and including murder, I decided to attend. That decision was made easier since the convention was paying for my travel and room. See, one of the traditions of WHC is that each Guest of Honor gets interviewed on stage in front of a crowd of people. Sarah wanted me to conduct her interview, and thus, the convention staff were very accommodating. Basically, they were paying for Sarah and me to drink wine and bourbon and run amok (possibly naked) through the streets of downtown Provo for a weekend, carving a vast swath of destruction and carnage in our wake. Maybe we'd even let Jeff Strand tag along. You haven't seen depravity until you've seen Jeff Strand in the depths of a spring water binge...

Unfortunately, due to other commitments that she just couldn't get out of, Sarah had to cancel her appearance at WHC at the last minute. Since they were already paying for me to attend anyway, the convention organizers asked if I'd like to be a replacement Guest of Honor. I said yes. And it should be noted, even though Sarah was unable to attend, the convention did a wonderful job of representing her throughout the weekend, with her books available for sale and prominently displayed in the convention registration area and dealers room. It is little touches like this that veteran authors like myself pay attention to, and as far as I'm concerned, this year's organizers deserve big props for that.

So, there I am, an accidental Guest of Honor, being driven from the airport in Salt Lake City to the convention in Provo. I'd been bounced around airports all day, and had my flight delayed twice. It was late, I was tired, and all I really wanted to do was check into my hotel room and maybe grab a drink and then go to sleep. The ride took about an hour. I asked my driver if any of the convention staff were concerned about whether or not holding the convention that far away from a major airport might impact attendance. What I found out was that, while it was certainly a concern, the bigger concern was the HWA's Bram Stoker Awards.

HWA stands for the Horror Writers Association. It is a non-profit organization founded in 1985, for the purpose of promoting the interests of Horror and Dark fantasy writers, publishers, and other professionals in the field. This is done primarily via the annual Bram Stoker Awards, which recognize superior achievement in the field of horror fiction.

WHC and the HWA are two completely separate entities, run by two completely separate organizations. Every year, sometime between the first week of February and the first week of May, professionals in our field attend WHC—the trade show for horror writers—wherever it is held. They also usually attend the annual Bram Stoker Awards banquet, which used to be held in New York City or Los Angeles, and usually in June. But at some point in the 00's, a decision was made to hold the Bram Stoker Awards banquet at the World Horror Convention. In my opinion, this was a mistake. If the purpose of the Stoker Awards is to recognize superior achievement in our field, and promote that superior achievement to the fans and the general public, then it should stand as its own entity, rather than being saddled to a trade show that we have already established (in the previous column) is decidedly NOT a fan convention. Joining the two events together only serves to dilute both brands.

And yet, that tradition has continued sporadically over the years. Various WHCs have hosted various HWA Stoker Award banquets. As a result, fans and the general public have now irre-vocably confused the two. Rarely a month goes by where I don't overhear a reader confusing them. Readers think the HWA gives out the Grandmaster Award. They think WHC gives out the Stoker

Awards. They see three letter abbreviations, both with an "H" in them, and think they are one and the same. Now, understand, this is not the reader's fault. Fans just want to read horror novels—they don't want to know about all the minutiae going on behind the scenes in the industry. When my toilet breaks, I call a plumber. I don't know which pipefitters union he belongs to. I just want him to fix the fucking commode.

As I said, from where I sit, hosting the HWA's Stoker Banquet at WHC is not good for brand recognition, and I think it does a disservice to both organizations. It also seems to invalidate the World Horror Society's stated Rules of Conduct for convention organizers bidding on the right to hold a WHC. They state, quote, "WHC should be held no earlier than the last weekend in February and no later than the first weekend in May. The reason for this interval is to avoid conflicts with the World Fantasy Convention, usually held around Halloween Weekend, and the HWA Business Meeting & Bram Stoker Awards, usually held around the beginning of June, both of which involve professionals from the horror field." End quote.

This year, the HWA did not hold the Bram Stoker Awards banquet in conjunction with WHC. That's a good thing, right? Well, yes and no. It's good that they are back to being two separate identities. WHC was in Provo. The Stokers were in Las Vegas. The problem is, the Stoker Awards took place May 12th—just two weeks after WHC. Now, I've been told by multiple HWA members that former President Rocky Wood, before his death, requested that the Stokers be held in June, like they usually are, so as not to compete with WHC. I haven't verified if this is true or not, because experience has taught me that I can spend a week verifying things and sorting facts from allegations, and after all that work, random halfwits on the Internet will ignore my findings anyway, so fuck that noise. I have better ways to spend my time.

I don't know if that gossip is true or not, but I have no problem believing it might be true, because Rocky Wood was a good man, who genuinely cared about WHC and cared about this industry. Even when he and I butted heads, I always appreciated and respected his love of this genre. So, I don't know. Maybe he expressed that desire. Maybe he didn't. Whatever the case, this year, WHC went up against the Stoker Awards, and professionals in this field had three choices:

Option A: Attend WHC in Provo.

Option B: Attend the Stokers in Las Vegas.

Option C: Find a source of income other than writing and have the money to attend both.

When we arrived at the hotel, it was clear to me that Option B was the clear winner. Yes, it was late. But lateness has never mattered at a World Horror Convention. In almost twenty years I have never walked into a World Horror Convention and not found the hotel bar packed. But it wasn't packed. It was deserted. So were the lobby and the hallways. Indeed, had it not been for the fact that the hotel had a room reservation in my name, I would have suspected I was in the wrong place.

The only two people from our tribe that I saw were Kelly Laymon (daughter of Richard Laymon) and a young man I didn't know, but recognized immediately as one of us. He was about the same age as my oldest son. Kelly introduced him as Wile E. Young. She made a point of telling me—before she went off to bed—that this was his first WHC, and that he was a big fan of mine, and that he had read *The Rising* in high school, and he wanted to be a horror writer, and that was my fault.

END OF THE ROAD ⬅

Remember how we talked in last week's column about the concept of Eternal Return? Well, suddenly it was 1999 again, and I was at my first WHC, meeting Kelly and her parents for the first time, and telling her father that I had read *The Cellar* in high school and that I wanted to be a horror writer. And Richard Laymon made me feel welcome and offered encouragement and advice and mostly let me know that there were other people like me. So did Jack Ketchum. And Ray Garton. And John Pelan. And Edward Lee. And F. Paul Wilson. And John Skipp. And dozens more over the years. And so, even though it was late, and I was tired, and I still wanted to grab a drink and go to sleep, I chose instead to stay up and talk to Wile E. Young and did all the things my mentors did for me at various World Horror Conventions over the years.

And I'm glad I did, because it was delightful.

Yes, the Stoker Awards definitely impacted WHC's attendance this year. It was the lowest attended World Horror Convention I've ever been to. But what it lacked in people, it made up for in intimacy. And look—I'm not bashing the HWA here. They absolutely have a right to hold their event wherever and whenever they want to. All I'm saying is that, from the perspective of a new, aspiring horror writer, you'd be hard pressed to get the kind of access that was available at this year's WHC.

As I said in last week's column, it used to be that when you attended WHC, you were among friends. You were among family. I had wondered if that would still hold true.

Brian, Stephen Kozeniewski, and Jack Ketchum. (Photo copyright Bryan Killian 2016)

Well, it does. I saw old friends—Jack Ketchum, Linda Addison, Michael Arnzen, Jeff Strand, Kevin J. Anderson, Michael Bailey, Bailey Hunter, and more. I made new friends—Dave Butler of Wordfire Press, Dale and Natalie Johnson from Cross Genre Books (who helped me fill some holes in my Arkham House and Gnome Press collections), Josh Hutton of Ammodillo Munitions, and others.

I also saw acquaintances, such as editor Jason Brock, who said he wanted me to know that all the terrible things he'd said about me a week earlier on Facebook were just that—terrible things said on Facebook, and that we should be cool, regardless. And I agreed with this because what else was I gonna do? Punch the guy, stomp his head in, and ruin WHC for everybody, including myself? Not even I am *that* much of an asshole.

I stepped outside of myself during my interactions. I watched Jack Ketchum and I talking alone together in a quiet hotel room. I watched Jeff Strand and I giggling over what he was going to say about me two weeks later when he emceed the Stoker Awards. I watched myself watching Michael Arnzen and Kevin J. Anderson, and marveling over the mentors they've become to others.

Wile E. Young and Richard Wolley, happy to join the family. (Photo copyright Brian Keene 2016)

But mostly, I watched the convention through the eyes of the newbies. I watched it through the eyes of Bryan Killian and Stephen Kozeniewski, two authors who are just now beginning to discover that they're not really newbies anymore, and they can do this shit, and aren't quite sure whether to believe it or not yet. I watched it through the eyes of Rachel Autumn Deering, a Harvey Award and Eisner Award nominated comic book writer who has fled that section of the industry for the safe harbors of horror literature, and has found acceptance and a much healthier scene. I watched it through the eyes of Amber Fallon, and Sara Tantlinger, and Wile E. Young, and Richard Wolley, and dozens of others who have just started down this path, who have just taken their first tentative steps. They are tinder and kindling, and all they needed was a spark. All they needed was a small flame of encouragement and acceptance, so that they begin to blaze.

Blaze, kids. Blaze. Set the world—and the genre—on fire. Light it up with your own unique glow.

I told you this nine-month series of columns would look at the genre twenty years ago, and look at it now, and examine the changes. Here is what I learned about the World Horror Convention. Twenty years later, most of the faces have changed. Most of the panel topics have changed. Most of the exhibitors have changed. But its purpose—and more importantly its spirit—remains absolutely the same. It is just as vital and needed and required now as it ever has been. It provides something that no amount of interaction on Facebook or Twitter can ever provide. It is my sincere hope that it will still be doing so another twenty years from now.

It is 7 p.m. on a Thursday night as I write this. The column is due tomorrow. Next week, I head back out on the road again. I don't know what I'll find out there, and that has me afraid. But for right now, for just this minute, I am enjoying the fire inside of me—a fire that others started, and a fire which I, and other authors of my generation, have in turn helped to spread to those coming up behind us.

A fire that, almost twenty years later, is becoming an inferno.

Eternal Return indeed.

Speaking of Eternal Return, and seeing old friends, and mentors, and the spirit of the World Horror Convention, I also ran into Richard Laymon at WHC.

This was a surprise because he's been dead since 2001.

More on that reunion next week...

CHAPTER SIX

OLD FRIENDS AND OTHER REVENANTS

In an earlier installment of this column, we talked about the early days of the Internet. I'm taking you back now to the year 1998. There were exactly four websites dedicated to horror fiction—*Horrornet* (run by Matt Schwartz), *Masters of Terror* (run by Andy Fairclough), *Gothic Net* (run by Darren McKeeman), and *Chiaroscuro* (run by Brett Savory). Think about that. Four websites devoted to horror fiction. By contrast, nearly twenty years later, Google horror fiction and see how many websites you get. But back in the olden days, we had four.

Richard Laymon used to hang out on *Horrornet* and *Masters of Terror*. You could find him in the chat room of the former, and he had his own primitive message board on the latter. Now understand, this wasn't some half-wit hack or some brash newbie just starting out. This was Richard fucking Laymon, the fourth head on the Mount Rushmore of Modern Horror, the guy that some would argue was outselling his friends Dean Koontz and Stephen King in the United Kingdom and Australia, one of the titans of what had yet to be branded as Extreme

Horror—and almost every single day he would take the time to inter-act with fans and newbie authors on both websites, answering reader questions and offering advice to budding writers.

Richard Laymon and Brian Keene in 2000.
(Photo copyright Ann Laymon 2000)

These days, we take that sort of interaction for granted. If you enjoy an author's work, you can probably tell them via Twitter, Facebook, Instagram, or a host of other social media outlets. But in 1998 we didn't have those things. What we did have, though, was Richard Laymon.

As I wrote for *Ginger Nuts of Horror* last year, Dick Laymon was a mentor and cheerleader and scoutmaster for so many of us working in the field now. When we were all just starting out, we could always rely on him for advice, encouragement, laughs, and even a gentle ass-kicking when we needed it. Even writers who didn't care for his work (preferring their horror quieter or their prose more literary) looked to him as sort of a guidepost as what to do and what not to do in this industry.

His autobiography, *A Writer's Tale*, is the seminal bible for an entire generation of writers—as essential and mandatory as Stephen King's *On Writing* and David Morrell's *Lessons From A Lifetime of Writing*. Stylistically, you see echoes of his influence in the works of writers like Bryan Smith, Steve Gerlach, J.F. Gonzalez, Monica J. O'Rourke, Brett McBean, Jonathan Maberry, and so many others, including myself.

What doesn't get acknowledged as much is his influence as a human being. Yes, his books were filled with depravities and atrocities, but the man himself was humble and good-humored and a monument to what it means to be a husband, a father, and a friend. As I said on my podcast a few weeks ago, there have been times in my life where I have regretfully failed to follow that example (a sentiment that my co-host that week, Geoff Cooper, agreed with for himself), but it's something to aspire to. With Dick, there was always another book or story to move on to and write, and with life, there always another chance to move on to and get it right.

No, we didn't have social media, but we had Richard Laymon.

Until Valentine's Day 2001, and then we didn't have him anymore.

I still remember getting that phone call. I was living in Maryland at the time, and had just come home from a lovely dinner with my then-wife (ex-wife now, but she still remains one of my best friends). This was before cell phones had become so prominent, as well. We weren't in the door a minute and we got the call that he had passed away—which pretty much ruined the rest of that Valentine's Day. And that's the reason why I'm not crazy about celebrating the holiday anymore.

I told you in the very first column that much of this tour is spinning out of my reaction to the deaths of J.F. Gonzalez and Tom Piccirilli. They're not the only friends I've lost in this business, but their deaths hit the hardest. The one thing that brought me a bit of peace in their cases was that I got a chance to tell them both what they meant to me. They knew for sure. But I never got that chance with Dick Laymon.

Until the last night of this year's WHC.

I shared a room with Rachel Autumn Deering and her wife, Jessica Deering. On Saturday night, we had a party in our room. Just a small gathering. In addition to the three of us there was (in no particular order) Jeff Strand, Michael Bailey, Jack Ketchum, Linda Addison, Bryan Killian, Michael Arnzen, Stephen Kozeniewski, Kelly Laymon, Wile E. Young, Richard Wolley, Sara Tantlinger, our friend "Jenny" (who wouldn't want her real name used here), and probably some other people I'm forgetting (and my apologies to them—I may have a brain disease brought about by bourbon and too much fun which makes me forget things from time to time).

Richard Laymon and Brian Keene (with Kelly Laymon) in 2016. (Photo copyright Michael Bailey 2016)

It was a delightful evening, hanging out with old friends and new friends alike. At some point during the evening, Kelly Laymon leans over to me and asks, "Would you like to go say hi to Dad?"

I glanced around the room, eyes hurriedly scanning the corners, half-expecting Dick Laymon's ghost to appear, tequila in hand, with that big old grin he often had in such gatherings. When this didn't happen, I turned to Kelly in confusion and asked her to clarify for me. Well, it turns out that Kelly was in the process of moving across the country. Wisely not wanting to entrust her father's ashes to the TSA or UPS or a moving company, she had packed Dick Laymon into the car with the rest of her belongings.

A few minutes later, Kelly, myself, Michael Bailey, and Jeff Strand stumbled out to the hotel parking garage... well, Kelly, Michael, and myself stumbled. Jeff didn't stumble because he'd been nursing a bottle of spring water all night. I often secretly suspect that Jeff Strand might be the smartest and most responsible of all our generation of horror writers, but please don't tell him I said that.

But I digress.

We got to Kelly's car, packed tight with all the stuff from her move. She rummaged around inside, moving boxes of books and other items, and then produced a lovely box with her dad's ashes inside. She handed it to me, and I took it in my hands and stared down at it, and—to paraphrase the lyrics from Lera Lynn's "My Least Favorite Life"—the blue pulled away from the sky and the station pulled away from the train. I felt time stop and fold back in on itself, collapsing and folding over and over again, until it was that proverbial flat circle we talked about in previous columns.

It was 1980 and I was riding my bike to the newsstand, where I would buy some comic books and a paperback called *The Cellar* by Richard Laymon.

It was 1991 and I was working a dead-end job in a foundry, and reading *The Stake* by Richard Laymon on my lunch break, and fantasizing about being a writer.

It was 1998 and I was meeting Dick Laymon for the first time online.

It was 1999 and I was meeting him in person, so star-struck that that I was rendered incoherent.

It was 2000 and he got me in as a plus one to the Bram Stoker Awards banquet and introduced me to his editor, Don D'Auria, and wrote an introduction for my first book, and blurbed another based on a partial manuscript, and then he and Edward Lee were polishing off my tequila and leaving hilariously obscene signatures in all of my copies of their books.

It was 2001 and he was dead.

And it was 2016 and here he was again.

Some of J.F. Gonzalez's ashes got spread at sea in California. Some of them reside at his home. And some of them are placed inside a wall in The York Emporium, one of his favorite bookstores. Any time I want to talk to Jesus, I just go to the store and do so. And then customers walk by and whisper, "Hey, isn't that Brian Keene talking to the wall over there? That's a shame. He used to not be insane."

I didn't speak to Dick Laymon out loud. At least, I don't remember doing so. I said some things inside my head, though. Then I handed him back to Kelly, and Michael and Jeff each took their respective turns. I also snapped a picture of the box and texted it to Geoff Cooper, Mike Oliveri, and Michael T. Huyck, and told them that Dick said hi.

He would have thought that was funny.

I said in the first of these columns that this tour was about saying goodbye.

But in this case, it was about saying hello again, too.

This weekend, June 10th-12th, I'm signing in Pennsylvania and Ohio. Friday night I'm doing a Meet and Greet at 7 p.m. (along with Mary SanGiovanni, Stephen Kozeniewski, and dozens more authors) at Bradley's Books in the DuBois Mall in DuBois, PA. Then, Saturday, we'll be signing books at that same location all day long. If you're near that area, come say hello and get a book signed.

On Sunday, I'm going to try an experiment—a pop-up signing somewhere near Youngstown, Ohio. I can't tell you where because I don't know where yet. I'm going to find a nice spot, put the location out there via Twitter and Facebook, and then wait for people to show up. It will either be really neat or it will fail miserably.

Either way, next week, I'll report back what happens.

CHAPTER SEVEN

SCENES FROM A MALL AND A PARKING LOT

The authors with the staff of Bradley's Book Outlet. (Photo copyright 2016 Vicki Haid)

In the song "Hello" (off Ice Cube's album *War and Peace Vol. 2*) Dr. Dre raps, "We came a long way from not giving a fuck, selling tapes out of a trunk to moving this far up."

The first book signing tour I ever did was for *4X4*—a book I co-wrote with authors Geoff Cooper, Mike Oliveri, and Michael T. Huyck. It was published in hardcover and paperback, is long out of print, and goes for quite a bit of money on the secondary market these days. The *4X4* tour consisted of two bookstore appearances—Dark Delicacies in Burbank and Borderlands Books in San Francisco—as well as an appearance and interview on local cable television. The four of us flew to San Francisco, were joined by artist Gak and author Gene O'Neill, and then drove to the other signing in Los Angeles.

At a rest stop along the way, I managed to sell passersby copies of the book out of the back of our rental car.

That was in 2001.

Last Friday and Saturday, I took part in the first Rural Pennsylvania Authors Expo, which was held inside a shopping mall in DuBois. It was organized by Vicki Haid, the manager of Bradley's Book Outlet. Other authors who participated included Mary SanGiovanni, Stephen Kozeniewski, Megan Hart, Sara Humphreys, Rob E. Boley, Krissie Gasbarre, Diana Farley, Jason Pokopec, and many more.

Here's a little secret for you beginning authors: Do you know who the most important person in your career is?

It's not your editor. As Warren Ellis once said, editors are like appendixes. Ignore them until they bother you and then remove them with knives.

It's not your publisher. Sooner or later, publishers are just another ex in your long string of soured relationships.

It's not reviewers. In 2016, thanks to the internet, every halfwit with a keyboard can call themselves a book reviewer and there is zero quality control or room for critical insight.

It's not even your readers. Oh, readers are important, sure, but they're not the *most* important person.

Nope. That role is reserved for booksellers and librarians. A good relationship with booksellers and librarians can make your career. A bad relationship with them can end it. They are your advocates. They are the people BUYING your book. They are the people SELLING it to readers. And when you find an exceptional, passionate, enthusiastic bookseller or librarian, hold on to that person for life.

Vicki Haid is such a bookseller, and she organized a phenomenal event. I don't know that I've ever attended a first-year event like this one that was so well organized, or where the authors were made to feel so vital and welcome. She did an outstanding, commendable job, and I will do whatever I can to attend and support her future events. I'll support her because she supports authors. If the other managers in the Bradley's Book Outlet chain are even half as creative and enthusiastic as she is, then that's a chain I want to do more business with.

That being said, I'm still not sure how the townspeople of DuBois itself feel about writers. The hotel staff were very excited to have us there, and Vicki's employees and the staff of the mall's other stores were all delighted and enthusiastic, but many of the mall's patrons seemed unsure of what a book was, let alone inclined to purchase one. Now, not all of them, of course. I want to stress that before some pinhead links to this column and says something like, "Brian Keene says everyone in DuBois is illiterate! See? I told you he was an asshole!" I'm not saying that at all. But I am saying that I noticed we sold more books to people from out of town than we did to people for whom going to that particular shopping mall is a regular Saturday occurrence.

The easiest way for me to illustrate my point is to simply reproduce the notes I made during the signing.

Friday night, we had a Meet and Greet. Megan had a fan show up. Sara had a fan show up. And I had a fan show up. I can't speak for Megan and Sara's fans, but mine was Ron Davis, a guy who has been reading my books for years, and whom I know through previous interactions. He's never had a chance to meet me or have his books signed, because I've never done an appearance near his home before. DuBois, it should be noted, is not Ron's home. He drove approximately two hours to meet me and get his books signed. We took care of that and I spent a few hours chatting with him, and made sure he had an awesome experience, because as I told you in our very first column, THAT'S WHAT THIS TOUR IS ABOUT. So, it doesn't matter to me if it was just Ron, or if there were fifty people. The only thing that matters to me is that Ron and I got to spend some time together—because we may not ever get a chance to do so again.

So, we came back to the mall on Saturday to sign books. Mary, Stephen, and I were at a table which had been placed directly in front of the kiddie rides. You know those things in the middle of every shopping mall in America—coin-operated cars with characters like Elmo and Spider-Man that kids can ride on? The one behind us was the Flintstones, and every five minutes it played the Flintstones theme song, regardless of whether or not a child was riding it.

Here are those notes I mentioned. Let us see what we can determine from them.

11:00 a.m. – "Flintstones, meet the Flintstones…"

11:15 a.m. – A DuBois resident looks at every book that Mary, Stephen, and myself have on the table. She tells us that she doesn't like horror but she loves vampires. I try to sell her a copy of *Seize the Night*, an anthology of vampire fiction edited by Christopher Golden and containing a story by me. I explain that it was the editor's intent to give vampires back their teeth, and make them scary again. She informs me that she only likes vampires that glitter. She also informs me that vampires should never be scary. She passes on the book.

11:20 a.m. – "Flintstones, meet the Flintstones…"

11:23 a.m. – An elderly woman approaches the table, clasps Mary's hand, and says, with no introduction or preamble, quote: "When I was a girl, I was told that Jesus gives you babies, so I didn't know it was through intercourse, and nobody told us about condoms. I have eighteen grandchildren. Did I ever tell you this before?" End quote. Mary assures the woman that she has not, in fact, ever told her this before, as this is their first meeting. The woman nods, and thanks Mary, and wanders away. Mary, being a much nicer person than I am, doesn't try to sell her a book.

11:30 a.m. – "Flintstones, meet the Flintstones…"

11:35 a.m. – "Flintstones, meet the Flintstones…"

11:40 a.m. – "Flintstones, meet the Flintstones…"

11:45 a.m. – "Flintstones, meet the Flintstones…"

11:50 a.m. – "Flintstones, meet the Flintstones…"

Noon – Rob E. Boley stops by our table to tell us about an elderly woman who told him that Jesus is apparently a stork, flying around and giving babies at random to people. Mary and Rob trade books, as they've been wanting to read each other. Rob heads back to his table.

12:15 p.m. – "Flintstones, meet the Flintstones…"

12:20 p.m. – "Flintstones, meet the motherfucking Flintstones…"

12:23 p.m. – A young man stops by and asks Mary what we are doing. She explains that we are authors and we are signing books. He then picks up a copy of her novel *The Triumvirate* and asks her if it is a book. He then does the same with the rest of her books. I am not exaggerating. "Is this a book? Is this a book? And how about this one? Is this a book?" Mary, who again, is much nicer than me, patiently fields these questions. Then, when the guy has exhausted all possible queries, he turns toward me. I put my cell phone to my ear, and pretend to suddenly have a call, at which point the young man zeroes in on Stephen Kozeniewski instead. He picks up a copy of Stephen's *The Ghoul Archipelago* and asks, "Is this a book?" I get up from the table, still pretending to be on the phone. As I'm walking away, I hear Stephen trying to convince the young man that it is, in fact, not a book, but some cleverly disguised magic beans.

12:42 p.m. – The young man has wandered off, heading toward Megan Hart. I make my way back to the table and listen to the dulcet tones of The Flintstones theme.

12:45 p.m. – "Fucking Flintstones, meet the goddamn, shit-eating, motherfucking Flintstones..."

12:46 p.m. – I unplug the Flintstones ride.

12:50 p.m. – A lost child approaches the table and tells Mary that she came to the mall with her cousins, but the police said her cousins aren't allowed in the mall, so they left and she doesn't know how to get home. Mary finds a security guard for her. The security guard's name is Scotty and he has the most epic mullet I have ever seen. Seriously. I am still in awe of it, seven days later. Scotty assists the little girl.

1:00 p.m. – A woman named Kim asks me to sign her books. I am delighted to do so, because I haven't yet had a chance to sign anything today. I ask Kim where she's from. She tells me she is from Bermuda. I'm not talking about a town named Bermuda. I'm talking about the fucking island. She has a sister who lives in the next town over, and she saw I was going to be signing in DuBois, so she flew eight hundred miles from Bermuda to Pennsylvania to visit her sister and meet me. I am so delighted by this that I don't even care about The Flintstones. Kim has made my day, and—much like Ron the night before—I hope that I have made her day, as well.

1:15 p.m. – I sadly say goodbye to Kim, who has to leave.

1:16 p.m. – A local man approaches the table. I greet him and offer to sign a book. He scowls, declines my offer of a signed book, and informs me that he is the custodian and he wants to know who unplugged The Flintstones ride. The only time it is supposed to be unplugged is if it is OUT OF SERVICE.

1:20 p.m. – "Flintstones, meet the Flintstones…"

1:25 p.m. – A local woman whose name I never caught, buys a copy of *Terminal* and has me sign it.

1:30 p.m. – If you guessed Flintstones, you guessed correctly.

1:32 p.m. – A passerby asks Stephen for directions to the restroom.

1:40 p.m. – I borrow a piece of paper and a magic marker, make an OUT OF SERVICE sign, hang it on Fred fucking Flintstone's fat fucking face, and unplug the ride again.

3:07 p.m. – Kenny arrives. He and his partner have driven all the way from Michigan. I want to hug them both. Kenny has brought the original painting for the Deadite Press cover of *A Gathering of Crows*. Kenny has brought along a copy of every single book I have ever written. I sign everything he brought into the mall, and then I accompany them out to their car to sign the rest.

3:30 p.m. – Mary and Stephen both text me to make sure Kenny hasn't bonked me over the head and stuffed me in his trunk. I assure them that he is fine, and we are happy, because we are. Again, as I told you in our very first column, THAT'S WHAT THIS TOUR IS ABOUT. It's about Ron and Kim from Bermuda and now Kenny. We spend some time together—because we may not ever get a chance to do so again.

4:15 p.m. – On my way back to the table, I pass the elderly lady, who is telling Scotty the Security Guard and the lost child all about how Jesus magically gives you babies.

4:32 p.m. – On my way to the restroom, I pass by Rob and see a local picking a book up off his table. I overhear the local ask Rob if it is a DVD.

4:47 p.m. – We give some books to Vicki's staff, because they are awesome.

5:00 p.m. – Megan, Rob, Jason, Stephen, Mary, and myself do a horror panel. The ratio of attendees to panelists is exactly even. The panel lasts ninety minutes, and is a lot of fun.

6:30 p.m. – I sign books for Aaron. Aaron and his wife were at the grocery store in Rochester, New York, when he happened to see a Tweet about the signing in DuBois. They left the grocery store and DROVE FIVE HOURS to get their books signed. I spend a half hour with them.

7:00 p.m. – The signing is over. I pack up my books and sign the store's stock. On my way out, I plug the Flintstones ride back in and remove the sign. I am incredibly grateful to Vicki and her staff for being so generous and kind, and equally grateful to Ron, Kim, Kenny, and Aaron, all of whom came from out of town, and to the local lady who also bought a book. As I explain to Mary and Stephen over dinner at Ponderosa Steak House, readers like Ron, Kim, Kenny, and Aaron, and booksellers like Vicki are why I'm doing this for the next nine months.

9:00 p.m. – Stephen and I meet up with Kenny and his partner, and share some bourbon and some laughs.

11:00 p.m. – I fall asleep happy, but dream about Fred Flintstone giving babies to old people.

On Sunday, I tried something new—a "pop-up" signing. I got the idea from Kanye West. I am fascinated by Kanye West because he is, in my opinion, the biggest douchebag working in entertainment today, and I find him a source of endless amusement. I was intrigued by how he could Tweet that he'd be appearing at a certain location in two hours, and two hundred people would show up. I decided to try something similar. I reasoned that if Kanye West could get two hundred people to show up at a surprise appearance, then I could get three or four people.

Some of the participants in the Youngstown Experiment. (Photo copyright Brian Keene 2016)

Another happy Youngstown fan. (Photo copyright Brian Keene 2016)

I spread the word via Twitter and Facebook that I'd be signing in the parking lot of a Quaker State and Lube in Youngstown, Ohio, at noon. Mary, Stephen, and I woke up and made the drive from DuBois to Youngstown. We arrived right at noon. Kenny and his partner pulled in behind us, which gave us all a good laugh. For a few minutes, I thought it might just be us, and that my experiment had failed. But then Travis arrived. Travis is another long-time reader whom I've chatted with online for years. And then Jason arrived, along with his daughter. I signed all of Jason and Travis's books, and spent some time with them, and took some pictures. Jason had to leave. I invited the others to lunch. While we were inside the restaurant, two more readers showed up, so I went outside and spent some time with them, and sold them some books out of the trunk of my car. And then, as they were leaving, another guy showed up and I did the same for him.

The theory of Eternal Return tells us that time is a flat circle, that events will occur and recur endlessly throughout the different realities.

In 2001, I am selling books out of the trunk of a car, and am grateful and indebted to every single good bookseller and fan I meet.

In 2016, I am selling books out of the trunk of a car, and am grateful and indebted to every single good bookseller and fan I meet.

I've come a long way from not giving a fuck, selling books out of a trunk to moving this far up—but in a way, it's not that far at all.

CHAPTER EIGHT

INTO THE BREACH

The day before I left for California, my eight-year-old son and I spent the afternoon in the woods. After hours of swimming in the creek, avoiding snakes, catching turtles and frogs and then letting them go, and pretending we were in a "real-life" game of *Minecraft*, we sat down on a big rock. Both of us got quiet for a moment.

Then I asked, "So, do you want to talk about me leaving tomorrow? I haven't done a tour like this since you were born. Is there anything you are wondering about? Are you worried or scared or feeling sad?"

He thought about it for a moment and then said, "Well, Dad, I'm worried you'll get lost."

I suppressed a smile because I didn't want him to think I wasn't taking his concerns seriously. After I explained to him that the airplane pilots knew where they were going, and that Jamie LaChance, Kasey Lansdale, and Tod Clark (all of whom will be driving portions of this leg of the tour) also knew where to go, he seemed better with it. Fears put to rest, he then asked me to bring him back Freddy Krueger and Jason action figures.

The next day, I told him goodbye. He took it well. Gave me a big hug. Playfully punched me in the belly. Gave me another big hug. Didn't cry.

On the way to the airport, I cried enough for both of us.

Things I always travel with:

Toshiba Laptop Computer.

Sony Digital Voice Recorder so I can dictate things while driving.

Three Blue Yeti Microphones so I can record a podcast interview if an opportunity presents itself.

Four Moleskine Notebooks in case I want to jot something down when not driving.

Kindle Paperwhite.

Chargers for all of the above.

Assorted pens and markers.

Pictures of both my oldest son, my youngest son and his mother, my girlfriend, and my cat.

Nobody carries photos with them anymore. Instead, we keep pictures on our phones. But I always bring these pics with me.

I miss them all already.

I always fly out of Harrisburg International Airport, which is right next to the Three Mile Island nuclear power plant. Those cooling towers loom over Central Pennsylvania like Lovecraftian monoliths, reminding all of us locals just how fucking close we came to dying many years ago.

They are always the last thing I see upon flying out.

While waiting to board the plane, I meet an opera singer and his wife. They are in their seventies, and on their way to Kansas City for vacation. I was unaware that people went to Kansas City for vacation, but whatever.

I'm not really in the mood to talk to strangers. I'm already missing my kid terribly, and I can still feel the psychic shadow of those cooling towers falling over me, and I'm pondering what it means. I've got *Mayan Blue* by Michelle Garza and Melissa Lason on my Kindle, and I'd really like to read it, but find doing so is impossible because the opera singer wants to talk.

"Where are you going?" he asks.

"Los Angeles," I reply.

"Oh, on business?"

I nod an affirmative.

"What line of work are you in?" he asks.

"I'm a writer," I admit.

Our plane is late, and he spends the time telling me all about the book he wants to write and maybe I can write it for him and we'll split the money, and how does that work anyway, and do I know Stephen King, and why are his movies never as good as the books?

We board the plane and as luck would have it, the opera singer and his wife are one row behind me and across the aisle.

I get no reading done.

One-hour layover in Detroit while I change planes. The opera singer and his wife are gone. I break out my Kindle and finally start reading *Mayan Blue*. It's off to a good start. Once again, I am blown away by the number of fantastic new horror writers that I've become aware of this year. 2016 has been a shit year for the entertainment industry, but it's been spectacular for horror fiction.

I sit in first class for this section of the trip. I like first class. Can't always afford it, but when I do, I enjoy it. One of the things I like about it is that usually, the people in first class aren't there to fuck around. They are serious business people and not prone to idle conversation. You can get work done in first class. I've never been able to write on airplanes, but I do use the time to get caught up on my reading.

Except, I get the one exception to the first class rule. I get a lady who wants to chat.

"On your way to Los Angeles, too?" she asks.

It seems like an odd question, since if I was on my way to Kansas City, I'd be sitting on a different plane with the opera singer—but I confirm that yes, I'm going to Los Angeles.

"Oh, on business?"

I nod an affirmative.

"What line of work are you in?" she asks.

I decide to lie. "I'm a political pundit for all three cable television news stations."

She leaves me alone for the rest of the flight, and I get to finish *Mayan Blue* and start Laird Barron's *Man with No Name*. I enjoy them both.

Eventually, I land in California.

Los Angeles is a weird mutant bastard of a city. It is both wonderful and terrible, but I am glad to be back in it.

On the way to the hotel, the heat blasts the cab. The driver apologizes for his faulty air conditioning. The windows are down, and the wind blowing through them feels like I'm standing in front of a hair dryer—warm and electric. We stop in traffic. A car next to us is playing Alice in Chains.

"So, I found myself in the sun, oh yeah. Hell of a place to end a run, oh yeah. California…somebody check my brain…."

Despite the heat, I shiver.

I think about dead friends, and I rummage in my bag, and pull out the pictures, and glance at them one by one. Then I put them back in the bag and look out at California flashing by, just in case I don't get to see it again.

CHAPTER NINE

AN ABUNDANCE OF BOURBON, OR, "WHISKEY RIVER TAKE ME HOME"

On Wednesday morning, I woke up in Los Angeles, forgetting that I was still on East Coast time. I stumbled outside in search of coffee and couldn't understand why it was still dark. Then I fumbled for my phone and glanced at the time and saw that it was only four in the morning. The only people awake were the homeless—and they weren't nocturnal by choice. They were just out to beat the heat.

Los Angeles is a city that runs on automobiles. Seriously. You can't get anywhere in Los Angeles without a car, and in truth, because of gridlock, you can't get anywhere with a car, either. I'm told that the city offers public transit, but much like Bigfoot, Chupacabra, and Dean Koontz novels that don't feature a dog, I have never seen it. There are reports of subways and trains and buses, but they remain mythical at best. One of the city's newest skyscrapers downtown is offering a giant slide, but that doesn't seem very practical—especially if one has simply ventured outside to retrieve a cup of coffee. Rocketing six stories down a giant slide while holding a scalding hot beverage doesn't sound like a good time to me. The slide itself doesn't seem like a very good idea, either. I mean, what's wrong with elevators and good old-fashioned stairwells? Is the slide supposed to appeal to the same infantile adults playing with toys at age thirty and still clinging to the desperate hope that Marvel and DC Comics stories still somehow "matter" rather than being nothing more than churn for the corporate intellectual property farms?

It occurred to me that DC Comics had moved to Burbank. I could have paid a visit and asked co-publisher Dan DiDio, except that I didn't have a car, and public transit was missing in action, and also because—according to friends of mine still at DC Comics—Dan doesn't want to talk to me because a) I have a bad habit of expecting to be paid the same amount as other writers, and b) I refused to sit next to *Superman* editor Eddie Berganza when I attended the New York City premiere of *Man of Steel*. And who could blame me for that second thing, really? Let's conduct an experiment. Google "Eddie Berganza Sexual Assault" and tell me you'd want to sit next to the guy. Seriously. I'll still be here when you get back.

(Hold Music)

See? I'm perfectly content with my decision not to sit next to that guy in a darkened movie theater filled with comic book industry professionals.

Another reason I couldn't drop by the DC Comics offices was because it was four in the morning and I hadn't yet procured coffee. Resolving to fix that, I redoubled my efforts—hiking seven blocks before I finally found a convenience store that was open. Supposedly they served coffee, although it looked more like tepid brown swamp water and tasted like the inside of a baboon's stomach.

I bought four of them.

The cashier didn't have a carrier tray, so I had to hike the seven blocks back to my hotel performing a juggling act that impressed even the most laconic and taciturn of the homeless who watched my progression. Soon enough, I offered two of them two of my cups, thus freeing me to better carry my caffeine fix and also getting bonus karma points.

"Hey," one of the homeless shouted at me, "this tastes like the inside of a baboon's stomach!"

Brian and Del Howison of Dark Delicacies. (Photo copyright Brian Keene 2016)

I was back in my room by five in the morning, and I wrote until my first appointment—a breakfast meeting with a film distributor. Over the last two years, I've served as Executive Producer on a feature length film called *I'm Dreaming of a White Doomsday*. Written and directed by Mike Lombardo, it's a movie that should easily be seen in theaters, as well as pay-per-view and other on demand outlets. To make this happen, we need a film distributor. The folks I was meeting with bought me $40 waffles and coffee, and also ordered a round of bourbon for the table. When I questioned this, they said they were big fans of mine and of the horror genre, and they'd heard that I liked bourbon.

"Sure, I do," I replied, "but not at..." I glanced at my phone. "Eight o'clock in the goddamned morning."

"Relax," advised a smiling Millennial whose clothes cost more than the Jeep I'd reluctantly left back home. Then he asked if he could take a selfie with me.

Several more rounds of bourbon and coffee and selfies followed, and no business was being discussed. Finally, in no mood for nonsense, I pushed ahead with my pitch: "*I'm Dreaming of a White Doomsday* is a post-apocalyptic *The Babadook*."

Everyone blinked at me. Apparently, the Millennials who love the horror genre and distribute movies had never fucking heard of *The Babadook*, despite it being one of the most successful and talked about horror films in recent years. You remember this when you're sitting through yet another *Nightmare on Elm Street* reboot a few years from now.

I stumbled to a cab and back to my hotel, where the girl at the desk informed me that another film distributor had sent me a package while I was out. The package turned out to be a bottle of bourbon.

Hal Bodner and Brian. (Photo copyright Brian Keene 2016)

Around eleven, author Hal Bodner showed up. We sat in my hotel room and recorded an interview which will air on my podcast. I drank the bourbon, because there were only two bottles of water and Hal was drinking those.

Wednesday evening, actress, author, director, and screenwriter Laura Lee Bahr showed up, and we hung out for a while, and then went over to author John Skipp's house, where we ate wonderful artisan pizza and watched the sun go down from Skipp's rooftop, painting the sky with fire. Skipp produced a bottle of bourbon he'd bought for me. When it got dark, I recorded another podcast interview with Skipp and Laura. They drank beer. I drank the bourbon. We talked long into the night, and Laura and I didn't leave until the bourbon was gone.

Thursday morning, I did the coffee walk. This time, the homeless people avoided me, perhaps warned about the strange middle-aged man from Pennsylvania who was handing out fetid cups of swamp water the day before. Then I had an early lunch with some executives from a Hollywood production company who were interested in optioning my novel *The Complex*. We had steak and bourbon. After fifteen minutes, I'd divined—using an arcane and mystic process that twenty years in this business has ingrained in me—that these guys would never get *The Complex* made. I ordered more bourbon.

That afternoon, Jamie LaChance and I drove out to Orange County to visit with J.F. Gonzalez's parents. Jamie is an attorney and a long-time reader. He's also been my driver while I'm here in Los Angeles. He's been a good friend to me, and was a good friend to Jesus, as well. Jesus's parents seemed happy to see us, and in truth, I was happy to see them, as well. They've always been very kind to me, and visiting with them brought about some closure and connection that I didn't even know I needed. They insisted on buying Jamie and me lunch. I was very grateful the Mexican restaurant where we went to eat didn't serve bourbon.

On the way home—which is what Southern Californians call "sitting in traffic"—author David J. Schow called and summoned me to dinner in North Hollywood. Now, I was stuffed to the brim with steak and Mexican food and bourbon, but when David J. Schow asks you to do something, you fucking do it. I would drag my balls across six miles of broken glass for David Schow and John Skipp if they asked me to. Luckily for my testicles, David was simply asking us to meet him and his partner, "Speedy," for dinner. So, we did. It was a very nice Italian restaurant. I had lasagna and several glasses of bourbon.

On Friday, I had three business meetings. I was offered bourbon at all three. For lunch, I stopped at a food truck, desperate to get the taste of bourbon out of my mouth. I ordered three tacos. By two that afternoon, I realized that the tacos had been a very bad idea. I ended up skipping a birthday party for singer, songwriter, and editor Kasey Lansdale because I couldn't get more than five feet away from the toilet. Most of Kasey's friends are singers and actresses, and I was certain they wouldn't appreciate me shitting myself while trying to make small talk. I ended up finishing the bottle of bourbon the company had sent me, because I was too sick to leave the room and buy replacements for the bottled water Hal Bodner had drank.

John Skipp, Brian, and David J. Schow. (Photo copyright Brian Keene 2016)

On Saturday, I did a signing at Dark Delicacies in Burbank. Proprietors Del and Sue Howison have supported me for twenty years, and I am always honored to return that loyalty and support them, as well. My first ever book signing was at their store back in 2001. It felt good to be signing there again. Sales were excellent. There was a pretty sizeable crowd at the beginning of the signing. They winnowed down into the second hour—right around the time Hal Bodner arrived. Cause and effect?

I was thrilled that so many friends came out to show their support. Hal, Skipp, Schow, Speedy, Laura, Kasey, Jamie, my friends Paul and Shannon Legerski, author Cody Goodfellow, and Cartoon Network's Dick Grunert, just to name a few. Thanks to all of them, and all of the readers and fans who showed up, and made it such a success. The store sold out of their copies of *The Complex*, and *Pressure* was their best-selling hardcover for the week.

I should also mention that during the signing, I was given two bottles of bourbon by two different readers.

I am not making any of this up.

Jamie gave me a ride back to my hotel after the signing, where the front desk informed me that there was another package with my name on it. An actress friend, currently on location and sad that she wasn't in town, had sent me a bottle of bourbon.

Later, Schow called and suggested I blow the hotel and spend the night at his place instead. I did. We stayed up late, sitting out on his balcony and looking down upon the city of Los Angeles and discussing everything from movie remakes to Lost Tales of the Splatterpunks, and do you know what he offered me to drink?

Beer.

Not bourbon, but ice cold, refreshing beer.

There is a special place in Heaven for puppy dogs and baby ducks, and a spot right between them that is reserved for David J. Schow.

Before going to sleep, I repacked my bags. Kasey Lansdale and I were heading out for San Diego early the next morning, and I didn't want to make us late. I ended up having to borrow a canvas tote to pack all my bottles of bourbon in.

Kasey Lansdale and Brian at Dark Delicacies. (Photo copyright Brian Keene 2016)

CHAPTER TEN

A BRIEF WALKING TOUR
OF BURBANK'S HORROR ROW

Unbeknownst to most fans of the horror genre, there is a two-block stretch of Magnolia Boulevard in Burbank, California, that serves as "Horror Row." What follows is a brief walking tour for those wishing to experience it.

We start at 3512 West Magnolia Boulevard, the current address of Dark Delicacies. In business since 1994, Dark Delicacies—operated by Del and Sue Howison—sells horror novels, horror non-fiction, horror vinyl, horror movies, horror toys, and horror-themed clothing and accessories. It's a popular hang-out and social spot for Los Angeles-based horror professionals, many of whom a visitor might happen to spot browsing the shelves. Dark Delicacies hosts in-store signings with authors, actors, directors, and musicians on a weekly basis. Their book selection is unbeatable—used mass-market paperbacks, new trade paperbacks, signed limited edition hardcovers, and offerings from both the mainstream and the small press. They are also a *New York Times* bestseller list reporting store, meaning strong sales there can boost a horror novel's success. More importantly, Del and Sue make sure that every visitor to the store feels welcomed and special.

Sticking to that side of the street, we next come to the Museum of Mystical Wonders, located at 3204 West Magnolia Boulevard. The Museum of Mystical Wonders is an art gallery, museum, and gift shop for those with a macabre inclination. Among the items on display are historical artifacts from fortune-telling, spirit or Ouija boards, carnival sideshows, psychic phenomena, magic, and more. Well worth a look, but be warned—time does strange things in the museum. You'll wander the displays, peering and staring, and swear that you've only been there twenty minutes when in fact, an hour has passed you by.

Gary Oldman's full head cast from Dracula, on display inside Motion Picture F/X Company. (Photo copyright Brian Keene 2016)

Continuing down the street, we come to the Motion Picture F/X Company, a full service special makeup effects supply house located at 2920 West Magnolia Boulevard. Think of it as a general store for special effects companies, the aisles filled with silicones, stones, clays, resins, polyfoams, make-up, and more. Of interest to those not employed in the movie industry, however, are the props on display to the public, running the gamut from a bust of H.P. Lovecraft to actor Gary Oldman's full head cast from *Dracula*. Stop in to look at those, but be polite and buy some fake vampire blood while you're there. The staff are enthusiastic, welcoming, and friendly, and happy to talk shop.

Creature Features storefront. (Photo copyright Brian Keene 2016)

Our last stop on this side of the street is Creature Features, a two-thousand-plus square foot emporium with an impressive storefront located at 2904 West Magnolia Boulevard. Selling books, movies, a massive soundtrack collection, toys, and hosting the occasional signing, the store is, at first glance, similar to Dark Delicacies. However, the interior layout is more like a flea market, swap meet, or antique mall, and the merchandise firmly skews toward the more science-fiction end of horror than Dark Delicacies does. Based upon my initial visit, the store also lacks the personality and helpfulness of Dark Delicacies. During the twenty minutes I spent inside, the staff ignored me, even when (in my opinion) I made it very clear that I wanted to spend money. Not a "Hello" when I entered. Not a "Goodbye" when I left. But maybe that was just my experience. It's certainly worth a stop, especially since you're going to cross the street right outside their store.

There's a gas station on the corner if you need a bathroom break. No? You're good? Okay, take my hand and let's cross the road. Carefully, now. Remember what I said in the last column. Los Angeles is a city that runs on automobiles.

So, now we're on the opposite side of the street. The first thing we'll encounter is not one, but three Halloween Town stores. Halloween Town is like a year-long celebration of our favorite holiday, selling costumes, masks, wigs, props, and more. They even dabble in books and DVDs. Their presence on this side of the street cannot be ignored. They pretty much dominate the entire block. Their first store, located at 3013 West Magnolia Boulevard, sells costumes and accessories for children and pets. Their second location, at 3021 West Magnolia, focuses on costumes and accessories for adults. Their third location, at 2921 West Magnolia, features clothing, props, accessories, and the like. Definitely worth a look, though be advised—they do not allow photography of any kind. Keep your smart phone stowed and just enjoy the visuals.

Next up is Bearded Lady Vintage and Oddities, located at 3005 West Magnolia. This is the sister store to the Museum of Mystical Wonders, and it is absolutely worth the stop. The staff were friendly and gregarious, and eager to talk all things genre related. More impressively, they also made sure to mention some of the block's other horror attractions, which I thought was pretty classy. Bearded Lady cannot be easily described. It's part store, part museum, and all cool. They sell "vintage oddities and collectibles," which means you can find Ouija boards, mint condition comic books, dried tarantulas, pig's eyes floating in jars, t-shirts, a book on magic tricks, and various sorts of other strange ephemera all in one store. I'm told that the production staff for Marvel's *Agents of S.H.I.E.L.D.* and *Agent Carter* buy some of their props from the store, because it's cheaper than manufacturing them.

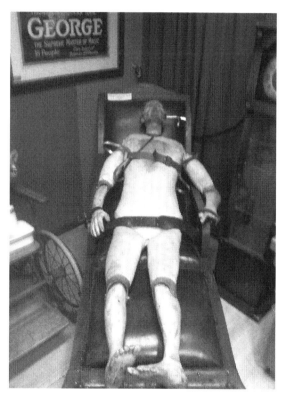

Inside Bearded Lady Vintage and Oddities. (Photo Copyright Brian Keene 2016)

Our final stop on the walking tour is Blast From the Past, located at 3117 West Magnolia Boulevard. Blast From the Past is a massive comic book store. Why am I including it on our walking tour?

Because a lot of their merchandise will appeal to fans of the genre. They have one of the biggest in-store selections of horror movie action figures and toys I have ever seen. When I left on this book signing tour, my eight-year-old had one request—bring him back a *Friday the 13th* action figure (no, I don't let him watch the movies, but to kids of his generation, Jason, Freddy, and the rest are akin to the Universal Monsters). I found him a Jason action figure at Blast From the Past. I also found action figures for *Scream, Halloween, A Nightmare on Elm Street, Alien, Predator,* and *Terminator* to go along with it. Blast From the Past also hosts a horror trivia night (which Dark Delicacies' Del Howison sometimes participates in). And the staff are friendly, helpful, and very aware of just what a cool place they work in.

That ends our walking tour of Burbank's horror row. I hope that you enjoyed it, and that it will prove useful when you plan a trip to Southern California. I'll see you back here for next week's column, in which Kasey Lansdale and I wreak havoc in a tea room.

CHAPTER ELEVEN

DRIVE ON

Early morning in Los Angeles, and after a week, I was still on East Coast time. As a result, while the rest of the household slept, I was sitting out on David J. Schow's balcony in the Hollywood Hills, looking down on the city, and drinking coffee. It was the first moment of reflective, quiet, alone time I'd had since leaving home, and I was enjoying it.

I watched the sun rise. I watched a coyote slink behind a neighbor's house far below. And I watched three big black crows alight on some electrical wires just beyond David's balcony. Squawking to each other, they looked out upon the world as if they owned it. And who knows? Maybe they did.

I sat there, quietly sipping coffee, watching three crows from the balcony of the man who co-wrote the screenplay to *The Crow*, and smiling at the universe's little joke.

Then, Kasey Lansdale swept in like the *Looney Tunes* Tasmanian Devil, and the spell was broken, and the coffee was finished, and we headed out to the next signing—at Mysterious Galaxy Bookstore in San Diego.

Kasey is, of course, the daughter of Joe R. Lansdale. I don't know what accounts for the talent in the Lansdale family. Maybe it's an atmosphere that fosters and incubates creativity and expression. Maybe it's something in the Nacogdoches water supply. Or maybe it's just really good genes. Whatever the case, the Lansdale clan has always struck me as a literary equivalent to the Carter Family of old. Joe's accomplishments need no recounting here, but he's not the only writer in the family. His wife, Karen, has written, edited, and was one of the original founders of the Horror Writers Association. His son, Keith, writes prose and comic books. Kasey has written prose and edited an anthology (*Impossible Monsters*). She also runs her own small press publishing company—Pandi Press. But perhaps more prominently, she is also a country music singer and songwriter. She's opened on tour for Wynonna Judd, worked in the studio with John Carter Cash, played a concert at Dodger Stadium, and traveled all over the United States and overseas, playing and singing.

And she busted her ass to get to that point.

Kasey has drive. The success she's had so far? She didn't get that overnight. She worked hard to achieve it. And that success pales in comparison to the future successes she's currently striving for. And make no mistake—she's doing this on her own. Yes, her father is there to help her if she asks for it (just like all good parents are—and just like I do for both of my sons), but she's achieving these things on her own, much like Joe Hill did, writing and submitting stories under that name, determined to get published based on his skills and talent, rather than who his father was. I remember back when only a small handful of us knew the truth, of how impressed I was by Joe's sincerity and drive, his earnestness at succeeding on his own. Kasey has embarked on a similar journey, and as her friend, it's exciting to see that dedication and determination finally paying off. Indeed, Kasey told me as we drove south toward San Diego that she'd just been interviewed a few days before, and for the first time, the interviewer didn't ask any questions about her famous father. Instead, the questions were all about *her*. That's an important distinction.

Drive.

You can teach an artist about the various rules and disciplines of their creative field. You can teach a writer about grammar and point-of-view and plot tropes. You can teach them to write every day and read every day. But you can't teach them drive and you can't teach them determination. Most of all, you can't teach patience. An artist either has these things or they don't. The artist who has these things will most likely achieve some degree of success.

A quick side-trip to the beach. (Photo copyright Brian Keene 2016)

With plenty of time to kill before our signing, Kasey and I stopped off at a tea room a friend of hers in Hollywood had recommended. I had a salad. She had a pastry. Neither of us had tea (unless you count iced tea) and neither of us were impressed. The staff weren't real friendly, and one thing led to another, and we started raising hell and then had to quickly leave. So, we made a quick side-trip to the beach, instead, before ultimately heading to Mysterious Galaxy.

Jonathan Maberry, taking a break from his own book signing tour, was on hand to lead a discussion, and I was impressed by the size of the crowd. A full house, with a very diverse audience, asked great questions and had us both sign stuff for them. I was given more bottles of bourbon and other cool things. A fellow Navy veteran gave me a Chief's badge and a trinket taken from around the neck of a dead ISIS fighter (more on that a few columns from now), both of which I was very touched by. San Diego is a military town. I was seventeen the first time I visited San Diego—and that was to undertake eight weeks of Navy boot camp, followed by another sixteen weeks of various specialist schools. I was humbled and honored by all of the current and former duty servicemen and servicewomen who showed up—everyone from mess cooks to active duty SEALS.

I was also stunned by how many writers were in attendance. In addition to Jonathan, Kasey, myself, and Bryan Killian (whose first novel I was lucky enough to blurb a few years ago), there were probably a dozen other aspiring authors. I soon found out that this was the work of bizarro writer and political activist David Agranoff.

Some of the San Diego-based authors. (Photo copyright Brian Keene 2016)

David has been making waves the last few years among readers of bizarro fiction (especially with his upcoming novel, *Punk Rock Ghost Story*, which was inspired by the strange case of the early-Eighties punk band The Fuckers), but just like Kasey, his success didn't happen overnight. I've known David from online interactions—and later in person—for well over a decade now, so I can attest first-hand how hard he has worked to achieve it with drive, determination, and patience. Perhaps more impressively, he hasn't used his talents to merely grow his own career. He's used them to grow the careers of others, as well. Discovering that a significant number of aspiring horror, bizarro, and other speculative fiction genre authors lived in San Diego, and dissatisfied with the offerings and current status of the HWA, David took it upon himself to found an independent writing organization—a collective of San Diego-based speculative fiction authors, made up of both beginners and professionals. He didn't have to do this. David is a political organizer, and here he is doing the same thing in his spare time for his fellow writers. That would be like if I was a plumber, and I fixed toilets all day long, and then in my off-hours I went around plunging the clogs out of other writers' toilets. But David doesn't see it that way. That's because he understands that in addition to drive, determination, and patience, an artist needs a community of other artists. We need friendships and interactions with others like us—simply because we're not like other people. We need like-minded people who share our drive. We need people we can talk to about what we do and how we do it.

At Mysterious Galaxy. (Photo copyright Brian Keene 2016)

Out here on the road, I've seen dozens of friends whom I've known for the last twenty years. You can call them a posse, if you like. The horror media used to call them a cabal. I just call them friends. I couldn't have done this without them. On days when my determination flagged, or my patience waned, they were there, encouraging me to drive on.

I'm older now. I've had a heart attack and my friends are dying and my beard has enough gray in it now that a tourist in Hollywood mistook me for Sean Connery. Some days, my drive falters. Just a little bit. But then I think about folks like Kasey and David and my transmission pops back into gear, and I floor the accelerator again.

And I drive on.

Which is exactly what I did the next morning. Feeling victorious after two wonderful signings at Dark Delicacies in Burbank and Mysterious Galaxy in San Diego, I rented a car, and drove off into the desert, heading for the next signing in Tucson...

...and ran smack into Donald Trump's wall.

More on that next week.

→ **CHAPTER TWELVE**

TOWER OF BABBLE

Hello. If you're just joining us, this is End of the Road—a weekly column in which I detail my nine-month cross-country promotional tour for my new novels *Pressure* and *The Complex*. I write about what I've learned out here on the road, and how the horror genre, and our industry, and our country, and myself have changed over the last twenty years. We now rejoin the column, already in progress.

The drive from San Diego, California, to Tucson, Arizona, is a lonely haul through a bleak and desolate stretch of sunbaked wasteland that resembles the set of a *Mad Max* movie. Or, at least, that's how it felt to me. So far on this Farewell Tour, I'd had partners to ride with, but Jamie LaChance and Kasey Lansdale had now returned home, and I was alone in the rental car with only my thoughts for company. This wasn't a good thing. Anyone who truly knows me will tell you that my thoughts do not, in fact, make for excellent company.

The desert flashed by at eighty miles per hour, featureless and bare, and yet simultaneously beautiful. It was a stark difference from the greenery and hills and trees of central Pennsylvania, and I couldn't help but be awestruck. Still, no matter how marvelous the scenery was, you can only see so many cactuses and boulders before you begin to grow bored. Usually on such a drive, I'd listen to my favorite podcasts—*Tell 'Em Steve Dave*, *Ground Zero with Clyde Lewis*, Kelli Owen's *Buttercup of Doom*, *Three Guys with Beards* (hosted by Christopher Golden, Jonathan Maberry, and James A. Moore), and Scott Edelman's *Eating the Fantastic*. Unfortunately, I had zero cell phone coverage, so I had to rely on terrestrial radio.

I used to work in radio, both as an on-air personality and in advertising sales. I haven't listened to terrestrial radio in over a decade, opting instead for satellite radio (at first) and ultimately, podcasts via streaming. When I left radio, back in the late Nineties, it was an industry full of uncertainty and gloom, similar to how publishing used to be, and how the comic book industry is right now. Back then, many were predicting the death of terrestrial radio, and while that hasn't happened yet, there's no denying that the medium is a thin shade of its former self.

What I found as I scanned the dial were country and pop music songs that sounded virtually identical, and lots of advertisements trying to convince listeners that terrestrial radio was still valid. But even more than these, I heard lots of people talking. And by talking, I mean babbling. And by babbling, I mean doing nothing more than scoring points for their particular political team by vomiting nonsense onto the listening audience.

I heard right-wing pundits insisting that young black men who don't immediately comply with a police officer's orders deserve to get shot. "He ran from the police," one talk show host shouted. "He ran from the police. They had no choice but to shoot him." This was news to me. When I first left on my tour, we still had something in this country called due process. But not anymore. Apparently, it had been done away with now, while I was out here on the road. We had learned to save money on pesky things like courts and juries and judges and fair trials, opting instead for just shooting people. In the process, we had also apparently changed the list of crimes for which capital punishment—the death penalty—was valid. The death sentence used to be for the really heinous crimes—slaughtering a family of five in their sleep or raping fifty people. Now, it was a valid and legal solution for innocuous transgressions like being black or running from the police or occupying a Federal wildlife reserve as a form of protest. These right-wing pundits went on to insist that the cause of all these troubles were, in fact, people on the Left.

I heard left-wing pundits insisting that the only way to fix things in the country and make it safe for everyone—black or white—was to further erode our freedoms. We should re-write the Constitution and the Bill of Rights, they said. If we did that, we'd be safer, and no one would ever hurt us again. This was also news to me. The Bush administration (a subsidiary of The Halliburton Corporation) had already rewritten the Constitution and the Bill of Rights with something called the Patriot Act. The Obama administration, whom the Left had put into power twice, had further eradicated those freedoms by renewing and expanding the Patriot Act, and terrorizing patriots who had risked everything to blow the whistle on how the NSA was using that expansion to spy on our *Pokémon GO* games, and using armed drones to target and kill American citizens without a trial (because remember, we no longer need trials or due process in this country; it's much easier just to shoot people). Despite all of this, it seemed to me that we were no safer. Indeed, the further our freedoms slipped away, the more dangerous things were becoming. I was confused as to how voluntarily giving up the rest of our freedom would make things better or safer, but the left-wing radio pundits insisted it would, and further insisted that the cause of all these troubles were, in fact, people on the Right.

The Left blamed the Right. The Right blamed the Left.

As I drove on through the desert, listening to the bullshit coming from both sides, I wondered if perhaps I was still asleep back in my hotel room in San Diego, or maybe still in Los Angeles, stoned off my ass on John Skipp's balcony, and all of this was just some crazed dream in which I wasn't driving through America, but instead traversing Judge Dredd's Mega-City and Cursed Earth landscapes. After all, in the *Judge Dredd* comic books, the police can summarily execute you for crimes like jaywalking and having a missing headlight, and the only people who have guns are the executioners themselves.

But no…no, I wasn't dreaming or hallucinating. This was the real world. I knew that because of the name I kept hearing repeated on my radio from both the Left and the Right. It was a name that I had never seen in a *Judge Dredd* comic book.

That name was Donald Trump.

Donald Trump scares a lot of my liberal friends—and he scares about half of my conservative friends, too. I'm not going to list the man's faults here, because he has many, and because you can and should investigate those things for yourself. People are scared of him because deep down inside, they suspect he's going to win. I suspect he's going to win, too—or at the very least, win the popular vote and land us in an Electoral College mess that will put the Bush-Gore fiasco to shame. But here's the thing. People are scared of Donald Trump for the wrong reason. Or, at the very least, a reason they can't articulate. A reason that lurks in the subconscious.

And that reason is anger. There is anger on both the Left and the Right, and even from the dwindling few like myself who walk firmly down the middle of America's political highway. Anger between the

Left and the Right. Anger between Black and White. Anger between the Poor and the Elite. Anger between Christians and Muslims. Anger over sexual orientation and gun rights and land rights and taxes and globalization and a host of other things. It used to be the Elite could keep the American public pacified on a steady diet of reality television and Kanye West records, but people are beginning to wake up—and regardless of their race, creed, religion, gender, or sexual orientation—they are fucking angry. They have good reason to be angry. The problem is they're channeling that anger at each other, rather than at the source of all their problems.

It's not Black or White. It's the people versus might. It's not Red or Blue. It's the State versus You. But when I try to explain that to my friends they accuse me of being a Left-wing nut or a Right-wing nut. Which is exactly what the people in charge want you to do. They want you to stay angry at each other, so you won't turn your anger on them.

That unfocused anger is what has led to the rise of Donald Trump, and that same unfocused anger is what might propel this dangerous populist demagogue into the White House this November. Which is frustrating to someone like myself, because Donald Trump is nothing more than one of those Elite. Yes, Hillary Clinton is certainly one of the Elite, but Donald Trump doesn't represent an alternative to her. Voting for either of those candidates is simply voting for business as usual in this country. Neither Clinton nor Trump will do anything about the increasing militarization of our local police departments. Neither will expand the national dialogue on economic disparity, globalism, gun control, LGBT rights, terrorism, or any other hot button political issue. Instead, all they will do is feed the anger people already feel regarding the issues, the same as Obama and Bush before them. Because that's all any Republican or Democratic candidate does.

Anger fills our airwaves. Angry people clamor for "change" via Trump the same way they clamored for "change" under Obama and "change" under Bush before him. The only thing that changes is they trick you into voting for one of them again.

Need proof?

Well, I walked out into the desert and found you some.

Out there between San Diego and Tucson, shortly after passing a border checkpoint, I parked the car along the side of the road and walked out into the desert. I made sure to stay in a straight line and not diverge from my path, because it gets well over a hundred degrees out there and shade is nonexistent. The car vanished from sight. The sounds of trucks rushing by on the highway faded. It was just me and the desert. I kept walking, found a few interesting rocks to take home for my son, snapped a few pictures, and kept going. I came to a small barbed-wire fence, the kind we use back in Pennsylvania to keep sheep and goats from wandering out of the field. I couldn't figure out who had put the fence out here in the middle of the desert, or what purpose it might serve. I stepped over the fence and kept going, taking more pictures and collecting more rocks. Eventually, I pulled out my phone to check the temperature. I saw that it was 112 degrees.

And then I saw that, according to my phone, I had inadvertently crossed over the border into Mexico. I wasn't sure how that was possible, but it seemed to me that if, in fact, that was what I had done, Border Patrol might have been better served having a checkpoint out here rather than the ones I'd repeatedly driven through miles back. Not a wall, mind you, but some type of border crossing station. Not a wall, because it's fucking silly to think a wall could be built out here.

Take a look.

Future Location of Trump's Wall. (Photo copyright Brian Keene 2016)

That's where Donald Trump wants to build a wall.

Half our country is so filled with anger over the anger from the other half of the country, that they are willing to believe a mentally ill construction magnate—whose key proposal is to build a wall in this inhospitable spot—is better suited to run our nation than the parade of pinheads who have done so before.

It's easy to sit at home in Kansas or Nebraska or Maine and say, "That sounds good! We should build a giant wall." But let me tell you something—regardless of which side of the immigration debate you reside, take a trip to the border and see it for yourself and realize just what an undertaking such a proposal would be. It's not something that could be achieved in a year or even four years. It's a job that would last at least a decade.

The proposed wall serves one purpose, and one purpose only, and that purpose is distraction.

It's just something else to keep you distracted, and while you are focused on building that wall, poorly trained police officers will continue to kill young black men and old white farmers without trial, and Presidents will continue to kill American citizens with drone strikes without trial, and politicians will continue to flaunt the laws, and corporations will continue to spy inside your bedrooms via your latest videogame app, and people will continue to slaughter innocents in the honor of whichever version God they think is better, and half our citizenry will continue to be denied basic human rights simply because of whom they love, but hey, at least we'll have a wall, and the construction magnates will be getting rich from building it, and if those other things anger you? Well, then, you can turn on the radio or the television and bask in similar anger from the side of your choice.

And the Tower of Babble will continue to grow, until it blots out the sun, and crushes us all beneath its massive shadow when it collapses under its own weight. And five-hundred thousand years from now, after we've slaughtered each other to extinction, some alien scientists will detect our signals, floating in the ether, and decode those ghostly remnants, and decide that Rush Limbaugh and Rachel Maddow must have been our supreme deities, and that it was probably a good thing that such an angry race of beings came to an end, because really, no other intelligent species is going to want that shit polluting the rest of the universe.

I got back in the car and headed for Tucson, and kept the car in the middle of the road—the most dangerous place to drive, but in my opinion, the only alternative route.

CHAPTER THIRTEEN

MISSING IN ACTION

I spent an afternoon recovering at the home of poet Linda Addison before my next signing at the Barnes and Noble in Tucson, and during that time, I'd begun to mull over something important.

Before I tell you what it is, we need to backtrack a bit.

A decade ago, you could find my books in any bookstore. Indeed, most Borders and Barnes and Noble carried a few copies of each book in my backlist, thus creating a Brian Keene shelf, right next to Stephen King, Dean Koontz, and Jack Ketchum. I can't tell you how crucial this was to increasing the size of my audience. If you're a customer browsing the horror section (or even the alphabetical K section) your eyes are naturally going to be drawn to an entire row of books written by the same person, rather than a lone book by a lone author.

Linda Addison, Wile E. Young, and Brian in Tucson. (Photo copyright Brian Keene 2016)

When myself, J.F. Gonzalez, Mary SanGiovanni, Bryan Smith, and others in our field killed Leisure/Dorchester to save the genre (and ourselves), those Brian Keene sections went away. Since then, readers have been unable to find my books in stores. That's because many of the publishers I have since signed with—Deadite Press, Apex Book Company, Thunderstorm Books, etc.—don't have distribution into those stores. And that's okay. In truth, I make more money from Deadite Press than I ever made from Leisure Books (and I was one of Leisure's top-paid authors) because of Deadite's distribution. They sell directly to readers and through Amazon, which means I get paid every month, rather than waiting ninety days or more for the bookstore chains to pay them. And since they are selling their books to readers at full price, rather than at a discount for the bookstores, I get paid a much bigger cut of the cover price.

And that's the way it has been for many years now, starting with the publication of my first post-Leisure novel, *Entombed*. I've released a dozen plus books since then, and none of them have been available in bookstores. Based on my sales and social media imprint, I had assumed all this time that my former bookstore readers had followed along with me, and were now buying those books via Amazon or on Kindle.

But I was wrong.

Yes, my post-Leisure sales stayed the same (and even increased, somewhat). But it wasn't older readers following me into the brave new digital publishing landscape. It was newer, younger readers discovering me for the first time. Many older readers hadn't followed me at all, because they were unaware I had continued writing and publishing.

I have seen the proof of this over and over again, at every signing. Readers age thirty-five and younger bring Deadite Press paperbacks they've ordered online, or pick up a copy of *Pressure* or *The Complex* and tell me they already read it on their Kindle, but want to get a signed copy. They follow me on social media, and are completely up-to-date on what I've been up to. Readers over the age of forty bring a stack of Leisure paperbacks for me to sign, and they comment that it's nice to see me back in bookstores again. (Keep in mind, *Pressure* is published by a mainstream publisher, meaning bookstores carry it, the way they used to carry my Leisure titles.) They are under the impression that *Pressure* is the first thing I have written since *A Gathering of Crows* (my last Leisure novel). They ask me if I'll ever write a third book in *The Rising* series, completely unaware that books three and four have been available for several years now. These are readers who are not social media savvy, who don't use Kindle or other e-book readers, and who vastly prefer to find their books the old-fashioned way—by perusing the shelves at their local bookstore. They are readers who I mistakenly left behind—readers who I didn't even know I had lost.

And now that I've found them again, I need to figure out how to reconnect.

I saw the same dynamics in play the next night at The Poisoned Pen in Phoenix. A standing-room-only crowd showed up to see Stephen Coonts, Ben Coes, Weston Ochse, and myself. Half the crowd were over the age of forty, and happy to see me apparently writing novels again. The other half were under age thirty-five, and happy that I had never stopped writing novels.

(And yes, I know there are people over the age of forty who are well-aware that I didn't retire, and have been buying all my stuff, but you guys are super-fans, and the data above doesn't apply to you. And bless you for that.)

Some of the crowd at The Poisoned Pen in Phoenix. (Photo copyright Brian Keene 2016)

The Phoenix signing was supposed to be over at nine p.m. but I signed until around ten-thirty, in order to accommodate all of the people that had shown up. Then I hung out a bit longer with Weston, Paul Goblirsch of Thunderstorm Books, and author Joe Nassise, who I hadn't seen in years. We had a spectacular time.

Then it was time to hit the road again. High school football coach Tod Clark was my companion for the next part of the drive. As he and I climbed into his truck and drove off into the desert, I presented him with my findings and data.

I had to stay with the independent presses like Deadite and Apex and Thunderstorm. But I also needed to stay with at least one mainstream publisher, lest people think I'd disappeared again.

An hour out of Phoenix, something large and hairy and bestial ran across the road, eyes shining in our headlights. It might have been a coyote. Or a Chupacabra.

Or an omen of things to come...

→ **CHAPTER FOURTEEN**

TIME BOMB

All roads eventually lead to... (Photo copyright Tod Clark 2016)

Last week's column ended with high school football coach Tod Clark and I leaving a triumphant, standing-room-only signing in Phoenix, and climbing into his truck to head for Albuquerque. We'll return to that in a moment. But first, I need to tell you about the bomb I was carrying with us.

Back in the eleventh installment of this column, I wrote: "A fellow Navy veteran gave me a Chief's badge and a trinket taken from around the neck of a dead ISIS fighter (more on that a few columns from now), both of which I was very touched by."

Well, here we are at "a few columns from now," still in Phoenix. Tod and I have not yet gotten into the truck. Indeed, we haven't even made it to that triumphant Phoenix signing yet. Instead, we are sitting in a hotel room with author Weston Ochse and publisher Paul Goblirsch of Thunderstorm Books.

How is that possible? Well, right now, we are traveling through time, you and me. That is what life is like out here on the road. I have spent the summer hopping back and forth across this country's different time zones—sometimes crossing three or four zones a day. At this point in our narrative, I never know what day it is, let alone what time it is. My phone automatically adjusts the clock to whatever state I'm in, but I am not a fixed point in time. Far from it. I am rocketing through time, and my two sons and my girlfriend, author Mary SanGiovanni, are the fixed points.

So far, I've been playing phone tag with those fixed points because when they are awake, I am traveling or sleeping, and when I am awake, they are sleeping. I get in a quick couple of texts with Mary before signings. A few FaceTime calls with my youngest son after stumbling out of bed. A lone phone conversation with my oldest son while waiting to be served in a diner. But none of these are in person.

I can no longer remember what my girlfriend's hair smells like. Instead, I smell the perfume and aftershave of strangers.

I can no longer recall the strength of my oldest son's handshake. I remember the first time I felt it, sure. The first time I felt it, that was when it really dawned on me that my first little boy was no longer a little boy, but a man. But I can't remember it now. Instead, my palm carries the impression of hundreds of handshakes with strangers.

And as for my second son, my pride and joy, known to listeners of my podcast under his on-air pseudonym of Dungeonmaster 77.1? I can see him on FaceTime. I can hear him and talk to him and tell him I love him and listen while he tells me about what he did at science camp and his latest creation in *Minecraft* and how he and his mother found a rare Pokémon while shopping at the Amish market. But all of these things are taking place through a video screen, and you can't hug an iPhone and feel it hug you back. An iPhone doesn't bury its face in your shoulder and squeeze you tight, letting you know how much it missed you. Instead, I am left with the hugs of strangers.

Time travel is a lonely occupation.

That is what life is like at this point in our narrative. That is where we are, one month into the end of the road. That is where I'm at, hurtling through time and space. I carry all of this with me. And I carry you with me, as well. I carry your well wishes and your delight and your excitement and enthusiasm. I carry the nice things you say about my books, and your accolades, and your personal stories of how *Ghoul* or *Dark Hollow* or *The Girl on the Glider* helped you in life, or how *The Rising* got you suspended in eleventh grade, or how *Dead Sea* felt like I wrote it for you. I cannot carry my loved ones with me, so I carry you with me instead.

Something else I'm carrying with me, according to Weston Ochse, is a bomb.

In the hotel room in Phoenix, Weston asks me how the signing in San Diego went. I tell him how awesome it was. He wonders how many people brought me bourbon. The four of us share a good chuckle over that. But then I tell him about the charm from the dead Islamic extremist that I was given, and Weston grows pale.

Here are some things you need to know about Weston Ochse:

1. He's one of my oldest friends in this business.

2. He's one hell of a writer.

3. He doesn't scare easily.

The public knows that Weston is retired military, and that he used to work in Intelligence (with a capital I). And some of you might know that he continues to work in Intelligence as a civilian. He doesn't have to. He could instead have a very nice life as a full-time writer. But once that world is in you, it's in you for life, and it's very hard for some men and women to walk away from that. I say this without hyperbole—Weston Ochse is a real-life Jack Bauer, and he's always my number one pick when my friends and I play "Draft Your Zombie Apocalypse Survival Group."

And right now, he's continuing to turn pale.

"Are you carrying that thing with you now?" Weston whispers, visibly shaken.

"Yeah," I reply. "It's in my kit bag, down in Tod's truck. It's pretty cool. A little leather cord with this red leather triangle on the end of it. There's something sewn inside the triangle, but the dude didn't know what. Want to see it? I can go get it."

"No," Weston shouts. "I don't want you to go get it! Jesus Christ, Brian, you've done some insane shit in your life, but this might be the craziest. What the hell were you thinking, man?"

"I was thinking that it was a very cool present for somebody to give me. He said the Taliban and ISIS fighters wear them as charms to keep away the Djinn."

"Oh, I know they do," Weston says. "I've seen my fair share of them. We call them do-rags."

"Do you have any?"

"No, I don't have any. And neither should you. Yes, they wear those to ward off the Djinn. But they're also supposed to bring bad luck to anyone else who takes them. You should send that thing to Rainy right now. Rainy can tell you if it's bad or not."

Author Rain Graves is a dear friend to us both, and an expert when it comes to real-life supernatural shit.

"Oh, come on." I pause, shocked by the dismay and concern etched into his face. "Do you really think it's that bad? You really think I'm going to be cursed?"

"Yes. I think whoever gave that to you could have unwittingly given you some terrorist shithead's version of a psychic suicide bomb."

Before I could respond, Paul and Tod noticed that we were out of bourbon, so I headed down to the truck to retrieve another bottle from the stash. Weston's words weighed heavily on me. I'm not a superstitious man, but I've also seen a number of things in life that I cannot scientifically explain—things that are therefore, by definition, supernatural. Did I believe that Weston was right, and that I could be cursed? Well, I wasn't sure. I don't generally believe in curses, and I've been told by people who know about these sorts of things that I have "a powerful energy" and that I unknowingly seem to "repel curses back on the people who cast them." Whether you believe in that sort of thing or not, you've gotta admit, it's a useful skill set to have.

So, even if Weston was right, and I was carrying the rudimentary equivalent of a psychic suicide bomb, how could I, in good conscience, send such a thing to Rainy? I know there's a portion of the Internet who think I'm an asshole, and yes, sometimes I am, but come on. Not even I would do something like that. Send a cursed trinket from the wasteland battleground of the Middle East to a dear friend? Include a letter that says: "Dear Rainy, Weston thinks this thing might be cursed. I hope it's not ticking. Thanks. Love, Brian."

No, I decided. *There's no such thing as cursed Taliban charms, and even if there is, that shit won't work on me. All magic, regardless of the school, is about projecting one's will over everything else. I may be getting older, but I've still got one hell of a lot of willpower.*

Which brings us back to the conclusion of last week's column. You'll remember that Tod and I were driving through the desert at night, and something large and hairy and bestial ran across the road. My first thought was to glance into the backseat, and make sure my kit bag was still zippered shut, and that the charm wasn't glowing or floating in mid-air or some shit.

Any other time, Tod and I would have stopped and investigated, but there was another signing to get to, so we drove on into the darkness, chalking the sighting up to someone playing *Pokémon GO*. We crossed another time zone in the middle of the night. About two in the morning we stopped at a motel out in the desert and grabbed four hours of sleep. Then we climbed back into the truck and headed for Albuquerque, where I was supposed to sign books starting at noon.

Night falls on Brian and Tod. (Photo Copyright 2016 Brian Keene)

The signing was a bust. There are a number of reasons why. First of all, from what I can tell and based on the accounts of others in the area, the store did little to market or promote it. There was a big sign out front advertising another author's signing for later that night, but no mention of me. Another factor is the fact that the signing was taking place at noon on a workday, and most people were probably, in fact, at work.

At no point did I chalk the attendance up to the cursed psychic suicide bomb in my kit bag.

In the end, four people showed up, and one of them had been at the signing in Tucson, and I'd signed for two others at the World Horror Convention back in April. Still, I was happy to see them. That's what this tour is about. I'll be honest—it was kind of a kick in the ego to go from a series of extraordinary signings with great turn-outs and high sales to this, but at the same time, it was awesome to get to spend that extra time with these four folks. I didn't want to do a reading, in case other people arrived, so I opted instead for a Q&A. I was pleased to talk to them for as long as they wanted. Then I signed their books, and signed the store stock, and Tod and I climbed back into the truck and started traveling through time again.

Albuquerque. (Photo copyright Tod Clark 2016)

Tod and his wife own a ranch on the outskirts of El Paso. We spent the night there, drinking and talking—taking a much-needed break from traveling. I'm a country boy. I'm used to the wide outdoors and dark nights and being able to see the stars. One of the reasons I've never lived in a city or suburbia for too long is because you can't see the stars at night. Until that night, the best stargazing I'd ever done was out in the middle of the North Atlantic Ocean. There are no lights there, and you can see stars you never knew existed. But sitting there at Tod's ranch, in what used to be an old-timey saloon, drinking bourbon and looking up at the stars...

...time stopped. That whirlwind I'd been on for the last month came screeching to a halt. I relived the entire tour—everything that had happened up to that point—in a second. In another five seconds, I'd relived my entire twenty-year career. Above me, the stars began to spin. I missed my sons. I missed Mary. Stars have always been our personal thing, and while I love Tod like a brother, and would gladly give him my kidney or take a bullet for him, I wished Mary had been there to share them with me. At that moment, it felt like she was a million miles away, and out there in the middle of the desert, there is no cell phone service. I was alone. Except for Tod. And the stars. And a feral desert cat named Millie who apparently hangs around the ranch, and who decided to be my friend for the night. I was glad for her company. The stars stopped spinning, and so did my head. I sat there, petting Millie and talking with Tod, and enjoying for one brief moment the stillness of time.

Tod and Suzin's Ranch. (Photo copyright Brian Keene 2016)

The next morning, I was back in the whirlwind, crossing another time zone, when I began to wonder if Weston hadn't been right.

More on that next week…

CHAPTER FIFTEEN

AD CAPERE TENEBRIS

So, I'm boarding an airplane in El Paso, about to traverse the time zones once again and fly to San Francisco, when it occurs to me that the ISIS fighter's psychic suicide bomb is still in my carry-on bag. The totem is snuggled up against my laptop, three Yeti microphones, my digital voice recorder, an assortment of pens and Moleskine notebooks, half a tin of Altoids, a few cigars, a cigar cutter, and a hardcover of David J. Schow's *DJSturbia*, which I bought way back in Burbank. The TSA are concerned with my cigar cutter, and debate among themselves whether I could hijack a plane with it. I helpfully point out that it is not on the list of forbidden travel items, and they concede. Nobody in the TSA thinks to question the ISIS trinket. Why would they? To them, it just looks like a small triangular wedge of red leather with a leather cord attached to it. But I know what it is, and now that I do, I can't stop thinking about the damn thing.

This in turn leads to unkind thoughts concerning my mother.

Allow me to explain.

My mother turns seventy this year. We have not always had the best relationship, but I love her just the same, simply because she is my mother. She's in good health, and will probably be with us for many more decades to come (her grandmother lived to almost one hundred and her mother recently clocked ninety-two). It is my hope that, should circumstances dictate it, she would live with my sister rather than me.

Because living with her would drive me insane.

In her golden years, my mother has discovered a latent talent—having prophetic dreams. In truth, it's not so much that she's discovered this talent now. She's always had it, ever since she was a little girl. The problem is now that she's retired, she has more time to hone it and use it. And the person she often uses it on is me.

A few weeks before I left on tour, she shared one of those dreams with my ex-wife and my sister and the ladies she meets for lunch every week. The only person she wouldn't share it with was me. This was upsetting since, according to my ex-wife, the dream was, in fact, about me, and that the dream did not end well. When I finally confronted my mother about it, she told me she'd had a dream that I was flying out of El Paso, and Marty Robbins was playing in the background, and I looked down at the ground. Then she trailed off, not finishing. I found out from others that in the dream, something bad happens. But nobody would tell me what the something bad was supposed to be. Finally, I gave up in frustration, mumbling in my best impression of *South Park*'s Eric Cartman, "Screw you guys, I'm going home."

And then I promptly forgot about the whole thing.

Until now, as I'm boarding the fucking plane. The flight attendant smiles at me. I try to smile back, but it feels more like a grimace.

I shuffle down the aisle, find my row, stow my gear in the overhead, and slump into my seat. I always go with an aisle seat, even

END OF THE ROAD ←

when flying coach. My seatmate has the window shade drawn, which makes it impossible for me to look down at the ground below. I cock my head and listen. I hear the flight crew telling us what to do in case of a water landing, but no Marty Robbins crooning "El Paso City."

It's okay, I think. *Weston is insane, and so is my mother. I have surrounded myself with crazy people. I need to fix that. I really need to look into a new career. I wonder if it's too late to become a forest ranger?*

The plane begins to taxi down the runway and I start to sweat. The worst part of any flight for me personally is the take off and the landing, since that's when most airplanes crash. I've mentioned before that I don't like flying. I have a bunch of rituals I go through on every flight. For example, even though I'm an agnostic, I believe that if there is a baby on the plane, the universe won't let it crash. However, if the baby starts crying, that's a sign that something is wrong. This is just one of my flight rules. I have dozens more. The number one rule is always drink several Bloody Marys in the nearest airport bar, before boarding the flight, but it is seven o'clock in the goddamn morning, and Tod Clark had no Bloody Mary mix back at his ranch.

(The worst flight experience I've ever had was one month after 9/11, when author Geoff Cooper and I were the only other passengers on a plane full of three boy scout troops and their chaperones, flying from Baltimore to Buffalo, and Coop—unbeknownst to either of us—had a nine millimeter bullet wedged into the treads of his boot, but that is a story for another time.)

Just as the wheels leave the ground, the passenger next to me opens the fucking window shade. I have to literally stop myself from reaching across her, snapping it back down, and shouting, "For God's sake, don't start singing 'El Paso City'!"

And then our flight continues and everything is fine and we land in San Francisco where I'm met by author and editor Michael Bailey. You'll remember him from an earlier column, when we unexpectedly ran into Richard Laymon's cremated remains. I like Michael. I refer to him as "a good kid." Mentored early on in his career by such veterans as F. Paul Wilson and Tom Monteleone, Michael is certainly one of the few at the forefront of this new generation of horror writers. He is possessed with an energy I used to have twenty years ago, and I like watching him work, because it reminds me of who I used to be, before alcohol and heartache and bitterness aged it all away and left behind the shambling corpse you see out here on this book tour.

But I digress.

Michael Bailey, Brian, and Gene O'Neill. (Photo copyright Michael Bailey 2016)

Michael drove me to the home of author Gene O'Neill, who lives high up a mountaintop in the beautiful Napa Valley. Michael told me on the way there that Gene's wife was out of town. She'd been worried about Gene spending time alone with me, because I am a bad influence.

"A bad influence," I squawked. "I'm a bad influence?"

END OF THE ROAD ←

"That's what she said." Michael shrugged. "She also said that she felt much better having me here to keep you from convincing Gene to get too wild."

Eventually, we reached the O'Neill residence. Gene greeted us at the door with a one-hundred-dollar bottle of scotch, and commanded us to hurry up and drink it, because he had three more bottles just like it. We complied, because Gene is older than us and you should always respect your elders.

I arched an eyebrow at Michael and muttered about bad influences. Michael giggled. Gene snapped at me to quit muttering and keep drinking.

Here's what I really respect about Gene, and it's a story people never pause to think about. Gene's got literary awards and an impressive body of work—over a dozen horror and science-fiction books, dozens of shorts stories, and much more. His seminal *The Burden of Indigo* (one of the finest post-apocalyptic dystopian novels ever written) would be enough to hallmark his career. He's also a mentor to not one or six but dozens of younger writers. And he's accomplished all of this in just a little over a decade. Most of what has happened in Gene's writing career has happened since his retirement from the workforce.

Gene is the same age as my mother, and he's possessed with the same drive and energy and talent as her—except that instead of tapping into the power of prophetic dreams to scare the shit out of his children, Gene is using those energy reserves and talents to craft a lifetime's amount of work in the time it takes T.E.D. Klein to finish a short story.

Carpe diem. It's Latin for "seize the day." I've known that since the sixth grade but most people didn't discover it until they saw the film *Dead Poets Society.* It's a good motto to live by, and one I've instilled in both of my sons. But my mother and Gene O'Neill and others like them, they have an equally admirable motto. *Ad capere tenebris.* "Seize the twilight."

I told you way back in the first installment of this column that I'm feeling my age. David J. Schow told me to shut the fuck up about that, because if I'm feeling old at forty-eight, then he must be positively ancient. But I won't shut the fuck up, nor will I apologize for it. When your friends start dying on you, it fucks with your head. That's why I'm out here. That's what this entire insane cross-country tour comes down to—trying to un-fuck my head.

But it occurred to me, sitting in Gene's kitchen and sipping really good scotch and listening to him speak with excitement about all the things he wants to write about in the future, that maybe the old adage is true. Maybe you really are only as old as you feel. And if I am, in fact, staring into my own approaching twilight, then maybe I ought to face that shit head on, the same way I've faced everything else in my life, with head held high and shoulders unbowed, fists clenched, witty comment forming on my lips, and just a hint of a sardonic smile.

Ad capere tenebris.

Seize the twilight, indeed.

→ **CHAPTER SIXTEEN**

A MESSAGE TO THE NEXT GENERATION

Brian, Alan Beatts, and Jude Feldman. (Photo copyright Brian Keene 2016)

Alan Beatts and Jude Feldman are absolute bad-asses. Alan is a former private investigator, bodyguard, firearms instructor, and motorcycle repairman. Jude is a former welder and computer micro-assembly technician. They also run Borderlands Books in San Francisco, a name inspired in part by William Hope Hodgson's horror-fantasy-science-fiction classic (and one of my favorite novels) *The House on the Borderland.*

I was introduced to Alan and Jude by Richard Laymon back in 1999. I first visited Borderlands Books in 2001, right after they'd moved to San Francisco's Mission District. Indeed, when I visited, they were still remodeling the place. I signed there later that year with Gene O'Neill, Mike Oliveri, Michael T. Huyck, Geoff Cooper, and Gak. And I've lost track of how many times I've signed there— or shopped there—since then. Doing some quick math in my head, I know I signed there at least twice with Jesus Gonzalez, once with a large group from the World Horror Convention, once with my ex-wife, once with Nick Mamatas, once with Mary SanGiovanni, and so on. Basically, anytime I'm in San Francisco, I stop at Borderlands.

I haven't stayed as in touch with Alan and Jude as much as I'd like over the years. They've been busy adding on a café to the store, and I've been busy cranking out books, but I've always considered them dear friends. Alan has always been a source of inspiration to me, and in the early days, his advice and counsel were what I counted on the most. It's not hyperbole to say I wouldn't be where I am today without Alan's guidance.

Signing there again on this tour felt like coming home, especially after the Albuquerque debacle. I spent the early part of the day in the city, having lunch with Gene O'Neill, Michael Bailey, and Nick Mamatas, followed by a walking tour of the Mission District (which has changed shockingly since my last visit, due to the overwhelming creep of gentrification—something I'll talk about at length in next week's column). Then we headed over to the store, where I spent money on books (in addition to the latest horror, science-fiction, and fantasy novels, Borderlands has a fantastic collection of Arkham House, Gnome Press, Ash Tree, Fedogan and Bremer, and other out-of-print titles) and then hung out in the café with Nick, Michael, and Gene.

Some of the crowd at Borderlands Books. (Photo copyright Nick Mamatas 2016)

When it was time for my signing, I was pleased to see a full house. My voice was shot by that point—the victim of a month on the road and too much bourbon and too many great conversations and cigars and laughter—so I opted to do a Q&A rather than a reading. The crowd asked great questions and we sold a lot of books. It was a fun, uplifting, and positive ending to the first leg of this tour.

"He's padding the column," someone is shouting right now. "Get to the gentrification rant, Keene!"

I will. Next week. And no, I'm not padding the column. I bring up Alan and Jude and their store and their place in this industry because I'm about to drop a big old truth bomb on you, and I don't want that wisdom to get lost amid a discussion of how Mamatas and I, fleeing from the crush of eighty-dollar hipster haircuts and a competing cacophony of cafés blasting world music out into the streets, descended into the city's subway system on a stairwell fashioned from bloody hypodermic needles. That's next week's column.

While catching up with Alan after the signing, I asked him if he ever got to read a transcript of my World Horror Grandmaster Award acceptance speech from 2014. He had not. So, I told him about it.

Back in the day, Alan and Jude would always host a party at the World Horror Convention. It was always the best party of the weekend, and usually attended by a crush of people—authors, editors, publishers, artists, fans, and perhaps one or two HVAC salesmen who just happened to be staying in the hotel, as well. During the party, Alan would get everyone's attention and have them look around the room and find one person that they did not know. Then he'd invite everyone to go introduce themselves to that person.

Alan imparting wisdom on a young Wrath James White and a young Brian in 2002. (Photo copyright James Futch 2002)

To illustrate why that was important then and why it is still important now, here is a partial transcript of my Grandmaster Award acceptance speech. Parts of it echo what I wrote very early on in these columns, but it won't hurt you to hear it again. You should also know that I've edited the speech here for space constraints—you can find the full version in my book *Trigger Warnings*).

I stand before you today expressing two things you probably didn't expect from me—humbleness and humility.

It's impossible to not be humble when you consider the previous winners of this award. Before writing this speech, I went back and perused the list, just to freshen my memory. Previous winners are (in order) Robert Bloch, Stephen King, Richard Matheson, Anne Rice, Clive Barker, Dean Koontz, Peter Straub, Brian Lumley, Ramsey Campbell, Harlan Ellison, Ray Bradbury, Charles Grant, Chelsea Quinn Yarbro, Jack Williamson, F. Paul Wilson, Ray Garton, Joe Lansdale, Robert McCammon, Tanith Lee, James Herbert, Jack Ketchum, T.E.D. Klein, and Dan Simmons.

And now me.

You know what that's like? It's like you go to the Rock and Roll Hall of Fame induction ceremony and you're looking at all of the previous winners—The Beatles, The Rolling Stones, George Clinton and the Parliament, Jimi Hendrix, Black Sabbath, Led Zeppelin, Metallica, NWA, Guns N' Roses… and then you find out tonight's honoree is Justin Bieber.

My name is Brian Keene and I am the Justin Bieber of the horror genre.

It's impossible to accept this award without humbleness and humility. I feel those things very deeply today. And those aren't the only things I feel. In the months leading up to this, it's been a struggle for me to feel that I was worthy of this honor, and to feel like I belonged to the canon of authors who received it before me.

I remember the very first World Horror Convention I ever attended. This was back in 1999, when the Internet was still relatively new and most of us were still sending submissions via snail mail with the required Self Addressed Stamped Envelope. Before attending that convention, the only author I'd ever met in person was Joe Lansdale, who I met during a signing he and Tim Truman were doing at a local comic book store. And that meeting didn't count because my conversation with him was limited to, "Holy shit. You're Joe fucking Lansdale," and, "Could you make that out to Brian," and finally, "Holy shit. You're Joe fucking Lansdale."

So, prior to World Horror Convention, most of my interactions with my peers had been conducted solely online, using Windows 3.0 and a very primitive chat room that took approximately twenty minutes to refresh every time you typed a response. On the airport shuttle, I met Gak, an artist whose name I recognized because we'd been appearing in the same fanzines together, and whose art, years later, is now indelibly inked across much of my back in the form of a large tattoo.

When we got to the hotel, Gak disappeared. My room wasn't ready yet, and I found myself standing in the lobby, not sure what to do next. There was a guy dressed all in black sprawled across one of the sofas in the lobby. He looked like the love child of Rob Zombie and Blue Oyster Cult's Buck Dharma. There's no one else around. And then this guy, maybe sensing that I'm lost or unsure, calls me over and shows me something he'd just bought in the dealer's room. To this day, I can't tell you what the item was, because it quickly dawned on me that the guy was John Shirley. He's trying to show it to me and have an intelligent conversation with me about it, and meanwhile, I'm standing there with my mouth clamped shut because I know if I open it, I'm going to shout things like "Dude, you wrote *A Splendid Chaos*! You're John fucking Shirley!"

Most of the weekend was like that. I quickly discovered just how open and welcoming this community of ours is, and in moments—be it having dinner with Brian Hodge and Yvonne Navarro, or socializing at a party with folks like Neil Gaiman or getting high with Ramsey Campbell —I repeatedly resisted the urge to shout at them about who they were and what they'd written and then melt down into a quivering puddle of fanboy goo.

It is fair to say that particular WHC changed the course of my life. It was at that con that I also met most of the peers I'd been talking with online. We all quickly became friends—and in the decade and a half that have followed, they remain some of the best friends I have ever had in life. Indeed, one of them (Mary) eventually went from being one of my best friends to the woman I love.

But it also changed the course of my life for another reason. Before attending that convention, I'd approached writing as a pastime—a hobby. I'd write things occasionally and send them out to zines, and sometimes they'd get published and more often they got rejected. Coming home from that first WHC, I was driven to write. Compelled to write. It changed my entire outlook and approach to this vocation. I began writing every evening, no matter how tired I was at the end of the day. The publication versus rejection ratio changed. I became more involved with our community. I finally began to view myself as a writer, rather than as a blue-collar guy who worked a succession of various jobs and wrote occasionally on weekends.

I'd always dreamed of writing for a living. Attending that first WHC was what finally gave me the gumption to actually strive toward it.

At my second World Horror Convention, Richard Laymon introduced me to his editor, Don D'Auria, and told him about a little zombie novel I was working on. Don talked about that in the introduction to this event. At my third World Horror Convention, Jack Ketchum sat down with me at the hotel bar and went over the contract for that zombie novel with a red pen and taught me everything I'd ever need to know about negotiating a publishing contract. I still have that red-penned original at home, and I still have the receipt for the bottle of scotch I bought him in return.

I've been coming to World Horror ever since. It's done a lot for me, and I hope I've done a lot for it.

World Horror is not a fan convention. It's a professional gathering—a trade show for those of us who are involved in dark fiction and publishing. But it's also a family reunion. Like any family, we don't always get along the rest of the year. But the drama seems to fall by the wayside when the family gathers here. As horror writers, we're used to having to defend ourselves from attacks. Writers from other genres belittle us, the media often excoriates us, our friends and family and agents wonder aloud when we're going to write something serious—we're used to having our backs against the wall. It has been my experience that when that happens, our family—our tribe—invariably bands together and stands firm. We have each other's backs.

As a full time writer, I can't count on retirement or a 401K or health insurance or even a steady paycheck. But I can always count on you, my tribe, and I'd like to think I've shown that you can always count on me. Trends change, publishers go under, and readers can be fickle, but at the end of the day, we still have each other, and we still have this wonderful genre for which we all share a deep and abiding love and appreciation.

You are among friends. You are among family. Horror writers have always been welcoming of anyone, regardless of race, creed, gender, or sexual orientation. Indeed, we've often been the first to do so. You will never find a more welcoming, friendly, and good-humored group than the people in this tribe.

And even though I still don't think I deserve it, the people of this tribe have decided that I should receive this award, and thus I do so with great humility and humbleness and honor.

In closing, I'd like to do one thing. Bookseller Alan Beatts used to throw an awesome party every year at WHC. During the party, he would get everyone's attention and have them look around the room and find one person that they did not know. Then he'd invite everyone to go introduce themselves to that person. I'd like to ask you to do that now.

As Robert DeNiro says in Brazil, "We're all in this together."

Look around this ballroom. Find someone you don't know, and go welcome them to the family.

Alan and Jude prepping for one of their legendary WHC parties.
(Photo copyright James Futch 2001)

These days, I'm usually the one throwing the party at World Horror on Saturday night, and I always stop the festivities at some point in the evening and have everyone introduce themselves to each other. But I didn't start that tradition.

Alan Beatts started it.

It is my sincere hope that someone else will continue the tradition when I'm gone.

→ CHAPTER SIXTEEN POINT ONE

End of the Road was first written and published (as a series of online columns) in 2016 and 2017.

The hardcover and e-book were published in January of 2020.

Some months later, in the summer of 2020, one of Alan Beatts's former girlfriends alleged that he physically assaulted her, and his own daughter alleged that he attempted to have sex with her.

I believe these women.

Alan Beatts has not denied these allegations.

To say that the genre was rocked by these allegations is an understatement. Many, like myself, were utterly shocked. Others stated that they weren't surprised, and recounted their own experiences in private. But to understand their emotional and mental impact these allegations had on our genre and industry, one only needs to go back and re-read the chapter you just read.

Suffice to say, I will never sign books there again, or support the store in any fashion. That was an easy decision to make. What is more difficult to reconcile is the fact that I used Alan's analogy of the horror family in my Grandmaster Award speech, and again in this book. Indeed, that outlook and idea is one of the cornerstones of how I have approached this business over the last twenty-plus years.

But you know what? Alan stopped going to World Horror Conventions after 2008 or so, and that tradition has continued without him. And I'm not the only one who has utilized it. In *Clickers Forever*, author Robert Ford writes about J.F. Gonzalez using those principles during their first meeting. I've watched peers like James A. Moore, Linda Addison, Maurice Broaddus, Weston Ochse, and Christopher Golden utilize those guiding principles. And I have used them, too. I used them earlier in this book, introducing folks like Wile E. Young, Stephen Kozeniewski and Rachel Autumn Deering not only to each other, but to veterans like Jack Ketchum and Michael Arnzen. In the few years since first writing about that, Young, Kozeniewski and Deering have become friends, and are following that trail, the same way I followed Ketchum's trail, and the same way he followed Robert Bloch's trail.

It's a good principle, and it occurs to me that although Alan Beatts was the one to prominently verbalize it back in the day, he wasn't the only one utilizing it. Richard Laymon, F. Paul Wilson, Rick Hautala, Joe R. Lansdale, John Skipp, David J. Schow, Charles Grant, Tom Monteleone, John Pelan, Ellen Datlow, the aforementioned Ketchum, and all the other folks who have mentored and guided us -- they were practicing and preaching that this genre is a family, as well.

So, I'm okay with keeping that tradition going at conventions and parties and gatherings. I think -- as the genre strives toward more inclusivity -- that it is more important than ever to continue that tradition.

We don't remember who invented the wheel. And we don't remember the pitchman who didn't invent but went out there and proclaimed it loudly to the other cavemen. But we use the wheel every day.

In another ten or fifteen years, most people won't even remember Alan Beatts.

But they will remember how welcoming and hospitable their peers in the genre were to them, and they will strive to do the same for others.

And in the end, that is what matters the most.

Especially at the end of the road...

→ **CHAPTER SEVENTEEN**

GENRE GENTRIFICATION, OR, "QUEERS HATE TECHIES"

Last week, I mentioned that I've visited San Francisco's Mission District well over a dozen times. One of those times was back in 2006, when Christopher Golden and I led a group of about two dozen writers on what was supposed to be a trip to James Simes's legendary Isotope Comics, but—due to the fact that none of our phones had GPS technology back in the ancient days of 2006—turned into a walking tour of the Mission District instead. Author Nate Southard refers to this fondly as "the sixty-block death walk."

Steven L. Shrewsbury, Brian, Christopher Golden, and James Moore – Isotope Comics, 2006. (Photo copyright Steven L. Shrewsbury 2006)

People (mostly out-of-towners who had heard sordid tales of how the Mission District was home to roving bands of homeless, drug addicts, and mentally ill people) admonished us to be careful. They didn't think such a pilgrimage was a good idea. We explained to them that if San Francisco's Alan Beatts was a bookselling demigod, then James Simes was his comic book counterpart, and we had to go pay homage.

"Stay in a big group," people then advised us. "Stay together or you'll get stabbed!"

"We'll be fine," author Maurice Broaddus assured them. "We've got Keene and James A. Moore and Steven Shrewsbury with us."

And you know what? We were fine. We walked among the residents of the Mission District—including the many homeless, drug addicts, and mentally ill people—unmolested, and had a lovely time doing so. Not because Maurice was right about Jim Moore or Shrews or myself being imposing figures. We're not. Jim may be big, but so is Barney the Dinosaur and *Sesame Street*'s Snuffleupagus. You may find me intimidating, but in my spare time, I enjoy kittens and Pinterest. And Shrews? Well, he's only imposing at two o'clock in the morning when, after trying to match my bourbon intake, he decides to do a public reading in a hotel lobby, and during one very animated action sequence, he puts his fist through a glass coffee table by accident, and then keeps on reading even though he's bleeding all over the fucking book. True story...

But I digress.

No, the denizens of the Mission District left us alone because we were in their home, and we treated them—and it—as such. We respected them and where they lived and were shown respect in return.

This is one of those simple life lessons that I try to impart on both of my sons. When you are a visitor in someone's home, you treat them and it with respect. You don't move their furniture around. You don't admonish them for their television choices or their selection of beverages. You don't force your will, your values, or your perspectives on them. You don't harangue them over their politics or lifestyle or religious affiliation. If you don't agree with their lifestyle, values, or perspectives, you shut the fuck up and listen politely and try to learn something. If you still don't agree with them after you've learned, you go back to YOUR HOME where you are free to practice those things, and leave them to THEIR HOME where they are free to do the same.

This is pretty much how I live my life.

This is pretty much the opposite of gentrification.

Gentrification is what happens when rich people move into a poor neighborhood and remake it in their image. They move the furniture around while imposing their will, their values, and their perspectives on the people who live there. It is most commonly associated with urban neighborhoods, but as a country boy, I can attest that it happens in rural areas, as well. Rent and property values soar, and the locals get forced out, losing their homes, their culture, and their identity.

Michael Bailey, Gene O'Neill, Brian, and Nick Mamatas take the Mission District. (Photo copyright Michael Bailey 2016)

Before my signing at Borderlands Books, Nick Mamatas, Gene O'Neill, Michael Bailey, and I walked around the Mission District for a few hours. As I mentioned in last week's column, I was stunned by the changes gentrification had forced on the neighborhood. My favorite Irish pub where I used to be able to get a double bourbon on the rocks for six bucks was now a café shop where you could get a cup of organic, grass-fed, free-range coffee for twice that amount—provided you could shout your drink order over the terrible world music piped through the speakers or the cacophony of upwardly mobile techies typing on their laptops—a sound that only stops when they pause to make sure people were watching them. What's up with that, anyway? Are selfies on Instagram and favorites on Twitter not enough for you? Are you so fucking starved for attention that you have to haul your laptop along to the trendy coffee shop and make sure everyone sees you typing in public? Is your conversation so goddamned important that you have to share it with the rest of us while you're walking down the street? Twenty years ago, when people in the Mission District strode down the sidewalk talking to themselves, they were probably schizophrenic. Now, it's just some asshole on a Bluetooth.

"There goes Keene," someone is shouting, "hating on the hipster techies."

Well, maybe so. But you know who else hates hipster techies? The people who used to call the Mission District their home. I know this because Nick pointed it out to me. On every single block a brilliant, politically-motivated graffiti artist had taken a stencil and painted QUEERS HATE TECHIES in big, bold, red letters. I saw it on walls and sidewalks, businesses and mailboxes. And every time I saw it, I smiled. It gave me hope. It was a sign that at least one person was still fighting back.

Everyone Hates Techies. (Photo copyright Brian Keene 2016)

We passed a building that, at one time, was a homeless shelter and soup kitchen, providing beds and food to the poor who needed them. Now it is a barbershop, providing eighty-dollar haircuts to the hipsters who need them. That is not a typo. Eighty dollars to get your hair cut like Matt Fraction's or to have your beard trimmed like Grizzly Adams.

After the signing, I bid farewell to Gene and Michael, and to Alan and Jude. Then Nick and I headed for the subway. As we shoved our way through hordes of hipsters and techies, I saw another person talking to himself on his Bluetooth, and I asked Nick where the locals had gone.

"I'll show you," he replied.

We descended down into the subway system on concrete stairs lined with used needles and bloody napkins.

"Watch where you step," Nick cautioned. "You don't want any of that on your shoes."

At the bottom of the stairs, I saw a man talking to himself. Unlike the man on the street above, he wasn't wearing a Bluetooth. He had a cardboard sign in front of him, along with a paper cup with some coins inside. I gave him ten bucks—all the cash I had on me. It wasn't enough to get a cup of coffee or a haircut, but if he walked to another part of the city, it might buy him something to eat.

It was midnight by the time I checked into my hotel. I had to be at the airport at four in the morning. Once that plane touched down back home in Pennsylvania, the first leg of this nine-month book signing tour would be over. Instead of sleeping, I lay there in bed, watching Adult Swim and pondering whether the gentrification of San Francisco's Mission District could be compared or contrasted with the post-Dorchester/post-Borders changes in the horror genre.

"Queers hate techies," I mumbled.

And then I smiled.

Yes, I decided. Yes, we could compare and contrast gentrification with the changes in our genre. And although I hadn't realized it, I'd been out there on the road for the last four weeks with a big old stencil and a can of red spray-paint.

What had I learned so far? Let's recap the previous sixteen columns, shall we?

After the collapse of Borders and Dorchester Books, most horror fiction went underground. The gatekeepers at Barnes and Noble and Books-A-Million weren't stocking the latest from Jack Ketchum, Mary SanGiovanni, Bryan Smith, Sephera Giron, or Wrath James White, which started the false narrative that horror fiction was once again on the wane.

Upon hearing this, the gatekeepers at the mainstream New York publishers opted to stop buying horror novels, focusing instead on coloring books and celebrity memoirs, thus further perpetuating that false narrative.

As a result, most of your favorite horror writers had opted for one of three alternatives—they'd switched genres, signed with a small press or indie publisher, or had begun self-publishing via Amazon. Some horror fiction fans followed them to these new outlets, but a significant portion of our readership—a segment who prefer physical books and only shop at the big chain stores—couldn't find these horror novels, and thus, bought into that false narrative that horror was dead...again. And even when the mainstream New York-based publishers put out a horror novel, it wasn't marketed as horror. Paul Tremblay, Joe Hill, Jonathan Maberry, Stephen Graham Jones, and myself were all out on the road this summer, promoting our various novels, all of which had a decidedly supernatural bent, and none of which were being sold as horror.

When horror fiction collapsed in the Nineties, its writers and readers were forced to go underground. Because this coincided with the birth of the Internet, it led to the rise of the small press as a viable alternative to mainstream publishing. I started my career and made a name for myself by preaching about that viable alternative to a mainstream audience who hadn't known about it.

Now, a little over twenty years later, we had been forced underground again, just like the denizens of the Mission District. This time, it had led to the rise of self-publishing and alternative distribution sources. And for the last four weeks, I'd been out here on the road preaching those alternative distribution sources to a mainstream audience who hadn't known about them.

History repeats itself, I thought. *But where do we go from here? What happens next? Will we see a rebirth, the way we did when we were starting out at the turn of the century...or are we doomed? Is this a renewal...or our last dying gasp?*

I lay there until my airport shuttle arrived, thinking about all that I had learned out here on the road. Thinking about the older writers whom I admired, and where they fit in amidst this brave new world. Thinking about the newer writers I'd adopted, and whether they could bend and shape this new world on their own. Thinking about the friends I'd seen at my various signings. Thinking about the friends who were no longer there with me on the journey.

Thinking about J.F. Gonzalez and Tom Piccirilli.

"I miss you guys," I told the empty hotel room as I left.

If they heard me, they didn't respond.

As I climbed onboard the shuttle and gave the driver my airline info, I was suddenly overcome with apprehension. I had the feeling that something was amiss—that things were about to take a severe turn. Most of my friends will tell you (when I'm not around) that I'm terribly paranoid—but they will also admit, if pressed, that when my sixth sense starts tingling, it's usually right.

Where were we going, as a genre?

I hadn't figured that part out yet.

But for the time being, I was going home.

CHAPTER EIGHTEEN

HOUSEKEEPING

If you're just joining us, this is End of the Road—a weekly column in which I detail my nine-month promotional tour for my new novels *Pressure* and *The Complex*. I write about what I've learned out here on the road, and how the horror genre, our industry, our country, and myself have changed over the last twenty years. Last week's column wrapped up the first leg of the tour. This week's column will be short—just a few notes and addendums and bits of housekeeping that apply to those first seventeen installments of this weekly feature. What's that? Yes, seventeen installments. There have been seventeen of these columns, and I haven't missed a deadline yet. Amazing, right?

So far, writing this column has been an interesting exercise in time travel. The events I recounted last week took place on July 1st. You read about them on August 22nd. In my mind, sitting here typing this on September 1st, they feel like they just happened yesterday and they feel like they happened years ago.

Back in the fourth installment of this series (which offered a brief history of the World Horror Convention), I talked about the theory of

Eternal Return—best typified by some of the works of Laird Barron, Alan Moore, and Thomas Ligotti, or Rust Cohle's "Time is a flat circle" speech on HBO's *True Detective*. I told you how it would be one of the major themes of this series, and how we would return to it eventually. And we did. And we are right now. And we will again. And all of these things will happen at the same time.

Next week's column will be published on September 9th, and will detail events that occurred the week of July 9th. While you are reading about July 9th's events on September 9th, I will be putting the finishing touches on assembling a team to help me steal a...well, you can read about it in November, unless of course my team and I get caught in the act, in which case you'll read about it in the news well before then.

I talked a lot in the third and seventeenth columns about the collapse of the mid-list and how it impacted prose genre, particularly horror. There's a similar yet different debate going on in the comic book field right now. If you want to read a bit about it, there is a great essay on *The Outhousers* website by the always entertaining and always incendiary Jude Terror. There's also a rebuttal by long-time comics journalist Heidi MacDonald.

Recently on Twitter, writers Cullen Bunn, Tim Seeley, and comic shop employee Aaron X were discussing Jude's piece, and our thoughts on it. I (mostly) agree with it. Tim (mostly) disagrees with it. Cullen is somewhere in the middle. My concern—and the reason I tend to agree with Jude—is that I see an awful lot of similarities between what happened to the prose mid-list earlier this decade and what's currently happening in comics. I also see a lot of similarities between the collapse of mass-market horror prose in the Nineties and the subsequent collapse of comics in the Nineties. We've seen the market correction occur in prose. I strongly suspect we're going to see it occur in comics, as well, within the next two years.

But that's an entire column's worth of material, and I'll write about it (or talk about it on my podcast) at a later date.

My old pal Seth Lindberg reached out to me in regards to last week's column, focusing on the gentrification of San Francisco's Mission District and how that correlates to the gentrification of the horror genre. The first thing he informed me of was that the "Queers Hate Techies" thing is by a well-known graffiti artist and tagger who follows the Gay Shame Movement—which, according to Wikipedia, is a protest of and opposition to the over-commercialization of homosexuality, gay pride events, and the ever-increasing diverse portrayal of gays in media. Proponents attack what they view as "queer assimilation" in what they think are oppressive social structures. As someone who has been fighting for gay rights since the 1980s, I can't get behind the Gay Shame movement. Thus, that certainly makes me reconsider my reaction to the "Queers Hate Techies" graffiti. I still think it's a great commentary on gentrification, but I'm not crazy about the beliefs of the person spreading the message.

Seth also said, in relation to last week's column, "What's happening in San Francisco is really complicated. As someone who has lived here on and off since 1995, there's a part of me that wants to assemble charts and go on rants while you patiently listen to me, but I'm not sure it would help your piece in any measurable way. Obviously, things are always more complicated than they appear.

But I will say, 'Gentrification' is useful to people for good reasons and bad. The good reasons you know—the bad is that it gets used as a safety blanket for people who fear change. It is, like many things, a tight-rope."

Food for thought, and something I hope to revisit later on, as well.

Okay, next week, the second leg of the tour begins. If you think the saga of the ISIS Psychic Suicide Bomb is over, you're wrong. There's also, in coming weeks, a very real visit from a dead friend, a storm, disarray at a publisher, a car fire, a store fire, an incident on and off a mountain road—with a cow, alligators, Edward Lee's lizard hallucinations, a wedding, a road-trip with John Urbancik, and much more. If you've enjoyed the first seventeen columns, the best is yet to come.

And if you think you know where this is going, you're wrong.

I know you're wrong, because I am traveling through time ahead of you.

Hang on to my hand, because shit's about to get really dark…

CHAPTER NINETEEN

ONCE UPON A TIME

For the last few months, this weekly column has focused on my current book signing tour for *Pressure* and *The Complex*. If I've done my job correctly so far, then you've gotten a good look at what such an undertaking is like for me at my age and at this point in our genre and industry's history.

You've also probably seen the ghosts of Tom Piccirilli and J.F. Gonzalez flitting around between the sentences—sometimes subtly, and sometimes not so subtly. They're going to start making their presences known more fully in the weeks to come. But before I begin recounting the second leg of the book tour, and telling you about what went down in July and August, I thought perhaps we should travel back in time to the year 2008.

Things were very different in 2008. I was at the height of my popularity as a writer (indeed, I may have peaked around then). The mass-market mid-list was still thriving. Dorchester and Borders were both still functioning entities. The small press was still healthy, if somewhat bloated. Horror fiction was still enjoying a resurgence in popularity. I was still married. My son was a newborn. And I was off on another book signing tour—this time to promote a comic book I was writing at the time for Marvel Comics.

I was due to sign at a comic book store in Wyoming, and since Tom Piccirilli lived just an hour away (in Northern Colorado) and since he was one of my best friends and indeed, the big brother I'd never had, I asked him if he wanted to tag along. He did.

The next installment of this series recounts what happened next. Tom wrote it back in 2008. It appeared in the 2010 World Horror Convention Program. I am reprinting it here with permission from his estate. And I am doing so because Tom does a fantastic job of capturing exactly what things were like then. If you read this, and then go back and read the first eighteen columns in this weekly series, you'll see just how much things have changed.

I need you to understand something: everything Tom writes in the first half of this essay is one-hundred percent true. The guitar, the AWOL soldiers, the granny in the wheelchair—all of these things really happened. The essay doesn't veer into meta-fiction until the helicopters and black SUVs show up. After that, it becomes fiction, obviously—but even then, Tom reveals some very real and poignant truths about us both, and who we were at that time in our lives.

Now Tom is gone, and I'm still here, a shadow of the person that he writes about in this piece.

One of my favorite works by Tom is the "Self" series—a mythology of interconnected short stories and one full-length novel about a reluctant magus and his demonic familiar (named Self). I always liked those stories because I've got my own such familiar. Oh, it's not a real demon or anything like that. It's just my other half. I call it the Beast. Every once in a while, the Beast wakes up and whispers in my ear, telling me how good, how justified, and how satisfying it would feel to blow this entire genre up, just like a pissed-off kid kicking over the Legos he spent all day building. The Beast tells me to burn it all to the ground and lay everything to waste, reduce the industry to a smoking crater, taking out friend and foe alike. The Beast tells me I should leave things the way they were when I found them back in the Nineties.

As I get older, and as this business takes more and more from me, I sometimes see the wisdom in this, and it becomes harder to ignore those thoughts. Sometimes, fellow author and partner Mary SanGiovanni talks me out of it, the way Tom Piccirilli and J.F. Gonzalez used to.

But even still...there are rare nights where I fantasize about it.

But on most nights, I just miss my friends and the way things used to be.

Here is one of those friends, telling you how those things were.

(And remember—this is completely true until the black SUVs and helicopters show up...but even after that, there's more truth than you might imagine.)

CHAPTER TWENTY

HOW BRIAN KEENE NEARLY CAUSED THE NUCLEAR APOCALYPSE AND YES, EVERY WORD OF THIS IS TRUE, MOSTLY

➤ **BY TOM PICCIRILLI**

This is how trouble starts, I thought. Riding into the wasteland side by side with my bud, my little bro, Brian Keene, with him hunched over the wheel as the empty terrain of Wyoming flashed by, talking Hunter S. Thompson and other dead heroes.

We'd known each other for more than fifteen years and learned there was a lifetime of difference between 29 and 45. Time and mileage had caught up. We were gray and balding. We were singed around the edges. We didn't show our teeth much when we smiled. Me because of a bad case of Bell's palsy that had left the one side of my face partially paralyzed. Brian—well, I wasn't sure. Maybe too much sorrow.

He had come out west for a book/comic signing/interview. My place was on the way so he breezed by in the airport rental and we fell into the old patterns of our friendship. We shot shit, we opened up about our lives. We whined a little louder to each other than we would most other folks. We admitted, we reminisced, we embellished. We talked word counts. We looked into each other's faces searching out the scars of our endeavors. We wonder who paid the bigger price. It was the middle age version of seeing who had the biggest dick. It was the poor man's version of who has the nicest car. We talked about Dick Laymon. We always talked about Dick Laymon.

As a mid-list, low-list, and no-list novelist over the course of my haphazard career, it was only with great difficulty that I managed to hold onto any self-esteem at all while riding shotgun during a five-hour signing/interview with Brian Keene. Note that when I say "with Brian," I wasn't signing alongside and I sure as hell wasn't being interviewed. I was just his wing man while hanging around a comic shop in Cheyenne, Wyoming, a small store run by a few friends who keep the place more as a labor of love than a business. I was out of my natural element. I was in Wyoming, man.

The store was a hole in the wall, but what they lacked in size and space they made up for in enthusiasm. They called everybody from their local high schools, newspapers, and cable stations to get the word out that Brian Keene was coming to town.

Now, you never know which way a signing is going to go. You might have 20 folks show up, or you might wind up flirting with the chick working the coffee counter at B&N because you're sick and tired of making puppy eyes at stone-faced customers walking past at a brisk pace. Occasionally, the coffee counter chick might front you a biscotti for your troubles. In general, though, my own book signings definitely fall to the puppy dog eye extreme.

END OF THE ROAD

Brian downplayed it. He hoped to fake me out. He tried to tell me nobody would show. He said I would be bored shitless. He mentioned I could take the rented car and go off and get lunch and try to keep myself entertained, go see a movie, find a holdover frontier whorehouse.

The shop had ordered tons of Brian's titles and issues of *Dead of Night: Devil-Slayer*, which had all been bagged and laid out on a table. They had signs up. They had pictures of Brian in full gangsta pose in all corners. They stopped short of having a life-size Brian Keene cut-out which you could pose beside. Or better yet, one with the face cut out saying YOU CAN BE BRIAN KEENE FOR A DAY.

Then the interviews began, the first conducted by store employee on camera. It consisted of many super-hero and super-villain questions. Like, "If you had to face down a zombie apocalypse, who would you want at your side?" Brian answered, "Wolverine." With a codicil, "Or maybe Galactus."

Next came the interview by a group of three young guys from the YMCA who apparently were putting this up on a website. They had a laptop with a camera set-up. They hit him with a load of questions, some sharp, some stolen from the previous list. Yes, still Wolverine, yes, still Galactus.

Then the cutie but professional high school reporter chick showed up and asked pointed questions about writing, his personal history, day jobs, his new baby boy, writer's block, inspiration, his parents. The local news channel wafted in and glommed on until Brian made an off-hand crack about religion in a red state.

The fans mobbed up and crashed the door. They swarmed. They overtook. They overpowered. They overwhelmed. They looked starved for brain juice nutrition. They were wide-eyed and slack-jawed. They explained and espoused to one another about Brian's writing, singing about how it was so powerful, immediate, and gripping. How he had a real blue-collar sensibility, a working man's approach to horror, emotional pain, loss, and thrills. It's why, they said, he speaks to such a large cross-section of the public.

I lived in Northern Colorado and never even knew Wyoming had this many people. Brian shook hands and signed books and bonded and kibbitzed and posed and dallied. He even signed a guitar. I'm not sure why anyone would want a writer to sign a guitar. I'm not entirely sure how you make the transition from "I love this guy's books" to "I need his autograph on my Fender." It doesn't matter. Despite my confusion, I watched Brian sign a guitar. I watched a young man cry "awesome" with tears pooled in his eyes.

But it was the three soldiers in full military fatigues that really caught my interest.

They came in with a flourish, stood in line with an even more excited air than the kid with the guitar, and called Brian "sir" and practically took an "atten-shun" stance while in his presence. They shook his hand while Brian did his verbal canoodling, and then they lined up for photographs. But afterwards they couldn't bear to leave the shop early. They hovered in the back near where I was sitting. Their gazes gleamed with respect, admiration, and a little nervous energy. They kept eyeballing the door. It got me paranoid. I started watching the door too.

I said, "What's the trouble, guys?"

"Nothing."

"You look a bit worried."

"Well, the truth is—"

"The truth is what?"

"We're probably about to get arrested," they confessed.

"Arrested?" I asked. "Why?"

"We're AWOL."

"You're AWOL?" This was a pretty major jump from the kid with the signed guitar. "You mean you left your post?"

"We left."

"You left? You mean you left…what, the nuclear missile silos?"

"Our commanding officer wouldn't give us permission to come see Brian. So, we left anyway."

This is what happens in Wyoming, I thought. *You stick these guys out in the middle of a thousand square miles of nothing but sandstone and longhorn cattle skulls, give them only comic books and Brian Keene novels to read, and then tell them to sit by the button in case planetary nuclear annihilation becomes a necessity. Trouble ensues.*

"But…Jesus, guys, who's watching the missile silos?"

"They're mostly automated. Unless we wind up under attack and somebody has to push a button."

"There's nobody around to push the button?" I asked.

"Well, we wanted to meet Brian Keene."

"There's nobody to push the button in case of nuclear attack? Well, shit, you got your Keene novels signed already. Get back to the silos!"

But we were in Wyoming. Boredom plays a large part of everyone's lives. These people are edgy. These people, they're on the cusp.

"We wanted to take Brian out for a beer and some shots of Knob Creek. It's his favorite liquor. He blogs about it all the time."

"Yeah, I know! But guys, Jesus, hold on–"

I worked my way through the crowd to Brian's table at the front of the shop. He paused long enough to notice the expression on my face. He frowned and asked, "What's going on?"

"Three of your fans just left the nation unprotected in case of a nuclear attack."

"What?"

"And it's your fault. They want to party with you."

Brian's face fell in along its usual planes and edges, his normal expression mostly moderate guilt and dismayed confusion. "What did I do this time?"

"I don't know but I vibe bad shit about to befall us, so let's wrap this up. Who knows what'll happen if the Army or the feds really want to make a case."

"The feds are in play now? Should we leave?"

"Maybe after you finish signing this lady's comic books."

So after Brian made his fond farewells, hugged his fans, kissed a few babies, wheeled a grandma around in her wheelchair, signed a saggy tit, promised to run for president in 2012 if the Mayans didn't kill us all with their evil prophecies, signed somebody else's guitar, signed a perky tit, shook hands with the three soldiers, sipped from their flask of bourbon, left a few weeping readers on the curbside waving their black lace handkerchiefs while singing a heartbreaking Mexican song of death and farewell, and we finally managed to split from the store and jump into the rental car.

We hopped onto I-25 and headed south back towards Colorado, where the cowboys aren't quite as bored or affected by the radiation from ten million stored nuclear warheads, and we could at least hope for a slightly elevated but still modicum degree of sanity. As always, I was in bitter jealous awe of the admiration Brian managed to generate in his readers. The interest they showed in him because of his willingness to commit so much of himself and the persona he'd created down to the page. He spiked himself there with ten penny nails. I cut my wrists open and write in red too. All writers who give a damn about the work do. But Brian's fans show up with bandages and bind his wounds for him, and that is something very special.

As we rode along discussing new creative projects and old publishing troubles, suddenly four black modified GMC SUVs tore up from behind us and quickly surrounded our vehicle.

Brian wagged his head in disbelief and growled, "Now what's going on?"

"I don't know, but I think they're–"

"Feds! What do they want with us?"

"Well, it is your fault that the nation was defenseless in case of nuclear war. They may suspect you're a terrorist. They're signaling for us to pull over."

"This thing has no pickup!"

"You'd better do what they want."

Brian's face filled with dread and shame. "Look, we can't stop."

"What do you mean?"

"I never told you about my Navy days, did I? And how once I was arrested by the shore patrol–"

"Yes, you've blogged about it."

"Well, I spent a night in jail. In the can. The joint. The big house. The bin. That's what we ex-cons call it."

"Yeah, you blogged about it, B–"

"Well, I never told anyone about what went on board that ship. About the horrible experiments that were done…down in the hold… to our prisoners!"

"Oh, Jesus Christ. What men do while they're out at sea should be kept among themselves, Brian, I'm not judging you."

His eyes shifted. "We have to get off the Interstate. Now!"

"How? It's fucking Wyoming. We just passed a sign for a town that said POP: 32. How are we going to hide out when everyone in town can fit in your living room?"

We were stuck in the wasteland. No matter which direction we ran we were trapped in road warrior territory. Utah, South Dakota, Nebraska, or northern Colorado.

Brian drove with a force of concentration I've never seen on anyone else. I wondered if this was how he wrote as well. Focused like a beam of light becoming a laser. Every so often he'd spit chaw out the window and onto the windshield of the feds' trucks. It must've miffed them good because they started trying to box us in then.

But desperation fuels incredible feats. Brian managed to get more action out of that car than I thought possible. We cut over to the shoulder and through a barbed war fence, Brian yanking the wheel so tightly that I thought for sure we'd flip over. Rotted fence posts exploded around us. The wire flapped in our grille. I didn't want to die on an empty plain of red rock. The SUVs came after us, but Brian managed to zig and zag and serpentine past the outcroppings of stone while the trucks barreled into them and bottomed out even with their reinforced undercarriages. A red dust storm swirled around us. Brian spun the wheel hard again and floored it. We were in some kind of vague and uneven trail heading through the craggy ridges.

"Maybe we can get to Denver," he said. "And lose them."

"I don't know. It's still a haul."

"But if we make it we can get lost for a while, get resettled, regroup, plan our way out of this. I never told you about the time Tim Lebbon and I went skinny dipping at World Horror Con and the cops threatened to–"

"Yes, you blogged about it."

"Are those helicopters?"

They were. Flying in low from the east where the empty silos stood waiting for our proud troops to return after reading their Keene comic books. "Government troops!"

"Holy fuck. I think those are black ops teams!"

"What kind of shit have you gotten us into now, zombie boy!"

"Don't call me zombie boy, motherfucker!"

"Watch out!"

We crashed through another barbed wire fence. I had no idea what all this fencing was keeping in or keeping out. We hadn't seen a horse or a cow or long-horned sheep since we set out. We hit the highway again and nearly roared into the side of an eighteen-wheel Freightliner. I braced my feet against the dashboard. I thought for sure our front end was going to get chewed up but Brian managed to downshift and barely avoid wrecking us. We were on the wrong side of the highway heading south in the northbound lane, but Brian didn't seem to mind. Traffic rushed toward us head-on as Brian adeptly and almost calmly jockeyed from one lane to the next, avoiding blaring vehicles.

I was a lapsed Catholic who was whining novenas and praying to all the saints and martyrs I could remember, even those with the really screwy names: John, Paul, Anthony, Ignatius, Basil, Benedict, Dominic, Catulinus, Abban of Murnevin, Theodore the Sanctified, Irwin. Was there a St. Irwin? I didn't care. I prayed to him anyway.

"Take the next exit!" I shouted.

"No shit!"

We rocketed up the entrance ramp and narrowly avoided a bright yellow rice burner motorcycle. Brian screamed out the window, "Buy American, bitch!"

"Are the helicopters still following?" I asked. I couldn't see them anywhere.

"I don't know. We've got to ditch this car."

"There's a truck stop up ahead."

We pulled in and I immediately felt safer being among hundreds of other cars, trucks, SUVS, and vans. Fatigued families dragged ass across the parking lot while kids screamed and old folks bitched about the weather and gas prices. "We've got to steal a car."

"Well, look for something that seems fast."

We ran up and down the aisles trying to figure out what looked fast. And it had to be American. I was sure Brian would only steal American. I kept thinking about crossing wires. Who the hell knew which wires you crossed, but I'd seen a million movies where they made it appear easy. I'd written about it a lot myself. I had plenty of car thief protagonists in my fiction. I was suddenly enraged at myself for not researching the subject more. Fucking Google made it all too easy.

I turned and saw a Mustang slowing down beside Brian. I started to call to him, to tell him to duck or run or do something dramatic because the spooks were upon us, but suddenly the car braked hard and the driver's door swung open. A teenage punk with a grin that nearly went ear-to-ear hopped out and practically into Brian's arms.

I thought, *What now?*

"Excuse me," the kid said, "but are you Brian Keene? It is you! I love your work! I read your blog faithfully!"

Brian turned to me as if to say, *Look at this, another fan shows up at the most inopportune time.* But he didn't turn the guy away.

I thought, *This is why they worship him. Because he always makes the time for them. Because he always gives them a friend when they need one, a mentor, a brother, a father figure. Whatever they're looking for, Brian provides it by opening up his chest and reaching in and pulling it out of himself. Even while in heavy pursuit he'd stop and chat and sell some books and make this mook's day.*

He shook hands while I searched out assassins.

"Mr. Keene, I love zombies! I can't get enough of the undead. I absolutely loved *The Rising* and *City of the Dead*–"

"I do more than zombies, man!" Brian said, more than a hint of impatience in his voice. "Haven't you read my slightly supernatural, quasi-crime thriller *Kill Whitey*? Or my end of the world books *Darkness on the Edge of Town*, *The Conqueror Worms* and its sequel, *Deluge*, which I've been offering on my blog for free?"

The kid hadn't really heard Brian's retort, his eyes gleaming with love and adoration, his slack mouth continuing to work. "–and *Dead Sea*...and *The Last Zombie*..."

"I do more than zombies, you little shit! How about *Castaways*, my Richard Laymon homage? You don't know about my Levi Stoltzfus series, my Amish mystic warrior?"

"Brian, we've got to split!" I called. "Steal his car!"

"And *The Rising: Selected Scenes From the End of the World*," the kid continued. "And *The Rising: Necrophobia*. And *The Rising: Deliverance*! Oh, Mr. Keene–"

"You little fucker! I don't just write about zombies!"

"Brian! Now!"

But Brian Keene could never bring himself to break away from a fan. So I rushed over, kneed the punk in the groin, gave him a swift kick in the stomach while he was down, and then jumped into the Mustang. I immediately felt comfortable behind the wheel, with the engine already groaning, the car hot and heaving. Brian threw himself head first into the passenger side and we squealed out of there.

We stewed in silence for a while as we raced down the interstate towards Denver. Everyone needs a little optimism in their lives, and I kept thinking that if we could just make it to the city we'd be free and our troubles with black ops teams would somehow vanish.

But the cops picked us up right as we blasted down into LoDo, the lower downtown area. Sirens filled the world again and swept over us like a hot screaming wind. A new set of black SUVs weaved in and out among state troopers. All the forces of justice descended upon us.

"Look," Brian said, "I never told you what happened when—"

"Yes, you've blogged about it."

"You didn't even let me finish!"

"You blog about every fucking thing!"

The Mustang's wheel felt good in my hands. I pulled shit out of that engine that had to have been blessed by St. Theodore the Sanctified. I was blessed by the Pope, the archangel Michael, and Christ himself. Panic was getting me back in touch with my Catholic roots.

All of the cops and black ops and feds slowed down and let us run out ahead of them. I knew that meant trouble, but I couldn't see it coming from above or ahead or from any direction. That meant it would hit from below. I slammed the brakes and the car screeched like a twelve-year-old Brian Keene fan getting a picture with him for the first time. We sat there trying to catch our breath, staring out over the rim of eternity.

"What the hell is that?" I asked.

"I think it's...the Grand Canyon!"

"Isn't that Colfax Avenue over there?"

"Maybe it's not the Grand Canyon," Brian admitted. "But it's big! It's a very big canyon-like hole in the ground."

"Shit."

"It's been a hell of a ride, man, let's not stop. Let's just keep on going."

"It's really not that big a hole."

"Come on, let's rock! Hit it!"

We clasped each other one last time.

"I love you, man!" I told him.

"I love you too, bro!"

"I'm sorry I called you zombie boy."

"Godammit, you prick!"

And we gunned it forward into legend.

CHAPTER TWENTY-ONE

HOMECOMING

Sunlight reflected off Three Mile Island's nuclear cooling towers as my plane landed. After three weeks of traversing California, Arizona, Nevada, New Mexico, and Texas, I was home for seven days. The first thing I did (after getting my Jeep out of long-term parking) was drive to my ex-wife's house. She and my son had been babysitting my cat while I was away. I hugged all three of them and then sat down on their couch and accidentally fell asleep for fourteen hours.

When I woke up, I reminded myself that I was only home for seven days. Then I'd be back out on the road again.

I tried to settle back into my regular routine, but that was easier said than done. One problem was the time travel aspect of touring. After bouncing back and forth between so many different time zones, my body no longer knew what time it was, or even what day.

Another difficulty was the balancing act of spending time with my sons and still getting work done. I suck at working on the road. The West Coast leg of the tour was no exception. I wrote a little bit in hotel rooms—a page here or there. I jotted some things down in a Moleskine notebook while riding shotgun in Tod Clark's truck. I tried recording some thoughts in the digital voice recorder Kevin J. Anderson had suggested I buy, but couldn't figure out how to use it. Now, I was home, and had access to my office and all of its familiarity and comfort—but I still found working impossible. It was clear to both me and my ex-wife that while our eight-year-old had done okay with me being gone so long, my absence had impacted him just the same, so spending quality time with him was my first concern. Less so my older son, who, at twenty-five, is used to Dad's touring.

For the next seven days, my eight-year-old and I swam in the creek and went on hikes and played Legos and video games and watched movies and read comic books and had a glorious time. Work—which I was already behind on—took a back seat. I knew I would pay for this later on, as deadlines loomed and publishers got justifiably pissed off at me, and fans wondered where the next book was, but I didn't care. Some things are more important. Writing was basically limited to evenings after my son had gone to bed. I attempted to check my email, but there were 4,987 unread messages in my inbox, and I found the prospect of answering them daunting, so I opted to just ignore them and hope they all went away.

Signing at The York Emporium. (Photo copyright Brian Keene 2016)

The next Saturday, it was time for another signing. I didn't have to get on a plane or drive eight hours because the event was local—taking place at The York Emporium, one of the biggest used bookstores on the East Coast. The building used to be an old factory. Now, every corner is filled with bookshelves and display cases. Genre fans can find anything there—mint condition Arkham House and Gnome Press titles, limited editions from Cemetery Dance and Subterranean Press, Zebra and Leisure paperbacks, and even old fanzines from a bygone era.

It's also the partial resting place of J.F. Gonzalez (hereafter referred to as Jesus). After his death, some of his ashes were spread in California. Some of them reside with his wife and daughter. And some of them were interred within the walls of The York Emporium, along with an unopened bottle of bourbon and a sealed letter explaining who he was so that five hundred years from now, when workmen tear down the building to make room for a new spaceport, they'll know who is buried there and what he meant to us.

The York Emporium used to be a regular hangout for us both. Indeed, it was sort of a social gathering point for all of Central Pennsylvania's speculative fiction writers. For years, Jesus, myself, Geoff Cooper, and Robert Ford had individual hiding places within the store—spots where we could stash books we really wanted but couldn't afford that week, so that the others couldn't buy them first. Jesus's ashes are interred in his hiding spot.

I hadn't been inside the store much since we'd sealed him in the wall. Part of that was time spent writing and being a father and a boyfriend. Part of it was the fact that I hadn't been home much, due to touring. And part of it was because the few times I had visited, I'd sat down in front of Jesus's spot, hoping to feel something—some connection, some sign—and found only silence and a deep,

189

abiding sadness within myself. I took this to mean that wherever he was, it wasn't here.

I mentioned in an earlier column that my idea of the afterlife is a hotel convention bar, and Dick Laymon, Rick Hautala, Phil Nutman, Graham Joyce, Charlie Grant, Tom Piccirilli, Jesus, and everybody else are hanging out there, waiting for the rest of us to arrive. If that was indeed where Jesus had gone, then it was pointless for me to sit there in a bookstore and talk to a wall. Even with the better awareness the public has for mental illness these days, people still look at you funny if you talk to walls—unless you're wearing a Bluetooth. So, I didn't visit much, mostly because doing so made me sad.

I wasn't thinking about any of this the morning of the signing. Indeed, as Mary SanGiovanni and I drove to the store, I was thinking about just how triumphant the first leg of the tour had been—how most signings had been well-attended, how both *Pressure* and *The Complex* were selling through the roof, how I had successfully re-booted my mass-market, mainstream career, and how, for the first time in a long time, I was genuinely happy. How, for the first time in recent memory, it didn't feel like doom was dogging my footsteps, following in my wake like some dark, ominous, and ever-expanding storm cloud.

That was in the first week of July. Writing this now, in mid-September, I remember how that storm cloud exploded in the weeks that followed, spitting down rain and hail and hellfire.

Other writers call that foreshadowing. I just call it life.

The signing itself went great. In addition to Mary and myself, Chet Williamson, Stephen Kozeniewski, Robert Ford, Kelli Owen, Lesley Conner, Jason Pokopec, Rachel Autumn Deering, and a few other authors were in attendance. We signed books and did panel discussions. I met new readers and reconnected with long-time fans.

I saw a lot of friends I'd known from high school. The only downside to the day was the heat. The York Emporium has no HVAC system, and by one in the afternoon, the temperature inside the store had reached the high nineties.

Brian photobombs Rachel Autumn Deering and Cemetery Dance's Frank Michaels Errington. (Photo copyright Frank Michaels Errington 2016)

At the end of the day, before all of us went out to dinner together, I decided to visit Jesus. I walked over to his section and stood in front of the wall, and silently reflected on things.

For just a brief moment, I thought I felt something—an impression of a warning.

Now, it's common knowledge that I'm paranoid. I admit it and accept it. But Jesus was paranoid, too. We both had good reason to be. Twenty years in this business will make anyone paranoid. But when Jesus had his haunches up, when his Spidey-sense was tingling and he thought something bad was coming our way—the collapse of Dorchester or the fall of Borders, for example—he used to give off this very particular vibe.

For perhaps twenty seconds, standing there in front of his resting place, I felt that vibe. I felt it as surely as I feel these laptop keys beneath my fingertips as I type this.

And then...it was gone. I chalked it up to the heat. I chalked it up to my imagination.

Then I left the store and went to dinner with my friends, and then spent a final evening with Mary doing boyfriend and girlfriend stuff that we hadn't had a chance to do for a month because I'd been gone.

Two days later, I hugged my loved ones goodbye, climbed into the Jeep, and headed back out onto the road for the second leg of the tour. The Jeep's cargo compartment had a dozen boxes of Joe R. Lansdale books (which I was transporting to a convention for him), my duffel bag, my laptop bag, and my emergency kit. I headed south down Interstate 81, passing from Pennsylvania into Maryland and then Virginia. I listened to music and the *Ground Zero with Clyde Lewis* podcast.

But mostly, I thought about that feeling I'd had inside the bookstore...and what it might mean.

→ **CHAPTER TWENTY-TWO**

THE TAO OF THE COW

The storm reached its peak somewhere near the border of Virginia and North Carolina. The rain seemed to fall almost horizontally, and the wind rammed into vehicles, pushing cars and tractor trailers alike across entire traffic lanes. I gripped the wheel until my knuckles turned white, and chomped my cigar—a Drew Estate Tabak Especial—a little harder between my teeth. My coffee, long since cooled, sat perched against my crotch. Eyes on the road, I switched off my radio, and Clyde Lewis's *Ground Zero* podcast vanished. I risked a glance in the back of the Jeep, making sure my cargo was safe and dry. Everything seemed fine. My duffel bag and laptop case were still there, as were the dozen boxes of Joe R. Lansdale's books, which I was transporting to a convention for him.

The rain beat on the windshield and roof, demanding entry. My wipers tried valiantly to fend it off, but they were losing the battle. On the other side of the highway a tractor trailer skidded, its back end swinging back and forth, nearly clipping an obscenely huge motor home. Another tractor trailer was on my ass with the same tenacity my editors display when I miss a deadline. His grille loomed in my rearview mirror. I debated the wisdom of brake-checking him given the current road conditions, and that was when it occurred to me that this would be a fine way to die—a high-speed collision while hauling a load of books for Joe R. Lansdale through a seemingly apocalyptic storm during the second leg of what I had cheekily called my Farewell (But Not Really) Tour. It would make a fine conclusion to the Wikipedia entry of my life. I could see the news articles in my mind. "Keene died as the result of a twenty-car pile-up he caused brake-checking a big rig on Interstate 64 while transporting books for Hisownself." They'd ask Joe Lansdale for a quote, and he'd say, "I liked Brian. He was a good kid. Wrote a few good books—*The Lost Level* and that thing about the giant worms. They were a lot of fun. He did some pretty stupid things sometimes, though. Brian could fuck things up faster than a duck going down on a tick."

Teaching some asshole trucker a lesson in keeping two car length's distance between himself and other vehicles seemed much more preferable than dying of cancer. I'd seen what cancer had done to Tom and Jesus, and I was scared to death that I was next on its hit list.

"Fuck you, cancer," I said around my cigar. "I'm choosing my own time."

The tractor trailer backed off and veered into the other lane. I felt a twinge of disappointment.

It occurred to me that perhaps I wasn't dealing with the deaths of my friends in a healthy manner.

And that was when the Jeep's radiator blew up. Steam gushed out from beneath the hood and my speed dropped from seventy to something that resembled a slow crawl. I managed to pull over to the side of the road, but just barely. I turned on the emergency flashers and then I sat there—rain slamming down and cars whizzing by—and finished my cigar in between cursing a lot.

After my cigar was finished, I cursed some more.

Then I called a towing service.

Then I decided to curse a little bit more while I waited for the tow truck to arrive.

By the time the guy had my Jeep secured on his flatbed, the rain had stopped. He took me to a little garage in a little town where there must have been an ordinance stating that every resident was required to have a TRUMP-PENCE 2016 sign in their yard. Either that or the townspeople had decided to grow campaign signs in lieu of flowers and shrubs. The tow truck driver unloaded my Jeep and I tipped him and offered my thanks. The mechanic told me he could get the Jeep fixed, and that there was another Jeep Cherokee in a nearby scrapyard with a perfectly good radiator, and the entire process would take about five hours. This sounded perfectly reasonable, but I know nothing about automobile repair, so he could have just as easily told me the Jeep needed new muffler bearings and that would have sounded reasonable, too. Author Geoff Cooper once tried to teach me how to fix cars. He told me the timing belt ran the clock on the dashboard and I believed him.

But I digress.

I hung out at the garage, dining from their vending machine and watching daytime talk shows. The talk show hosts seemed convinced that Clinton would win the election. I glanced outside at all the Trump signs in front of the homes lining Main Street and wondered if the talk show hosts knew about the hot new landscaping trend this summer.

Then I called author and musician Ryan Harding. My original plan had been to spend the night at Ryan's house in Tennessee and interview him for my podcast. That plan had now gone terribly awry, which was unfortunate. Part of this Farewell Tour involves saying goodbye and thank you to my readers, but it's also about seeing old friends one last time—just in case it is the last time—and Ryan is one of my oldest friends in this business.

When the Jeep was fixed, I checked my GPS and did some calculating. My family cabin in West Virginia wasn't too far away. I could spend the night there, recover from my ordeal, and head out from there for my signing in Chattanooga the next day. So that's what I did.

Our family cabin sits on a bit of land that's been in my family for generations. My cousin still farms it. Down yonder in the hollow is a spot where my grandfather used to make moonshine back during the days of Prohibition. Some say moonshine still gets made there today, but if I wrote about that, we'd have to call this nine-month series of columns "meta-fiction" instead of "non-fiction" and I don't want to do that because so far, everything I've told you is the truth.

And also because I don't want to confess to making moonshine.

But I digress again.

I sat there that night, trying to write, but the words would not come. Instead, I opened a bottle of bourbon, defrosted some venison, and made myself dinner. I sat quietly, listening to the woods and drinking and thinking.

What had Jesus been trying to warn me of, back at the bookstore in Pennsylvania? The storm I'd driven through? That my radiator would take a dump and make me miss time hanging out with Ryan? No, that didn't seem right. What seemed more plausible, and more logical, was that the entire thing had been my imagination. Jesus's spirit wasn't there in that bookstore. He wasn't flitting about on the other side, trying to send me a message. He was dead. My best friend was dead, and the entire thing was my subconscious, eager to talk to him one last time, desperate for one last laugh or one last moment of contact. The whole thing had been a trick I'd played on myself.

No, I decided. I was not dealing with the deaths of my friends—especially Jesus's death—in any way that was even remotely healthy. I'm not a New Age kind of guy, and the last time the people in my life convinced me to try talk therapy, they regretted it because I didn't shut up for six months. I wasn't sure what the grieving process was supposed to entail, but I figured it probably wasn't abandoning my loved ones and traveling across the country on some fucking book tour, and drinking my own weight in bourbon, and playing chicken with tractor trailers on rain-slicked highways.

Jesus hadn't been trying to warn me about anything, because Jesus was dead. The experience in the bookstore was a warning from my own subconscious.

I got up at four in the morning and left the cabin, heading for Chattanooga. The mountains were thick with fog, and darkness seemed to cling to everything. There are no street lights in that part of West Virginia, and houses are sparse and shuttered at that time of morning. Even the moon was concealed. I drove in darkness, watching the mist swirl in my headlights, and tried not to cry. I missed my friend, and I was angry at my subconscious for being cruel.

Suddenly, something loomed in my headlights, seeming to materialize out of the mist.

When he was alive, Jesus and I had a long-standing joke about cows. It started with our mutual appreciation for the vampire cow of Marvel Comics—a villain from the Seventies run of *Howard the Duck*. It extended to the laughs we used to share over a story his former co-writer on the first *Clickers* novel, Mark Williams, had once written—a tale about a zombie cow. Mark passed away before ever publishing the story, and years later, Jesus and I were able to re-work it into the final *Clickers* novel, the appropriately named *Clickers vs. Zombies*. But our shared cow jokes really kicked into high gear when Jesus moved from Los Angeles to Central Pennsylvania. Having never been a country boy, he found himself living across from a dairy farm, and he was perplexed, bewildered, and more-than-a-little frightened of the cows next door. The second day after he moved here, he called me up in a panic and said, "What's wrong with these cows? What are they doing? They're possessed! They're making noise and riding on top of each other!" I explained to him they were making baby cows, but Jesus was unconvinced. Until the day he died, part of him suspected the cows were possessed.

All of that came flashing back to me now because there in my headlights, fog swirling around it, stood a cow. I slammed on the brakes. The new radiator kept working. And the cow didn't move. It simply stood there in the middle of the road, glancing at me as if to say...well, I don't know what it would say, because it was a fucking cow.

Tao is a Chinese word signifying the "way" or "path" or "route."

And just like that, I knew.

I understood.

The experience in the bookstore wasn't a warning from my own subconscious about my lack of a healthy grieving process. It really had been Jesus, trying to warn me about something else. This cow—this inexplicable cow standing in the middle of a deserted road at four o'clock in the morning—was his way of assuring me that it was really him.

Grinning, I grabbed my cell phone and snapped a picture. (Later, when Jesus's wife saw the picture, she said, "Jesus is on the road with you." And she was right.) Having captured the moment on film, I reached into the console, pulled out a cigar, clipped the end, and lit it.

Then, I drove around the cow and continued on down the road.

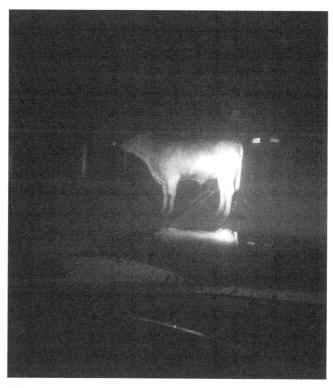

(Photo copyright Brian Keene 2016)

CHAPTER TWENTY-THREE

CONFLUENCE

The fog burned off with the sunrise, the new radiator worked fine, doing what radiators are supposed to do, and the storm was now yesterday's memory. I reached Chattanooga in record time, arriving at noon. I was due to sign at a wonderful independent store called Star Line Books at three that afternoon. With time to kill, I checked into my hotel, and then met up with friend Eddie Coulter and journalist Gavin Dillinger for conversation and a quick bite.

Eddie is a long-time fan. I've known him for close to twenty years. I even killed him in a short story ("The Fall of Rome" from *The Rising: Selected Scenes from the End of the World*). Gavin is a young writer who has penned some amazing opinion pieces for my favorite comic book news website, *The Outhousers*. (Disclosure/Disclaimer: I used to write for *The Outhousers* under a pseudonym, until the former editor spiked one of my stories in what I felt was a politically motivated decision. That being said, I have nothing but love for the full staff, and read the website daily.) We talked books and comics for a while. Eddie and I reminisced about Tom and Jesus, and told

Gavin he should read them. I declined to mention that Jesus had sent me a cow as some sort of warning. When it was time, we headed over to the store.

Like the vast majority of signings on this tour, the Star Line Books appearance went very well. There was a long line of people, and most of them had brought books from home, as well as picking up copies of *Pressure* and *The Complex* in the store. One couple had an adorable baby in a homemade *The Rising* onesie. Several people brought me bourbon—four bottles in total. In addition to readers, old friends showed up, as well, including Mark Hickerson (who moderates the forum on my website), and author Cherie Priest. A good time was had by all.

The owner of the store, Star, was very happy with the results. I was, as well. Once again, I found myself reflecting on how successful the tour had been so far. Big turnouts at all but a few stores. Big sales. Enthusiastic response from fans, readers, and attendees. It was hard being away from my loved ones for so long, but the results were apparent. This tour was having a demonstrable impact.

"I don't know what you're worried about, Jesus," I mumbled to myself during a quick bathroom break. "Everything is fine."

Then I realized there was a man three urinals down from me. He stared straight ahead at the wall, pointedly ignoring the crazy guy in the black and white Hawaiian shirt who talked to himself in public restrooms.

"Hi," I said, grinning. When he didn't respond, I went, "Moooooo…"

He hurried out, not even taking the time to wash his hands. I laughed.

Several of us went out to dinner after the signing. Cherie and I talked publishers, and the craft, and shared apocryphal Warren Ellis stories. We talked about her desire to be thought of occasionally as a horror writer, and my desire to be thought of occasionally as not a horror writer. During dinner, more readers showed up to get their books signed, so I went back over to the store and signed their books and posed for some selfies and thanked them for coming out. Then I returned to the restaurant, bid goodbye to my friends, and retired to my hotel for the evening.

Which was where shit began to hit the fan.

I'd turned on Adult Swim and kicked back on the bed with my laptop, intending to clear through some of the thousands of unanswered emails that had collected in my inbox. I saw one from Jabberwocky Bookshop in Massachusetts, where I was due to sign the following month. The email informed me that they were cancelling my signing because it was Alumni Week at the local college and they needed room in the store for books that would appeal to alumni...or something like that. To be honest, this was back in mid-July, and I'm writing this in late-September and I'm still not sure I understand why the signing was cancelled. All I know is that I had set this signing up early in the year, advertised the store prominently on my website and in promotional materials, included them in paid Facebook advertising, and even listed them on the back of the tour t-shirts—and all of that was now pointless. I'd heard from a number of fans who were looking forward to attending. We could have sold thirty to fifty copies of *Pressure* without even trying. Not to mention I'd planned an entire leg of the tour around that particular signing, and would now have to scramble and reroute.

"Okay," I muttered. "Fuck it. This tour has been a success and I'm not going to let one hiccup derail my mindset. Next email."

The next email was from my editor at Macmillan, the publisher of *Pressure*, informing me that she and her boss—the two people who had brought me on at the company—were moving on up the St. Martins corporate ladder as of tomorrow. In the writing business, this is called being "orphaned," and it can often be the worst thing that can happen to a writer. Let me explain why.

Early on in my career, I didn't want to be known as just a horror writer. I wanted to write all kinds of things—crime, westerns, literary fiction, political non-fiction. My first novel, *The Rising*, was an unexpected bestseller, and quickly put me on the literary map. I followed it up with two novels—*City of the Dead* and *Terminal*. *City of the Dead* was another horror novel, a sequel to *The Rising*. However, *Terminal* wasn't a horror novel. It had supernatural underpinnings, but it wasn't a horror novel by any means. Instead, it was a crime-noir novel. The editor who bought it had big plans. He brought myself and Tom Piccirilli to the publisher—Bantam/Random House—and gave us both two book deals. He told us to write whatever we wanted, genre be damned. He was our advocate. I can't stress how important that is. Mass-market publishing houses are huge, labyrinthine companies with hundreds—and sometimes thousands—of employees. Writers are a very small cog in their wheels. You need to have an advocate at the publisher. Somebody who will push your book. Somebody who believes in you. Somebody who won't let you slip through the cracks. If you don't have this, you and your book are doomed.

Which is exactly what happened with *Terminal*. During the final round of edits on the novel, the editor who had been my advocate left the company. Indeed, he left publishing altogether and became a bartender. I was orphaned. The new editor was very nice, but told me point blank that she didn't "get" my stuff, and preferred fantasy instead, and had me revise the novel considerably. *Terminal* was released with little fanfare and even less advocacy, and it bombed.

Had *City of the Dead* also not been in stores and selling well, my career might have ended right there. Luckily, it didn't, but for the next twenty years, there have been many beyond our genre who saw me only as "the horror writer who tried to write a more mainstream novel and failed."

Now, it was happening again. Just like *Terminal*, *Pressure* was intentionally written to be a more mainstream novel. Yes, there are horror elements, but again, just like *Terminal*, it was crafted to appeal to people who don't like horror—readers of Michael Crichton or Steve Alten, for example. My editor and her superior had both been wonderful advocates for the book. And now, while I was out here on the road, busting my ass and missing time with my sons and my girlfriend and losing my mind talking to dead friends all in an effort to promote the fucking thing, they were leaving. Just like the last time I had tried to reach beyond my genre and go mainstream, I was orphaned. What would happen next? Would I get a new editor who believed in me and the book? Or would I be assigned an editor who didn't "get" me again?

I would have to wait to find out...

Sighing, I shut down my email and checked social media. Fans were posting pictures from the signing, talking about what a great time they'd had. I was glad somebody was having fun. A reader posted about how she and her daughter had missed the signing. I told her to meet me in the hotel lobby the next morning, and bring her books along, and I'd be happy to sign them. And even though it felt like the world was coming down around me, I was happy to make that offer.

Readers don't know what's going on behind the scenes. They don't know that you just got orphaned, or that a bookstore just cancelled on you, or that you're getting messages from your dead friend, or that you miss your loved ones so much that you're sitting in a hotel room in Chattanooga, Tennessee, after a successful signing and dinner with good friends, crying and getting drunk on the four bottles of bourbon people brought to your signing.

Readers should never know any of that. They should just know that you appreciate them.

I finished the first bottle while I talked to Mary on the phone. She was supportive. She reminded me that I'd survived this once before and I would survive it again. She pointed out that I was "Brian Fucking Keene." She said that maybe the new editor would be awesome and supportive. She told me she loved me.

I started the second bottle and asked Tom and Jesus what they thought I should do next.

Outside, it began to storm again. On the television, there was a cow...

→ **CHAPTER TWENTY-FOUR**

BALANCE

Welcome to End of the Road, a weekly column in which I talk about my ongoing cross-country promotional tour for my new novels *Pressure* and *The Complex*. If you're just joining us, a quick recap—everything was going swimmingly and our hero was triumphant until he received a dire warning from what is either the spirit of his deceased best friend, or his subconscious tricking him into thinking it is the spirit of his deceased best friend. Since that warning, things have gone from swimmingly to terribly awry. Our hero—having consumed two bottles of bourbon after learning that a major signing has been cancelled, and he is now orphaned at his mainstream publisher (who published one of the books he is currently out on the road promoting)—is currently passed out drunk in a hotel room in Chattanooga, Tennessee.

We now rejoin the column, already in progress...

When my alarm went off, I woke up happy. I remained happy for thirty seconds. Then I remembered everything from the night before, and my mood quickly soured. I glanced over at the empty liquor bottles and thought about having another. I wasn't hungover—which was troubling. I know my tolerance for bourbon has reached mythic proportions online, but I don't give a shit who you are—you drink two bottles of Knob Creek by yourself and you should be hungover, if not dead.

It occurred to me that I might be turning into an alcoholic. I never drank like this at home, except for that short period after Jesus's death.

This is how it starts, I thought. *For musicians and writers and any other kind of artist. This is how they become an alcoholic. An addict. You put them out on the road for months at a time, away from their family and friends, sleeping in one hotel room after another, with nothing to eat than whatever chain restaurant happens to be in the next town, and then you start canceling gigs and knocking out their support system at the music label or publisher, and they inevitably turn to the free booze and drugs their fans were kind enough to supply them with at the last appearance.*

Fans. The word bounced around in my head, looking for something to connect with. Then it hit me. I was supposed to meet with Jennifer, a fan from Tennessee who had been unable to make the previous night's signing. We'd made plans to meet in the hotel lobby, where I would sign books for her and her daughter. And that was supposed to happen at nine. I squinted at the clock, then put on my glasses and squinted at it again.

"Eight forty!" I climbed out of bed, because at age forty-eight, jumping out of bed is not advisable. "This is no time to wallow in self-pity. I have a job to do. Never mind all this bad weirdness. I am a professional."

Signing books in the hotel lobby. (Photo copyright Jennifer Compton White 2016)

I showered, dressed, gulped a coffee along with my daily baby aspirin and Gingko Biloba, and was in the lobby at nine. Jennifer and her daughter were waiting for me, and they were super excited. I've honestly never heard somebody make an actual "squee" sound, but darned if they didn't. Their happiness and exuberance were exactly the tonic I needed. No, I didn't have a hangover, but my soul was in turmoil and my head was full of doom and gloom. Sharing a few minutes with these two women, listening to their kind words, seeing the happiness in their expressions, and giving them my gratitude cured all my psychic ills. I signed the books and comics they'd brought from home, and presented them with a few more I'd brought down from the room. We chatted for a bit and took some selfies. Then, I bid them farewell, collected my gear, bought another coffee, and hit the road again.

"It's all good," I said aloud. "Everything balances out."

Both my mood and the weather were considerably brighter as I drove across Tennessee. I sang along to the radio and tapped my fingers on the wheel and smiled at the other drivers.

Thirty minutes later, Alabama greeted me with fire.

I saw thick curling plumes of black smoke in the distance as I rolled past a sign welcoming me to "Sweet Home Alabama" and inviting me to "Share the Wonder." In the distance, I spotted an SUV fully ablaze along the side of the road. I pulled over and was just about to offer assistance when a slew of emergency vehicles arrived on the scene, so I wheeled back out into traffic and kept going.

Although I couldn't articulate why, the car fire left me feeling apprehensive. I wasn't in a black mood, like I'd been the night before, but I was unsettled.

Alabama welcomes you! (Photo copyright Brian Keene 2016)

My next stop was at the home of fans Alicia and Chris Stamps. Earlier in the year, filmmaker Paul Campion had run a successful Kickstarter campaign for *The Naughty List*, a short film based on my story "The Siqquism Who Stole Christmas." For their pledge, Alicia and Chris had won a visit from me. I spent a few hours with them, and that unsettled feeling vanished again. I befriended their dog, signed Alicia's books, marveled over her substantial horror and bizarro library and her impressive Richard Laymon collection, and talked—one fan to another—about a genre we loved. Then, as evening fell, it was time to get back on the road again. I was due to sign at independent bookstore Tubby & Coo's in New Orleans the next day. My plan was to drive to Louisiana, get a hotel room and some sleep, and be refreshed and ready for the signing.

Balance, I thought, driving across a levee in the dark. *A signing got cancelled and there is disarray at my publisher, but then some very kind readers balanced me out. Then there was a fire, but again, some very kind readers balanced me out.*

What I didn't know at the time was that Tubby & Coo's, the store where I was due to sign in twelve hours, had just caught on fire.

CHAPTER TWENTY-FIVE

END TIMES

To get to New Orleans, you're pretty much going to have to drive across a bridge. That's what I was doing the morning of July 16th, on my way to sign at Tubby & Coo's Mid-City Book Shop. I was still thinking about warnings from dead friends, and about balance and patterns and nice fans and fires and the theory of Eternal Return.

I don't like bridges. I don't like them for the same reason I don't like flying. It's not a fear of heights. It's a loss of control. On an airplane or a bridge, your fate is taken out of your hands. When I drive across bridges, I tend to stick to the middle lane, as far away from either side as I can, and stare straight ahead, not looking down, not thinking about how I'm fucked if there's a wreck or the bridge suddenly collapses.

Driving into New Orleans, it is impossible not to cross those bridges and think about the damage and devastation in the wake of Hurricane Katrina, particularly the seemingly post-apocalyptic aftermath. It's impossible not to think about the hundreds of thousands of people who sat there, suffering, waiting for the government to help them—only to discover that help was not forthcoming and they would have to help themselves. It's impossible not to think about the lawlessness and savagery on display in the weeks following that disaster—a brutality perpetrated by both civilians and the law enforcement and military who were there to ostensibly help and assist them. What we don't tend to remember is how it wasn't just New Orleans that Katrina devastated. Surrounding towns, parishes, and states were hit just as hard, but the media tended not to focus on them, because a flattened town of poor people in Mississippi isn't as telegenic and good for ratings as a flattened city full of trapped tourists.

I remember Katrina. I remember it because I listened to it happen live. I was out on tour, just like I am now. I had just completed some signings in Canada, and I was driving from *Rue Morgue* magazine editor Monica Kuebler's house in Toronto to a signing in Chicago. I had satellite radio and I listened to coverage of Katrina during the entire long drive. I had friends in New Orleans and the surrounding areas. Some of them got evacuated. Others were trapped inside. Those who were trapped were irrevocably changed.

All because of those goddamned bridges.

Take a bridge away, and people become islands. That's what has happened in this country now. The bridges that used to exist between us have been swamped and destroyed. Those bridges are overrun. They are burned down and blasted. And now, all across America, every day is post-Hurricane Katrina. We are divided along social, political, and religious lines. We have formed our own little islands, dependent upon which team we identify with. With our bridges gone, so is our dialogue and any chance for mutual respect or middle ground. Now we're just islands. Law enforcement. Civilians. Black. White. Latino. Republican. Democrat.

Conservative. Progressive. Christian. Muslim. Jewish. Atheist. Marvel. DC. Pepsi. Coke.

I got to the store a few hours early. Rather than stopping by and checking in, I decided to grab some lunch and check my email. Over a burger and fries, I learned that yet another signing had been cancelled—this time in Spokane. That feeling of impending doom returned.

First, I'd been orphaned.

Then a bookstore had cancelled on me.

Now another venue had cancelled on me.

"At least there aren't any more fires," I muttered.

When I got to Tubby & Coo's, I learned that the store had caught on fire earlier that morning.

It was an electrical fire, and although there was no flame or heat damage, the interior smelled like smoke and there was no electricity. The owners were heartbroken and apologetic. I could tell they'd been counting on this appearance to make some money. I knew there would be a crowd showing up. And I was goddamned if I was going to lose yet another in-store appearance.

"Can you use your cell phone to ring up credit card transactions?" I asked.

They confirmed that they could. So, I told them that I'd be happy to sign books outside the store, and that's exactly what we did. This was mid-July in New Orleans. It wasn't just hot. It was fucking sweltering. But I didn't care and neither did my hosts. I sat out there in the sun and the heat and signed books and took photos with everybody, and by the end of the signing, the store had sold out of *Pressure* and *The Complex*. We had a steady influx of people. Some were local. Others came from as far as Texas. I saw old friends and made new ones. I was given eight bottles of bourbon, a six-pack of craft beer, four books, a t-shirt, and a compact disc. I also got to see the interior of the store, and even though the power was off, and it was hot inside, and there was very little light, I was impressed. If you are ever in New Orleans, please do stop by and support Tubby & Coo's. It's a two-story building, and the second floor has been converted into an awe-inspiring children's section with a wonderful, curated selection of age appropriate horror, fantasy, and science-fiction titles.

The stairs at Tubby & Coo's. (Photo copyright Brian Keene 2016)

One of the murals in Tubby & Coo's children's section. (Photo Copyright Brian Keene 2016)

When the signing was over, I hopped back in the Jeep and headed out back across the bridge. I was facing an eight-hour drive to author John Urbancik's house. I was tired, running on caffeine and stubbornness, and wondering what else would go wrong, and how I would salvage it when it did.

During that drive, I saw Trump signs and Clinton signs. I saw homes that had been foreclosed on and shuttered businesses. I saw four—*four*—police cars parked behind a lone black man in a BMW along the highway, and several passersby who had stopped to film the proceedings with their cell phones. I saw gut-wrenching poverty and obscene wealth. I saw bumper stickers proudly proclaiming the driver's child was an Honor Student and other bumper stickers gleefully announcing that their kid beat up the Honor Student. I saw support for various professional sporting teams, but no support for each other as individuals. I was informed that #BlackLivesMatter and #BlueLivesMatter and #AllLivesMatter, and when I turned on the radio, I heard people arguing about which lives mattered the most. I saw signs telling me to repent because the end was near and billboards asking me if I knew Jesus Christ as my personal savior and graffiti telling me that there was no God and even if He had existed at some point, He was dead now.

I crossed many bridges between New Orleans and Tallahassee, but I crossed them alone.

Night fell and so did my spirits. Dread seemed to loom everywhere, suggesting itself in the most innocent of scenery. I became convinced that this tour was pointless, doomed to failure, and that nothing I did mattered.

I thought about Charles L. Grant, dying broke in a hospice. I remembered when I was younger, and I'd attended a party at author Matthew Warner's house. Myself, Mary SanGiovanni, Matt, Brian Freeman, and a few others of our generation had been standing in the kitchen, talking about how unjust Charlie's method of passing seemed to us. And I remember the absolute gravity and fear in Douglas E. Winter's voice when he stared at me and said, "Now you know what keeps us up at night, kid."

I thought about J.N. Williamson, dying in an old folk's home with only his sister, Gary Braunbeck, and Maurice Broaddus at his funeral service, which was presided over by a preacher who informed them that J.N.'s life's work had served the devil.

I thought about Richard Matheson, still trying to write even as dementia ate away at his ability to do so (or so I've been told).

I thought about Richard Laymon spending the morning writing and then collapsing in his kitchen.

I thought about Pic and Jesus, and I thought about how it never ends well for us writer types. Nobody gets out alive, of course, but is it too much to ask that just one of us goes in our sleep with the knowledge that what we did actually mattered, and that we touched people's lives with our stories about zombies and ghosts and vampires?

What the hell was I doing out here? It was the middle of fucking summer and I should be at home, playing with my son. I was wasting my life writing stupid pulp novels that would entertain people for a few days and then languish on the shelf of some used bookstore, quickly forgotten.

I, too, was an island.

When I reached Tallahassee, it was well after midnight. John was awake and waiting for me. I've known John over twenty years. He is one of my oldest and closest friends in this business. He was happy to see me. He had a glass of bourbon waiting for me. And he'd made cookies.

Five minutes spent in his company, and my gloom had passed. I hung out with my friend, talking and laughing, and enjoyed the bridge over troubled waters, a bridge that only the bonds of brotherhood can build—and that no storm can tear asunder.

John Urbancik and Brian build a bridge. (Photo copyright Brian Keene 2016)

CHAPTER TWENTY-SIX

CAMELOT

"**S**o," author John Urbancik said as we drove across Florida from Tallahassee to Land O' Lakes, "let me see if I understand this correctly."

(That's how John talks. If you're writing dialogue for John Urbancik, he would never say something like, "Let me get this straight" or "You've gotta be fucking shitting me." He would say, "Let me see if I understand this correctly.")

"You're on the second leg," John continued, "of a book signing tour for *The Complex* and *Pressure*. In the first week of this second leg, you've been orphaned by the publisher of one of those books, and you're waiting to hear the outcome of that. You have also seen three previously scheduled signings unceremoniously cancelled by the venues. A bookstore and a vehicle caught on fire, the radiator in your Jeep blew up, and you are running low on money, hope, and gas—and running even lower on fucks to give."

I gripped the wheel and stared straight ahead. "Correct."

"Also, you believe Jesus Gonzalez is sending you dire messages from beyond."

"Either that, or I'm going insane."

"Well, it would hardly be the first time you've done that."

"You are being less than helpful, John."

Grinning, John waved off the comment. "So, if things are that bad, what are we doing out here on the road?"

I shrugged. "I'm out here for you guys. And for the fans. I mean… between Pic and Jesus, who knows how many more years we'll have? Hell, just look at the heart attack ratio alone—you, me, Edward Lee, Jack Haringa, all while in our forties. I'm out here to say goodbye, I guess. To let people know it's been fun, and I appreciate it. I don't know why you're out here."

"I'm writing a new book," John replied. "It's called *On the Road with Brian Keene.*"

And he did. John rode with me across five states—Florida, North and South Carolina, Georgia, and Virginia, and during that time, he wrote a book called *On the Road with Brian Keene*—handwritten in a Moleskine notebook, scribbled from the passenger seat of the Jeep and in various hotel rooms along the way. Ask him about it on social media. Publisher inquiries welcome.

We reached Land O' Lakes, which is the home of Camelot Books. Run by Tony and Kim Duarte, Camelot Books is a titan among horror, science-fiction, and fantasy booksellers. Most of their sales are done online, but they do have a physical store which customers can visit by appointment. If you have money to spend, and you are traveling through Florida, I strongly encourage you to make an appointment to visit because it's not just a bookstore—it's a museum dedicated to this genre and the books we all love. The walls are lined with original artwork and paintings from book covers, including the original art for Camelot's edition of my novel *Entombed*. (In addition to being a bookseller, Camelot has also published books by myself,

Edward Lee, Mary SanGiovanni, Wrath James White, and others.) Shelves stand floor to ceiling, overflowing with trade hardcovers and signed limited editions. John and I walked those aisles, gasping in awe at pristine volumes from Arkham House, Gnome Press, Fedogan & Bremer, Cemetery Dance, PS Publishing, Thunderstorm Books, Subterranean Press, Ash Tree Press, Silver Salamander, Dark Harvest, and so many more. We saw books that cost more than we make in a year. We saw books that cost as little as $20. We got to hold books that we have only ever seen online or behind glass. And we spent money on some of them.

Original cover painting for "Entombed." (Photo copyright Brian Keene 2016)

While we were browsing, our friends began to stop by. Edward Lee showed up, looking fit and trim, along with David Barnett, the owner of the legendary Necro Publications and a fine author in his own right. Accompanying them was K. Trap Jones, a young author who I had never met before. Jeff Strand and Lynne Hansen arrived soon after, and hugs and handshakes abounded. I sat back, taking it all in and smiling. It felt good to be among friends. I hadn't seen Lee in over a year, and it had been almost a decade since I'd seen Dave. I had, of course, seen Jeff and Lynne at the start of this tour, but it was always good to see them again. I don't know that I've ever run across a couple that delight me in their togetherness more than Jeff and Lynne do. They just seem so perfect together, and their mutual love and respect is infectious and intoxicating.

Much like Tom and Michelle, I thought. *And Jesus and Cathy.*

My smile faltered.

Careful, Keene, my subconscious warned. *This is supposed to be a good time. Don't ruin it for everybody by getting maudlin.*

Oh, yeah? I thought. *That's easy for you to say, subconscious. You haven't lost your partner. Cathy and Michelle did.*

No, my subconscious countered, *but I do have to live inside your fucking head twenty-four seven, and believe me, pal, that ain't no picnic. If you're going to be depressed, have the decency to do it alone. Go out to the Jeep and drink one of those dozen bottles of bourbon that people brought to your signings in Chattanooga and New Orleans and let everybody else have a good time. You've been skirting the edge of alcoholism for thirty years now. You might as well grab the bull by the horns and give in. That's what people want from you. The party guy. The fun guy. The public figure. They don't want this sad little fucker who misses his friends. That guy sucks.*

Shut the fuck up.

No, you shut the fuck up.

And then my subconscious and I started punching each other, which happens more than you might think. Mary says it is particularly prone to happening when I am asleep. I don't know if that's true or not, because I'm asleep when it happens.

Kim, perhaps seeing the wrestling match taking place in my expression, wisely suggested that we start signing books, so that's what we did. Unlike the other book signings I'd done on this tour, the signing at Camelot Books didn't involve the public. Instead, John, Lee, Jeff, K. Trap Jones, and myself signed books for the store, which had pre-sold copies to their customers. We also signed store stock which could later be sold on their website. I inscribed a giant stack of *Pressure*, *The Complex*, *The Chinese Beetle*, and others. John signed a stack of his new novel, *Stale Reality*. I'm not sure what Lee, Jeff, and K. signed, because I couldn't see over the stack of books in front of me.

(Top Row, L to R) John Urbancik, Jeff Strand, K. Trap Jones, Edward Lee, Lynne Hansen. (Bottom, L to R) David Barnett, Brian Keene. (Photo copyright Kim Duarte 2016)

When we were done, the group went back to Tony and Kim's house. They value their privacy, as do I, so I won't tell you anything about that. Suffice to say, we had a wonderful afternoon full of food and laughter and sunshine, and we talked about a genre that we all love. Tony and Kim were wonderful hosts, and I can't tell you how grateful I was for everything. I talked with Tony and Kim about *Hole In The World*, a novel I owed them which was unforgivably overdue because I'd had a nervous breakdown while writing it, and yet they were gracious about the delay and understanding. (That was in July. As I write this, *Hole In The World* has four chapters left to be written and should be finished by mid-November.) I talked with Dave about an anthology he was putting together for Gerard Houarner's seminal *Painfreak*. (That was in July. As I write this, the deadline has passed and I hope to get the story finished this weekend.) I talked to K. Trap Jones, and got to know him, and was reminded of what it's like to just be starting out in this business. And I had a heart-to-heart with Lee, as we talked about our missing friends and how we both feel about that and how the days seem to be growing shorter and how there are things we still want to do—need to do—and how we might not have time to do them all.

And while Lee and I talked about those things, we watched small lizards darting back and forth across the landscape. Apparently, lizards are to Florida what squirrels are to Pennsylvania.

"Alligators, too," Lee reminded me. "You know how you have all those deer running around? Down here it's alligators."

Brian and Edward Lee but no lizards. (Photo copyright Brian Keene 2016)

At sunset, the party broke up and everybody headed home. More hugs and handshakes abounded. Then John and I climbed into my Jeep and hit the road again. Driving through rural Florida, I stopped at a swamp and got out. John followed after me.

"What are we doing?" he asked.

"I want to see an alligator," I replied.

"You've never seen an alligator before?"

"In zoos. But I want to see one in the wild. Lee says they're all around here."

"Lee also hallucinated lizards earlier today."

"The lizards weren't hallucinations. I saw them, too."

John frowned. "How much did you and Lee drink?"

"Look," I said. "I'm not drunk. And Lee wasn't drunk either. I don't think I'm asking for much. I just want to see an alligator."

"Well, we can do that from the safety and comfort of your Jeep. Wading out into the middle of a swamp isn't a good idea, Brian."

"Nonsense! What's the worst that could happen?"

"For starters, you could get eaten by an alligator!"

I grinned. "No worries. I've got my switchblade."

I stood there at the water's edge, swatting at mosquitoes and studying the bog. Peat floated atop the dark water. Frogs croaked. Birds chirped. If there was an alligator lurking off the shore, however, I didn't see it. I snapped some pictures of the swamp. Later, John's longtime partner Mery-et told me that there is indeed an alligator in the picture, and that I was nearly on top of it, and if I had taken a few more steps I would have probably seen more of it than I wanted to.

Can you find the alligator in this picture? (Photo copyright Brian Keene 2016)

I have looked at that picture over and over again in the months that have followed, and I still don't see an alligator.

But I do still hear from the other side.

At the time, I was under the impression that those communications had to do with the bad luck that seemed to bedevil this tour in July.

By August, I would discover that they were about something else entirely.

We'll get to that point later. There's no hurry. Time, as they say, is a flat circle.

But it is also a motherfucker.

CHAPTER TWENTY-SEVEN

TEXT MESSAGE FROM JOHN URBANCIK TO MARY SANGIOVANNI

➜ CHAPTER TWENTY-EIGHT

TIME BUBBLE

And thus began the most grueling part of the book signing tour since Tod Clark and I had driven across the American Southwest. John Urbancik and I spent five days in mid-July crisscrossing Florida, Georgia, South Carolina, North Carolina, and Virginia. That no doubt sounds romantic and adventurous to some of you. Hell, up until a few years ago, it would have sounded romantic and adventurous to me, as well. It would have been my idea of fun. Sadly, it's not so fun when you're approaching fifty. At that age, sitting behind the steering wheel of a Jeep for eight hours a day really puts a crimp in your fun. It also puts a crimp in your back and your neck and your butt and anywhere else arthritis and carpal tunnel have invaded your body. Indeed, if a career as a full-time writer hasn't cursed you with arthritis or carpal tunnel (and sooner or later, it will) then you can expedite things by heading out on a promotional tour and driving like idiots across most of the Southern United States.

Tired doesn't begin to describe it. I was beyond any word you can think of to describe exhaustion. Things like time and mileage and the days of the calendar ceased to exist. The world became the interior of the Jeep, with occasional excursions into bookstores or dingy hotel rooms. Poor John had to not only fill the role of my wingman and best friend—he also had to be my therapist, as well. He served admirably, and when not playing the confessor to my sins or signing books for people, he worked on his latest—the aforementioned *On the Road with Brian Keene*. (I wasn't kidding about that last week. Publisher inquiries are welcome.)

In short, things became a blur—a scattershot, bourbon- and caffeine-fueled kaleidoscope of meetings and moments with no true narrative sense, no beginning, no ending, and often, no sense.

The bubble forms.

Time is a flat circle and everything is connected.

Everything has happened before.

Everything is happening now.

Everything will happen again.

Time collapses in on itself.

Witness…

Brian Keene and Jeff Strand—PRESSURE WAR! (Photo copyright Brian Keene 2016)

Mojo Books and Records delivers a large, enthusiastic crowd. Among them are my old friend Mike Bracken, Jeff Strand, and Lynne Hansen (again), and a reader named Laurie who shares a very personal anecdote about her life and my work that nearly moves me to tears.

It is 1998 and Mike Bracken, John, and myself, along with Tom Piccirilli, J.F. Gonzalez, Mike Oliveri, Geoff Cooper, Ryan Harding, Regina Mitchell, Michael T. Huyck, Brett Savory, Cullen Bunn, Tim Lebbon, Mary SanGiovanni, James Newman, Feo Amante, and everyone else from those halcyon days of the early Internet are going to be successful writers someday.

It is July 2016 and some of us did go on to become successful writers, and some of us didn't, and some of us aren't here anymore. Here's something about success that they don't tell you—if you become successful at something, you will carry a lot of guilt about it. You will wonder why you, and why not your friend, and surely they deserve it more than you do. Now multiply that by a dozen and welcome to yet another reason why Brian drinks. But never mind all that, because it is July 2016, and I am seeing Jeff and Lynne over and over and over again. I am so numb from bourbon and traveling that I try to divine some hidden meaning in this—expecting to reveal a fundamental, universal truth. Instead, Jeff and I just sign copies of *Pressure* (as we have both written novels with that title), which are later auctioned off for the Scares That Care charity.

It is July 2016 and Laurie's words are nearly moving me to tears but it is also November 2016 and I still think about them and her and hope that she is doing okay.

It is July 3, 1996, and I am the general manager of a home electronics store. I'm working fifty-hour weeks and writing when and where I find the spare time. I take a rare night off to see a movie called *Independence Day*, and am blown away by how much fun it is. The film becomes one of my go-to favorites—something to put on in the background and make me happy.

It is July 2016 and I take a rare few hours of solace from the road to see the sequel, *Independence Day: Resurgence*, which turns into a massive exercise in frustration and disappointment. John and I both agree that our time would have been better spent sleeping in the Jeep than watching that travesty.

On the trail of Danzig. (Photo copyright Brian Keene 2016)

It is July 1995, and my girlfriend and I are about to see Danzig in concert at the York Fairgrounds. Unfortunately, she gets ill, and we leave the concert a few moments before Danzig hits the stage.

It is July 2016, and that girlfriend is now my second ex-wife (but remains one of my best friends); and the owner of a record store in

Florida is so enthusiastic about our visit to his store that he takes John and me into the store bathroom, where every inch of conceivable wall space is filled with the signatures of visiting musicians, and asks us to sign the stall door next to Danzig's signature. I have still not seen Danzig in concert, but our signatures are now next to each other's at a store in Florida. In my head, I hear Tom Piccirilli expressing confusion about why I get asked to sign guitars and the bathroom walls in music stores.

It is March 2004, and I'm doing my first signing at a Barnes and Noble store. The manager is a big supporter of the horror genre, but B&N corporate rules forbid him from creating an actual horror section in the store, so he does it stealthily. It was this type of ground level effort that led to the post-1990s horror boom at the start of this century.

It is July 2016 and John and I are signing at a Barnes and Noble in Orlando. The manager, Chris, is a big supporter of the horror genre, but B&N corporate rules forbid him from creating an actual horror section in the store, so he does it stealthily. It is this type of ground level effort that will lead to the horror boom coming as we head into the 2020s.

It is 2001, and Geoff Cooper, Mike Oliveri, Michael T. Huyck Jr., Gak, and I are driving across California on a book signing tour for *4X4*, and I am so drunk that the neon lights of a passing gas station have vapor trails.

It is July 2016 and John Urbancik and I are driving across the American southeast and I am so exhausted that the neon lights of a highway attraction called South of the Border (located on the line between North and South Carolina) has vapor trails. I recall author Armand Rosamilia telling us the day before that we have to stop at South of the Border, but John and I are zombies at this point, and almost simultaneously mutter, "We can't stop here. This is bat country."

Brian, Lincoln Crisler, and John Urbancik at The Book Tavern in Augusta, Georgia. (Photo Copyright Brian Keene 2016)

It is...2006 or maybe 2007 and I'm meeting a young aspiring author named Lincoln Crisler who tells me he is inspired by my work.

It is July 2016 and Lincoln shows up at a signing John and I are doing in Georgia—and I'm glad he has because the crowd is sparse—except that he's no longer a kid and he's no longer an aspiring author. He's a professional. I feel very proud. And very old.

It is 1992 and Los Angeles runs riot in the aftermath of the police viciously beating black motorist Rodney King. The smoke and fires and chants and violence frame the current Presidential election between two absolutely loathsome candidates—George H.W. Bush and Bill Clinton. No matter who is elected, things will only get worse.

It is 2016 and America's cities run riot in the aftermath of multiple police shootings of unarmed black men. The smoke and fires and chants and violence frame the current Presidential election between two absolutely loathsome candidates—Donald Trump and Hillary Clinton. No matter who is elected, things will only get worse.

Time begins to expand again.

Everything is happening again.

Everything is happening now.

Everything has happened before.

Time is a flat circle and everything is connected.

The bubble pops.

A week has gone by, and John and I arrive in Williamsburg, Virginia, where we are greeted by dear friends and fans who love us and have missed us. Some of them we haven't seen in a very long time, and yet…it hasn't been any time at all.

→ **CHAPTER TWENTY-NINE**

SCARES THAT CARE

Scares That Care is an IRS approved 501(c)(3) horror-themed charity that I donate my time and name to. We fight the real monsters of childhood illness, cancer, and more by financially helping families experiencing these overwhelming hardships. Each case is unique. We provide money, toys, utilities, and other items to help sick children and their families. We do the same for women fighting breast cancer. And we also partner with actor Kane Hodder (the *Friday the 13th* series) to aid children who have suffered serious, life-altering burn injuries.

Brian and Scares That Care Founder and CEO Joe Ripple. (Photo copyright Brian Keene 2016)

Our Board of Directors are all fans of the horror genre, and some of us also work within the industry. We consider ourselves to be Ambassadors of Horror, and thus, show the public that fans of the genre are not just black-clad weirdos fixated on serial killers or hanging out in the cemetery, smoking clove cigarettes and listening to Type O Negative and pretending to be fucking vampires. We are a completely volunteer organization. None of our staff, our board members, our directors, or our organizers draw a salary, and no paychecks are issued to them. This allows us to maximize the donations of our supporters and give it directly to the families who need our help.

In addition to year-long donations from our supporters in the general public, we organize a number of fundraising efforts, including the annual Scares That Care Weekend Charity Event. Ostensibly, this is a horror convention—but I can say with some pride that it's unlike any other horror convention you'll ever attend. Most horror conventions only focus on one particular aspect of the genre—movies or literature or comic books. The Scares That Care Weekend Charity Event focuses on the entire genre. Movie and television celebrities, filmmakers, authors, publishers, haunt enthusiasts, comic book creators, paranormal investigators, make-up and special effects artists, cosplayers, and much more—all gathered together under the same roof for a weekend. And it works great every year. Not only does it raise money for the charity—it helps the genre grow and expand. I see it happen every year. I hear the testimonials from fans who have attended. They've never read a book in their life, and they've come only to get Ken Foree to sign their *Dawn of the Dead* poster, and by the end of the weekend, they're buying books from Armand Rosamilia. Or they don't watch many movies or television programs, preferring instead to read, and by the end of the weekend, they're posing for a picture with William Forsythe.

We do good for the families we help, but we also do good for the genre.

If this week's column is beginning to sound like a public service announcement, well, I guess it is. However, that's necessary. Disclaimer: I serve on the Board for the Scares That Care Weekend Charity Event. Specifically, I book the authors who appear at the convention, make sure they've got a place to sign books and take photos with fans, oversee all of the author programming (readings, signings, panel discussions), and more. Next year, I'll be doing that, plus the same thing for podcasters, as we add a podcasting programming track. And I'll be running the Celebrity Room. And when I'm not doing those things at the convention, I'm helping out where needed—judging the costume contest or helping out in the autograph room or handing out bottles of water to people stuck behind vendor tables or just working the crowd and making sure everyone is feeling welcome, feeling safe, and having a good time.

The event runs Thursday night through Sunday afternoon. I average four hours of sleep per night during that time. It is exhausting. But I love it. I love helping the families. I love hamming it up for our attendees. And I especially love the people I work with. I've known some of the Scares That Care team for nearly twenty years now. We've worked other conventions together. These people are my dear, dear friends. CEO and founder Joe Ripple, Karen Novak, Andrew Ely—I've known these folks most of my professional career. We've laughed together, cried together, fought in the trenches together. We've seen each other through some pretty deep lows and lifted each other to some unimaginable heights.

So yeah, it's tiring—and as time now speeds up again, and we pick up where we left off in last week's column, as John Urbancik and I arrived at the third annual Scares That Care Weekend Charity Event looking disheveled and dirty and absolutely exhausted—I didn't care. I was happy to be there. Happy to see my friends. And ready to go to work.

In addition to my regular duties that weekend, I was also supposed to perform the wedding ceremony of author Bryan Smith and his fiancée Jennifer. The wedding was to take place Saturday. We arrived in Williamsburg, Virginia (where both the convention and the wedding were taking place), on Thursday.

On Thursday night, I realized that the speech I'd written for the wedding was somewhere between Chattanooga and Biloxi...

You ever heard of a crowd being described as "an ocean of people"? That's what the third annual Scares That Care Weekend Charity Event was like—an ocean of horror movie and television celebrities and their fans, filmmakers and their fans, authors and their fans, publishers and their customers, haunt professionals and enthusiasts, comic book creators and their fans, paranormal investigators and their fans, make-up and special effects artists and their fans, cosplayers, and everyone else—all descending upon the convention hotel in Williamsburg, Virginia, to raise money for burn victims and children and women with cancer.

I was exhausted, but I had no choice but to cast myself into that ocean, to dive into that sea of humanity and hope I wouldn't drown.

And I didn't.

Brian with Fox Mulder's nemesis. (Photo copyright Mary SanGiovanni 2016)

For four days, the ocean buoyed me, held me aloft. I floated on the surface, signing books and posing for photographs. I dived into the depths, having late-night conversations with Tom Monteleone or whiskeys with guitarist Matt Hayward. I even got a chance to enjoy something I rarely get to do anymore—go complete and total fanboy when Mary and I got our picture taken with William B. Davis, the actor who portrayed the Cigarette Smoking Man on *The X-Files*.

To recount everything here would take up several more columns, and we don't have time for that. It's mid-November as I write this, and the events I'm chronicling took place in late July, and we still have to get to the ghost and the heist and all the other stuff between then and now, so instead of giving you a blow-by-blow of the convention, let me tell you about a few of my favorite moments.

Jennifer Smith, Bryan Smith, and Brian. (Photo copyright Mickey Gould 2016)

Believe it or not, I am a licensed agnostic wedding officiant. Sometimes, when royalty checks are slow to arrive and I need money, I'll perform a few weddings. On Saturday evening, I had the absolute honor of performing the marriage ceremony of author Bryan Smith and his fiancée, Jennifer. Bryan met Jennifer on my message board forum, and both are big supporters of Scares That Care, so when they asked me if they could get married there, and if I could perform the ceremony, I was delighted and enthusiastic, as were Joe Ripple and the Board of Directors.

Like Jesus and Pic, Bryan is one of my best friends in this business. I always figured he kinda felt the same way, but Bryan is not the kind of guy who would normally tell you that. Which is why, on the day of his wedding, when he reiterated that he thought of me as one of his best friends in the business, I was incredibly moved. I made an excuse to run to the bar and get another bourbon, but what I really did was go outside and stare at the sky for a few moments—reflecting on the fact that, yes, Jesus and Pic might be gone, but not everyone was dead yet. There were people still here who gave a shit about me, and whom I gave a shit about in return.

That was when I remembered that I still needed to rewrite my officiant speech (the original of which was lost) for Bryan and Jen's wedding—which was due to take place just a few short hours from then.

"Shit!"

I found Mary and we ran upstairs to the hotel room and hid for an hour. During that time, she guarded the door and kept people from finding me while I wrote the wedding speech. I read it verbatim at the ceremony, before the exchange of vows (accompanied on violin by music producer and horror fan Jonathan Yudkin). Here is what I wrote:

Good evening. As you all know, we are gathered here this weekend to raise money for three families who very much need our help. For many of you, this is the third Scares That Care Charity event you have attended, and in doing so, you have become family.

Tonight, two members of our family are going to cement that even further. We are also gathered here this evening to unite Bryan and Jennifer in marriage. They met through a mutual love of our genre, and they are a part of our family, and they have chosen to share this very special moment with not just their immediate family members, but with the rest of you, their extended family, as well. So, thank all of you for being here as we celebrate the love between Bryan and Jennifer with a public and legal joining of two souls who have already been united as one in their hearts.

Although I am not a religious minister, and tonight's wedding is not a religious ceremony, I would like to begin with a bit of wisdom from the Bible. There is a passage in First Corinthians Chapter 13 that begins, "Love is patient, love is kind." And that is true. Love is patient and love is kind. But love must also be fearless, and strong, and trustworthy.

Love is knowing how your partner takes their coffee, and making it that way for them when they haven't even asked. Love is a shared Netflix queue. Love is knowing how your partner likes their feet rubbed, and doing so while you binge-watch Ash vs Evil Dead. Love is laughter. Love is talking. But love is also quiet sometimes. Love is listening. Love is communicating through a shared glance or a knowing look. Love is acceptance of our partner's quirks and foibles and insecurities, and gratitude that they accept our own. Love is calmness.

Love is how we feel about our partner, but love is also how our partner makes us feel about ourselves.

As fans and practitioners of the horror genre, we are sometimes asked, "Why do you watch that stuff or read that stuff?" We are asked, "Why do you act in those movies or write those books?" Sometimes, liking horror can be a lonely sort of fandom. Detractors of the genre can, knowingly or unknowingly, make us feel bad about our enthusiasm for it, and thus, make us feel bad about ourselves.

But love does not do that. Let me repeat: Love is how we feel about our partner, but love is also how our partner makes us feel about ourselves.

What is love? This is love, right here. These two people. And let us now celebrate that love.

Bryan and Jennifer have written their own vows, which they will recite while exchanging their rings. Do we have the rings?

*(**Recitation of the wedding vows and exchange of the wedding rings**)*

We have celebrated your love with this ceremony. Now that I have joined you in marriage, let no man or woman or slasher or demon or giant radioactive monster or inbred mutant cannibal or serial killer or ghost or Cthulhu tear it asunder. I now pronounce you husband and wife. You may absolutely kiss the bride.

So, that was the wedding. Jen looked beautiful and so did Bryan. That's one of my favorite memories of the weekend.

Weston Ochse, Brian, and Joe R. Lansdale. (Photo copyright Mary SanGiovanni 2016)

My other favorite part of the weekend was Joe Lansdale. It's no secret that I'm a fan of the man's work. And not just his horror stuff, either. I celebrate and collect the man's entire bibliography. Over the years, I've been incredibly lucky to count him as a friend and mentor of sorts, as well. As it turned out, spending the weekend hanging out with Joe and his wife Karen was pretty much exactly what I needed—even if I didn't know I needed it at the time. Their company, the shared laughs and conversation, the advice and knowing looks—it lifted my doldrums in a way nothing else could. Somebody (I think it was either Weston Ochse or Jonathan Janz) brought up me taking down Dorchester, which prompted Joe to tell us a riotous story of his own encounter with the publisher years before, which involved money owed and an editor ducking his call and Joe eventually pretending to be Norman Mailer. In moments like that, I wasn't thinking about my dead friends, or how the tour was coming off the rails, or the money I was starting to hemorrhage. Instead, I just laughed and was happy.

Indeed, at one point, Joe, Karen, Mary, and I were driving around Williamsburg in my Jeep. Joe and I were up front. The girls were in the back. And Joe and I were just chatting like two old hens. Mary told me later that it had been a long time since she'd seen me as relaxed and happy and alive as I'd been during that drive. She said it was nice to see me letting down my guard, and trusting people, and just being me.

And it was.

On Sunday, Joe, Jonathan Janz, and I were talking, and the conversation turned to Jesus, and Joe said some wonderful things about him as both a writer and a man. They were the kinds of things that Jesus would have loved to have heard—a validation that I know would have meant the world to him. I know they meant the world to me, as well.

Tom Monteleone and Brian. (Photo copyright Mary SanGiovanni 2016)

Monday morning, Mary, director Mike Lombardo, and myself climbed into my Jeep and started home. I'd be in Pennsylvania for three days. Time enough to hug my boys and tell them I love them. Then I'd be back out on the road. I missed my sons terribly, but all my other troubles seemed to have dissipated. Thanks to John Urbancik, Weston Ochse, Yvonne Navarro, Ron Malfi, Jonathans Janz and Yudkin, Tom Monteleone, Matt Hayward, Armand Rosamilia, and everybody else I'd seen that weekend—especially Joe and Bryan—I was at ease with the venue cancellations and the financial bleed. The physical and psychological toll of constant touring had eased.

I still missed my dead friends, but—I told Mary and Mike as we drove—I had finally made my peace with their deaths. The cows and fires and all the other signs? They weren't Jesus calling out from the other side, warning me of dire things to come. They were just my subconscious, desperate for some link, some contact. But it was alright.

Everything was going to be okay now.

The next day, Jesus let me know that it wasn't my imagination, and that things weren't okay.

And this time, there was a witness to verify that I wasn't going crazy...

→ **CHAPTER THIRTY**

DICKENS'S GHOSTS

"The allegorical nature of A Christmas Carol leads to relatively simplistic symbolism and a linear plot. The latter is divided into five Staves, each containing a distinct episode in Scrooge's spiritual re-education. The first Stave centers on the visitation from Marley's ghost, the middle three present the tales of the three Christmas spirits, and the last concludes the story, showing how Scrooge has changed. The Ghost of Christmas Past represents memory. The Ghost of Christmas Present serves as the central symbol of the Christmas ideal--generosity, goodwill, and celebration. Appearing on a throne made of food, the spirit evokes thoughts of prosperity, satiety, and merriment. Within the allegory, the silent, reaper-like figure of the Ghost of Christmas Yet to Come represents the fear of death, which refracts Scrooge's lessons about memory, empathy, and generosity, insuring his reversion to an open, loving human being." – Spark Notes

After a month on the road, I was home again for three days. My youngest son, who is eight, gave me hugs of a quantity and ferocity that he hadn't given me since he was six, back before third grade had taught him that it wasn't cool to hug your dad. He'd missed me, and told me so—verbally and via his actions. We played all day, and I showered him with all the little presents and trinkets I'd picked up during my tour of the south.

When he was asleep that night, his mother and I discussed things, and whether or not we thought my travel was having an adverse effect on him. Nothing seemed apparent, other than his clinginess, which could be chalked up to having missed me.

Still...I felt guilty as hell. Not since that drunken night in the Chattanooga hotel room had I been so riddled with self-doubt. Sure, I told myself. He seemed okay, but how could we know for sure? He was eight years old. You know what I remembered from being eight years old? My father never being home. My Dad worked seven-days-a-week shifts at the paper mill. If he wasn't there, then he was sleeping or working the farm (we had sheep, a cow, chickens, and beehives). I saw him for one meal a day.

Since the beginning of this tour, my son had seen me even less than that.

But, I told myself, my father had worked that grueling schedule to earn a living—to keep me fed and clothed and secure. This tour was accomplishing the same thing for my son.

That's what I told myself.

I just wasn't sure I believed it anymore.

When my father worked himself to the point of exhaustion, there was a paycheck at the end of the week. In my case, not only was there no paycheck, I wouldn't get paid royalties on the books sold thus far on the tour until mid-2017—provided I'd earned out my advance by then.

I wasn't broke, but I was beginning to hemorrhage money. Replacing the Jeep's radiator in West Virginia, the gas wasted during me and John Urbancik's alligator-hunting side trips, my bar tab for Scares That Care, postage spent shipping bottles of bourbon home when there was no more room left in the trunk—these things had taken a toll on my savings. In two days, I had to head back out on the road again, travelling to Morgantown, Beckley, and Pittsburgh. I'd need money for gas, food, and lodging.

Luckily, I knew where to get some.

I've written earlier in this series about The York Emporium and its owner, Jim. He and I had a standing deal. Whenever I needed quick cash, I'd sign a dozen or so foreign editions of my work, and sell them to him. Jim would then resell them online. For years, this has been the only way for my readers in Germany, Italy, Spain, France, Poland, and elsewhere to get signed editions of my books. They benefit from the arrangement, Jim benefits from the arrangement, and I benefit from it, as well.

Mary and I loaded up a box of German and Italian editions and headed for the store. While Jim went through the box and worked up a price for me, I walked back to the horror section to visit Jesus. I hadn't checked in on him since our signing there earlier that month. I vaguely recalled the strange feeling of doom that had overcome me before, but it seemed like something from another lifetime. Standing there now, facing the wall behind which a portion of his ashes were interred, it all came back to me now—the cow, the fires, and everything else.

Mary was browsing through the True Crime section. Jim was up front at the counter. Nobody else was around. I cleared my throat, and spoke aloud.

"Hey, brother. I'm home for a few days. I got your message. Damn near ran over that fucking cow."

You know how your limbs feel when they fall asleep? That tingling, pin sensation? My entire body began to feel like that. I glanced around. The Horror section was still empty, except for me. The tingling sensation grew stronger.

"Jesus...?"

I can't say I heard his voice. That would be a lie. I didn't hear his voice. I didn't hear anything. But all of the sudden, I had an impression of his voice—a distinct visualization of words in my brain. It wasn't a conversation. It wasn't a back and forth exchange. It was more like he was putting images of words and emotions in my head. I got "Hey" and the names of his wife and daughter. I also got "lonely" and "old man" and "home."

I reached for the wall. Both the tingling and the impressions grew stronger. "Lonely." "Home." Then his wife and daughter's names again, so strong that had they been spoken words, he would have been shouting. The "old man" bit confused me, but then I remembered that multiple people have reported the ghost of an old man haunting the aisles of the Emporium over the years.

I tried to speak, and couldn't.

I tried to breathe, but I couldn't do that either.

This isn't really happening, I thought. *This is fucking wish fulfillment. I miss him. I know he's buried inside that fucking wall, and therefore, I think he's trying to communicate with me.*

That was when Mary rounded the corner, pressed close to give me a kiss, and then paused.

"Wow," she gasped. "Do you feel that?"

"What do you feel?" I asked, not wanting to lead her.

"It's Chuy."

(Chuy was Jesus's nickname—one he normally hated—but there were a small handful of us who could get away with calling him by it.)

"Do you...do you hear anything?"

"He's happy to see us." Mary paused. "And he's...lonely?"

"He wants to go home."

"Or maybe he just misses everybody."

"I need to test this," I told her. "It could be both our imaginations, right?"

HOME. The impression jackhammered into my head.

Jim called out from the register, telling me he had cash for me. Mary grabbed my arm.

"Do you want me to stall him?" she asked.

I shook my head. "Go on up. I'll be there in a minute."

After she was gone, I bent down next to the wall. The tingling sensation engulfed me.

"I want to believe it's you," I said, "but you've got to give me proof, brother. If this is really you, and not my imagination, give me a sign."

I waited. The tingling sensation subsided. The impressions ceased. The moment passed.

I got my cash from Jim and went home.

The next day—my last day home before heading out again—I picked a new book off my "To Be Read" pile after my son went to sleep. Turned out I had selected Chet Williamson's short story collection *A Little Blue Book of Bibliomancy*. I wasn't really in the mood to read, but I enjoy Chet's stuff, and I needed a distraction.

I opened the book at random, and the page I landed on was Chet's tribute to Jesus, written shortly after his death.

"Fuck me..." I gaped, staring at the page.

Shaking my head, I flipped to the front of the book and began to read Chet's Introduction. The book begins as such: *"Erstwhile editor Tom Monteleone came up with 'Bibliomancy' in the title of this Little Book, and it appealed to me instantly. Bibliomancy, after all, is divination by book—letting a text fall open and dropping your finger at random upon a passage, which will then tell you what you need to know."*

Sighing, I closed the book, took off my glasses, closed my eyes, and pinched my nose.

Then I opened my eyes again and nodded.

"Okay, brother. I believe."

The next morning, I kissed my son and my girlfriend goodbye, climbed into the Jeep, and headed back out on the road—wishing that the tour was over, because my heart was no longer in it.

I had work to do.

CHAPTER THIRTY-ONE

GOD AND COUNTRY

The audience in Morgantown, West Virginia, was small—easily the smallest since Albuquerque—but the dozen or so people who showed up were enthusiastic and engaged. One guy, Jarod Barbee, had traveled all the way from Texas. It is December as I write this, recounting events that occurred at the end of July, and I've been going back through these columns, collecting them into manuscript format so Cemetery Dance can eventually publish them as a book. Many recurring things jump out at me as I re-read them.

One of those things is the number of displaced signing attendees. Starting way back in April, a woman from Bermuda travels to a signing in Pennsylvania. That story plays out again and again—so much that I didn't even write about them all. At most of the signings this year, there was at least one person who had traveled far from home. I am at a loss as to explain why, but I find the phenomena very humbling.

Some of the attendees in Morgantown. (Photo copyright Paul Synuria 2016)

I was due to sign at a Books-A-Million in Beckley, West Virginia, the next evening, so after I finished up in Morgantown, I drove to my grandmother's house in the mountains near Lewisburg. My grandparent's home is a three-bedroom structure built in the Seventies with thirty-two acres of land attached to it. My great-grandparents' home still stands nearby, as well—a weathered, rustic, World War I era structure of the type popularized by Mother Abigail's home in Stephen King's *The Stand*. If you go down yonder in the hollow, you'll find the stone foundation of an even earlier home, built long before the Civil War. My family has lived on this mountain for generations, ever since we first got off the boat from Ireland. It's a remote location, far from any town, and bordering national forestland, so it will never be developed.

Every American town I've visited this year looks like it was purchased at Ikea, with the same retail options and fast food joints and tax services. A Wal-Mart in El Paso sells slave-labor-produced jeans for the same price as a Wal-Mart in Boston. McDonald's in Los Angeles tastes just as shitty as the McDonald's in Trenton. The Game Stop in Seattle has all the same merchandise as the GameStop in New Orleans. Pick a Barnes and Noble—it doesn't matter where. None of them are going to have a horror section, and the only reason you'll even find my books there this year is because I'm on tour. There will be somebody dressed up in a Statue of Liberty costume outside your local tax preparation service this year, regardless of whether you live in Portland, Oregon, or Portland, Maine.

Every town is the same. Yes, the architecture and foliage may change. A suburban housing development in San Diego, California, may have stucco buildings and palm trees, while one in Lancaster, Pennsylvania, may have rancher buildings and tall, broad oaks—but the people living there all shop at the same places. They buy the same food, the same clothing, the same entertainment and media. They get their news from the same corporate-approved sources, and all of them—every single neighborhood—have Trump signs in their front yards. It is July, and I've been telling my friends and peers all summer that, based on what I've witnessed while traveling this country, Trump will win the Presidency. They all laugh at me. Even the ones who identify as Conservatives laugh at me. Then, it is November, and they all whisper, "How did you know?"

I was on tour. While everyone else was staying at home, and letting the Internet tell them what was going on in America, I was actually out in America, seeing things for myself.

Everything is the same. Small town America is a thing that exists in the memories of people of a certain age, and it's a nice setting or plot device for movies and novels and comic books, but it is no longer the norm in this country. I suspect it hasn't been for a very long time. Don't believe me? Ask yourself this—how many of your neighbors do you really know? Go to your local Target or Burger King or Pier One and ask yourself, "Who are all these people and where did they come from? Where do they live?"

There is no such thing as small town America. We live in an era of Stepford Towns.

But not so my grandmother's home. Because it borders national forestland, it will never be developed. There will never be condominiums or big box retailers or a strip mall filled with nail salons and fast food joints. It is a place of solace for me, and I go there whenever I can. I find peace there, and contentment.

For the most part.

There's just one drawback. My grandmother is very religious. In truth, my entire family is religious. Every Sunday, my parents go to the same Methodist church they've been attending their entire adult lives. They repeat things aloud from the liturgy, and listen to a sermon and sing three songs and then repeat the process again on the following Sunday. My sister and my brother-in-law go to one of those big modern, non-denominational churches, the kind where services are held inside an old Saturn dealership, and five hundred people show up, and instead of a choir, there's some dude with a guitar who moonlights in a Pink Floyd cover band.

These things give them peace and solace—the same sort of peace and solace I get from writing.

Me? I'm not religious. I call myself agnostic, because it's a simple term that most people seem to grasp. I believe there is more to this universe than we can possibly understand, and I believe that the supernatural is a real thing—something science hasn't gotten around to explaining yet. But I don't believe in God or Allah or Yahweh or Krishna, and I think their books were all ghost-written by human beings, and while I think Jesus Christ's teachings were excellent rules to live your life by, I don't expect him to come back anytime soon. Why would he? Last time he was here, a bunch of assholes nailed him to a cross because he had the audacity to walk around saying, "Hey, maybe we should all try to respect each other."

I'm not a Christian, but I'm not a Christian-basher, either. As a rule, I tend not to disparage other people's religious beliefs, because religion is a personal, intimate thing. It's as personal as making love, and who am I to make fun of what you like in bed or what religion you believe in. What makes you cum may not work for me, and vice versa.

I've talked in previous columns about the tribalism that has infected our national discourse. Democrats versus Republicans. Progressives versus Conservatives. Coke versus Pepsi. The Jets versus the Ravens. Marvel Comics versus DC Comics. Religion had that problem long before any of these other things. For my entire life, I've seen Christians bashing Muslims, and Muslims bashing Jews, and Jews bashing Catholics, and everybody teaming up on the Mormons. And when they're not bashing each other, then they're bashing others around them, having a go at the LGBT community or atheists. And then the LGBT community and the atheists bash back, and on and on we go in this vicious fucking circle.

Me, I don't care who you worship, who you fuck, or who you voted for. I don't care what you do or don't believe—as long as you extend me the same courtesy.

But I don't tell my grandmother any of this. My grandmother is ninety-two years old, and as far as she knows, I'm a born-again Christian and have been since the age of eleven, when I figured out that maybe if I pretended to be such, my family would leave me alone about Jesus and let me get back to reading comic books. I don't tell my grandmother this because, despite what you may have read about me online, I'm not an asshole.

In many ways, my grandmother's faith is all she has left. She was always a believer, but something happened back in the late-Sixties that I suspect made her faith more fervent. Her son, my uncle Mark, died in a car crash. I was a baby at the time, and have only vague memories of him. I remember him holding me, and I remember us playing with plastic farm animals, and that's pretty much it. Everything else is faded black-and-white photographs, and his books that I inherited—a first edition paperback of Heinlein's *Starship Troopers*, a paperback collecting the works of Poe, and a few other works of weird fiction. My family tells me that Mark was an outstanding Christian boy, and maybe he was, but I also know, based on the books I inherited, that he was reading Lovecraft and Poe and Brunner and Heinlein, and maybe I would have had more in common with him than the rest of my family, had he lived. Maybe I wouldn't have sometimes felt so alone, growing up.

I think my grandmother felt alone, too. Her son was dead, her daughter was married and living in Pennsylvania, and her husband was active duty Air Force and never home. It was a time of societal upheaval, not unlike what this country is experiencing again now, and I think she clung to the one thing she had left, the one thing that hadn't changed—that never changes. She clung to her faith in God. Who am I to wave my hand at that or disparage it? That's what religion is for—to bring peace and contentment to troubled souls, right? I'm glad that her God was there for her in that time of despair.

And now? Now she lives alone on a mountain, and her husband has joined her son, and her daughter still lives in Pennsylvania, and she despairs that her daughter, son-in-law, and granddaughter all voted for Clinton, and her grandson is one of those crazy political Independents (because even though I've never come out of the religion closet with my family, they all know I'm neither a Progressive nor Conservative), and the world she exists in has changed to the point of being unrecognizable. The only thing that has remained the same, the only thing she can identify with, is that faith in God.

And that's okay with me.

I thought about this, as Grandma cooked for me. (Ninety-two years old and she can still rule a kitchen and would run rings around any of these so-called celebrity chefs you see on television.) We ate venison tenderloin and biscuits and mashed potatoes and green beans, and blueberry pie for dessert. As always, Grandma had cooked enough for an army, even though it was just the two of us. We sat there at her dining room table, FOX News droning softly in the background, and talked about current affairs and family members and the weather and the possibility that Jesus Christ would, in fact, return soon. She hoped he would. She hopes he will every day. My grandmother begins and ends each day on her knees in prayer, asking the Lord to deliver her. I thought about that, sitting there eating with her around that dining room table. It seats eight people, but there was only the two of us.

And most days, it's just her.

She won't move. She'll stab you if you mention a retirement community. And in truth, she doesn't need it. At ninety-two she's still mentally sharp and physically capable. But as I said goodbye the next day and headed for the next signing, I thought about how lonely she must get.

That loneliness, that quiet house...it's no wonder she talked to God.

I couldn't have said anything about that even if I wanted to. After all, only two days before, I'd had a conversation with what I believed to be the ghost of my dead best friend.

→ **CHAPTER THIRTY-TWO**

THE DARK HIGHWAY

"Everybody thought it was a big joke...It was so funny, I just kept on going...Everybody thought I was just going to go on tweaking the Major's balls to the very end. Which was what I did. Then one morning I woke up and I was in. I was a Prime Walker...So I guess it turned out the Major was tweaking my balls." — Stephen King, *The Long Walk*

"First of all, if Bush's popularity points were two points off, Obama would have never been elected. But Bush had crossed the line. He'd gotten so blatantly and brazenly disgusting... And then, what does Obama do, he acts pretty much like Bush, you know? Signs the same letters, continues the same ban on torture photographs. Power never turns power down. So, this country's going to go down, and its problem is, it won't change its name, the documents will remain in place, it'll look like the same country, but it'll go

down… if you got onto an airplane and heard an announcement that said, 'We're going to pick the pilot from business class today,' you'd get off the plane. Well, that's what we do with the country." — Richard Dreyfuss, 2009 Interview

Last two days of July.

Last two signings of the second leg of the Farewell (But Not Really) 2016 Tour in support of new novels *Pressure* and *The Complex*.

Last hundred dollars.

But thanks to the generosity of my readers, I still had bourbon aplenty.

On the last two days of July, and America was devouring itself in a frenzied, perpetual state of what Hunter S. Thompson called "Fear and Loathing." Unarmed black youth and armed police officers were both being gunned down. The shootings became standard fodder for the twenty-four-hour cable news cycle, as dependable and familiar as those insipid local interest reports you see on your hometown news station. "FOX 43's Carl is at the craft fair. CBS 21's Alicia is on the scene of the spelling bee. In Cincinnati, police shoot a black motorist fifty-seven times. In Buffalo, a black motorist shoots fifty-seven police officers. Now sports and weather, and a look at this year's fall fashions." Everywhere I traveled, Trump banners hung from barns and factories, and sprouted from yards like grass. Given the racial tension that was rife in the country at the time, it is perhaps easy to understand the insistence of some on the Left who clung to the belief that anyone who supported Trump was a racist. It wasn't true, of course—no truer than the insistence of some on the Right who clung to the belief that Obama was a secret Muslim born in Kenya. But as we've already covered in this column, logic and critical thinking had flown the fucking coop for eighty percent of those on the Left and the Right, leaving those of us in the middle to stare and gape in horror and confusion.

Saying all Trump supporters are racist is like saying all Clinton supporters are Socialists, or all Muslims are terrorists, or all Jews covet money, or all clergy molest children, or all horror writers are alcoholics. Yes, there was a racist contingent that certainly—and loudly—supported Trump that summer, but there was an equally loud and racist contingent supporting Hillary Clinton, as well.

Boiling it all down to racism was a willfully stupid act, because it ignored the mood that was happening in this country—a mood that had taken hold shortly after the start of the Iraq war, and had deepened through the rest of the rotten Bush-Cheney Gang's tenure, and the equally rotten Obama tenure that had followed. That mood had nothing to do with being registered a Republican or a Democrat, and everything to do with the growing, sweeping awareness that the entrenched members of both parties—the Pelosis and McConnells and Grahams and Reids and McCains—were serving themselves, rather than the people. And like Richard Dreyfuss said in the eerily prescient 2009 quote at the start of this week's column, a growing number of Americans were willing to kick the pilots off the airplane and pick someone from business class to fly it instead. Never underestimate the lure and empowerment that the ability to say "Fuck you" has on the average American—even if they know it might be detrimental to them.

The signing in Beckley, West Virginia, went well. We sold about two dozen books, which is good for a town that size under the current economic conditions. I've known Anne-Marie—the manager of the Books-A-Million there—for most of my career. She was one of the first retail chain managers to give me a signing, way back in 2004 when my first novel, *The Rising*, came out in paperback. That was also in Beckley, but she was managing a Waldenbooks back then. Waldenbooks is long gone now. It has vanished just like West Virginia's coal mining and logging industries have vanished. The state populace voted for Democrats and Republicans—both of whom promised to save those jobs—but in the end, the Democrats and Republicans just argued with each other while the jobs went away. The people of West Virginia are resilient, however. They found other jobs. And so did Anne-Marie, moving from Waldenbooks and Borders to Books-A-Million, and managing to stay in the same town.

Not all West Virginians were so lucky. Some moved from logging and coal mining to welfare or the grave. Some turned to meth, as either a manufacturer, supplier, or user. Or sometimes all three. A few were lucky enough to find other work. As of 2011, the state's four largest private employers were Wal-Mart, West Virginia United Health System, the Charleston Area Medical Center, and grocery chain Kroger. The U.S. Bureau of Economic Statistics loves to report that, despite coal exports continuing to decline (a loss of $2.9 billion in 2013), West Virginia's economy grew. Well, sure it did. On paper. Some folks were lucky enough to get jobs at Wal-Mart and Kroger, where they then spent their paychecks. And the meth business kept the medical industry busy. In 2013, West Virginia ranked last in the nation with an employment-to-population ratio of only fifty percent. That means fully fifty percent of the population was unemployed.

Trump signs dotted Beckley that July like Christmas decorations.

Months later, in November, West Virginia voted to give the guy from business class a chance to fly the airplane.

After the signing, I went to a steakhouse with authors Michael Knost and Brian Hatcher. We had wonderful meals and lots of whiskey while we talked about writing and publishing, swapped industry gossip and rumors, and had a great time catching up.

Brian, Brian Hatcher, and Michael Knost. (Photo copyright Michael Knost 2016)

The next morning, I headed for Pittsburgh. It rained the entire way. I'm not talking some spring shower, either. No, this was one of those apocalyptic summer storms of the same size and quantity that I'd begun this leg of the tour with. The synchronicity was not lost on me. At the beginning of the month, I'd departed for a tour of the southern United States. While wending my way down the coast, a death storm had forced me off the road, and ended up putting my Jeep in the repair shop. Now, a full four weeks later, a twin deluge was occurring as I crossed back through the state.

I managed to reach the state line, but the storm's ferocity only increased. At one point near Pittsburgh, I found myself coasting through cattle chutes—cement construction barriers that turned an otherwise busy highway into a one-lane traffic nightmare. A long line of cars crawled ahead of me, their speed reduced to single digits because of the lack of visibility and the force of the winds. It was around noon, but the highway was pitch black, and not even my high beams were cutting through the gloom. Water churned along the roadway, funneled by the construction barriers. I watched it creep over the tires of the car in front of me. The wind hammered at vehicles, bouncing them back and forth. I watched a tractor trailer up ahead as its back end swerved, sideswiping the barrier. For one terrifying moment, I thought he was going to jackknife, stranding all of us in this gauntlet of death. But then he straightened his trailer out and headed on. Gripping the wheel, I stared straight ahead into the darkness and kept driving.

What else could I do? What can any of us do in that situation? Pulling over to wait it out is an impossibility. Your only option is to drive forward, focusing your energies on making it through to the other side.

Darkness enshrouds our nation. I'm writing this in mid-December, and the country is collectively holding its breath. And let me make something very clear—it would have been dark under Clinton, as well. I know members of certain organized crime groups who are in awe of the power of the Clintons. But it would have been a familiar darkness—the same type of darkness that has gripped this country since...well, I guess most would argue since Bush Senior, although I would argue it goes back to the death of Kennedy. Donald J. Trump is a different kind of darkness—or at the very least, he's done a masterful job of convincing people he is a different kind of darkness; an anti-globalist warrior standing up against the New World Order, an agent of change against the machinations of the elite, a wall against the corrupt malaise of the old-boys-and-girls-beltway-association. Personally, I don't believe he is any of those things, but he sure tricked a lot of folks into thinking otherwise.

Donald Trump didn't win the election because of Russians or racism or any of the other reasons the talking heads on television pontificate about. He won because half the nation has had it with the bullshit from Washington, and are fed up with the elites in both parties. Donald Trump was a chance for people to go into their voting booth, and when nobody was looking—not their neighbors or their friends or their spouse or their employers—they could lob a Molotov cocktail and say "Fuck you." Donald J. Trump was their chance to engage in a little safe anarchy, a chance to smash some fucking windows without having to risk arrest. Donald Trump was a chance to lash out in anger, a chance to throw a Molotov cocktail, a chance to kick the pilots off the plane and give the guy from business class a chance to fly, even if our destination was a nosedive into a mountain.

And as a result, now we've got a new kind of darkness to contend with. Drive forward, focusing your energies on making it through to the other side…

…or stay in the cattle chute and wait to drown.

I signed in Pittsburgh at Rickert & Beagle Books—a genre staple and historic store which is pretty much the Dark Delicacies of the East Coast, specializing in horror, fantasy, and science-fiction titles. Like all independent bookstores, they've been struggling this year. But so has Pittsburgh itself.

Now, everyone knows the bad times that were visited upon Pittsburgh when the steel industry underwent the same changes that besieged the logging and coal mining industries. But unlike West Virginia, Pittsburgh was able to turn things around, shifting to technology, robotics, health care, nuclear engineering, and financial industries. Pittsburgh is the poster child for managing industrial transition. *The Economist's* Global Liveability Ranking placed Pittsburgh as the first- or second-most livable city in the United States in 2005, 2009, 2011, 2012, and 2014. Google, Apple, Bosch, Facebook, Uber, Nokia, and IBM are among the almost two thousand technology firms generating $20.7 billion in annual Pittsburgh payrolls. The area has served also as the long-time federal agency headquarters for cyber defense, software engineering, robotics, and energy research. The nation's fifth-largest bank, eight Fortune 500 companies, and six of the top U.S. law firms make their global headquarters in Pittsburgh.

That's why Pittsburgh has been chafing over the last year under a new urban renewal plan proposed by Democratic mayor Bill Peduto, a politician in the tradition of that old guard I mentioned above. His project, known as P4, is a confusing and contradictory set of sliding criteria for subsidized development project approval that, according to many experts, downplays the need for job-producing, growth-enhancing, and economy-bolstering enterprises while increasing taxes and then wasting that taxpayer revenue.

Trump signs dotted Pittsburgh that July like Christmas decorations. Months later, in November, Pennsylvania also voted to give the guy from business class a chance to fly the airplane.

I did my part to help out Rickert & Beagle, signing books and encouraging first-time customers to return to the store again, and dropping my last hundred dollars on a signed and personalized Isaac Asimov hardcover for Mary's father. You can do your part, too, by checking them out online. They ship books anywhere.

When the signing was over, I got back in the Jeep and back onto the road, finally heading for home. The storm had abated, but another one was brewing on the horizon. The sun set, and there was no moon or stars to light my way.

I drove forward into darkness, determined to seek my own light.

Two hours later…

"Siri…" I cleared my throat, double-checked that I wasn't using the phone registered to me, and then tried again. "Siri, look up Pennsylvania State Laws regarding theft of a corpse."

"Hang on while I look that up for you."

Johnny Cash drifted from the Jeep's speakers, singing about seeing a darkness, and desperately pleading for someone to save him from it…

→ **CHAPTER THIRTY-THREE**

THE YEAR THAT ROARED

"It's hard to love. There's so much to hate Hanging on to hope, when there is no hope to speak of. And the wounded skies above, say it's much too late. So, maybe we should all be praying for time…" George Michael – "Praying For Time"

December 27, 2016

This past weekend saw the deaths of singer George Michael and actress and author Carrie Fisher, and actress Debbie Reynolds. I was a fan of both Michael and Fisher. As Princess Leia, Fisher was one of my first big celebrity crushes (along with such other eponymous Seventies starlets as Farrah Fawcett and Olivia Newton-John). More importantly, I have a lot of female friends my age who found inspiration and direction from her example. It's a similar situation with George Michael. I have a lot of gay friends my age who found strength and inspiration through Michael's lyrics over the years, and while I am not gay myself, I am a sucker for a good, heartfelt ballad, and his songs always scratched that particular itch for me.

As I'm writing this, 2016 has only four days left on the calendar. It is very possible that another celebrity may die within those four days. Or maybe not. Maybe George Michael and Carrie Fisher and Debbie Reynolds will be the last for the year. But here's the thing...

I think 2016 had a four-day head start.

December 26, 2015, saw the death of Lemmy Kilmister of Motörhead fame, a musician considered by many to be the last of the truly great rock stars. Dave Grohl, of Nirvana and Foo Fighters fame, once said of Lemmy: "We recorded his track in Los Angeles in maybe two takes about a year and a half ago. Until then I'd never met what I'd call a real rock 'n' roll hero before. Fuck Elvis and Keith Richards, Lemmy's the king of rock 'n' roll—he told me he never considered Motörhead a metal band, he was quite adamant. Lemmy's a living, breathing, drinking, and snorting fucking legend. No one else comes close."

Now, why am I mentioning Lemmy's 2015 death in conjunction with the seemingly abnormal number of celebrities who have died in 2016? Because Lemmy died only four days before 2016 began. I propose that Lemmy's death was 2016 cracking its knuckles, whispering "Here I come," and then charging forward with a roar.

And what a roar it was.

The Year That Roared devoured musicians such as David Bowie, Prince, Maurice White, Glenn Frey, Merle Haggard, Christina Grimmie, Phife Dawg, Keith Emerson, Guy Clarke, Ralph Stanley, Matt Roberts, Leonard Cohen, Leon Russell, and dozens more, including legendary Beatles producer George Martin. It mowed down actors such as Alan Rickman, Gene Wilder, Anton Yelchin, Garry Shandling, Patty Duke, Doris Roberts, Chyna, Alan Young, Kenny Baker, Kevin Meaney, Florence Henderson, Robert Vaughn, Alan Thicke, Joseph Mascolo, Zsa Zsa Gabor, and again, dozens more. To personalize this a little bit more for Cemetery Dance readers, it also cut a swath through the horror genre, with the passing of Ed Gorman, Robert E. Weinberg, A.R. Morlan, George Clayton Johnson, Angus Scrimm, David Hartwell, Mark Justice, Steve Dillon, Earl Hamner Junior, Frank D. Felitta, Robin Hardy, Gary Reed, Ted V. Mikels, Jon Polito, John Vulich, and Herschell Gordon Lewis.

I knew some of these people personally. Others I only ever knew through their music or films or writings. And a few of them I never knew at all. I heard about most of their deaths while in transit. It seemed like with each passing month and each celebrity death, I'd get a text while either on my way to a signing, during a signing, or on my way to a hotel after a signing. Many times, it was horror novelist Robert "Bob" Ford who tipped me off. I'm not sure why. It started with Prince—a musician for whom both Bob and I share a deep and abiding appreciation and love. I found out about Prince's death via a text message from Bob. And for the rest of the year, he kept me updated on the passing of other celebrities, as if he were some sort of hippie horror writer storm crow—or perhaps a more fashionably-dressed Gandalf the Grey, sending me grim and gloomy dispatches whilst I wandered this country on some ill-fated quest to reinvigorate my love of this genre, and take the industry's pulse, and figure out what my place was within it.

A friend of mine wrote something earlier this week. I'm not going to tell you who she is, because she values her privacy, but I want to share one bit of truth. She wrote: "2016 has not been difficult because some celebrity dies. It has been difficult because we all have real life things happening to us."

That's a big fucking truth bomb, right there.

2016 roared throughout the first and second legs of The Farewell (But Not Really) Tour. Those roars continued throughout the month of August, when the third and final leg began, but by that point, I barely noticed them any longer. 2016 could roar all it fucking wanted. I had real life things happening to me. I was burned out and broke, behind on deadlines, and trying to crawl my way through a swamp of exhaustion and muster the stamina for four more months of signings and touring. 2016 could take all the celebrities and icons and strangers and friends it wanted. I would deal with those deaths in time.

Because I was still very much trying to deal with the friends 2014 and 2015 had taken from me.

August 3, 2016

We finished recording the latest installment of my weekly podcast around noon. When my co-host Dave "Meteornotes" Thomas signaled me that we were out (meaning the microphones were no longer recording), I leaned back in my chair and sighed.

"That was fun," Dave's girlfriend Phoebe (who is also an occasional co-host) said happily. "It's good to see you two back in the studio again."

I nodded in agreement. It was good to be recording with Dave. I'd built a recording studio in my home specifically for the podcast, but it hadn't gotten much usage for most of that summer, due to my tour schedule. Instead, I'd been recording interviews out on the road, and then Dave recorded his segments back at home, and we spliced them together. But now, here we were, reunited.

I sighed again.

Mary, who was also sitting in the studio with us, frowned. "What's wrong, baby?"

I turned to her. "Are you okay with me telling Dave and Phoebe about what happened to us at the Emporium?"

Mary nodded. "I'm okay with it if you're okay with it."

"What happened?" Dave asked. "Did some nut back you into a corner and holler about the ending to *The Rising* again?"

"No." I shook my head, and waited a moment before continuing. "We think we had…well…an encounter with Jesus."

Dave and Phoebe looked at us. I gauged their expressions. Both were serious and attentive. I saw no hint of disbelief or disregard. I glanced at Mary and she nodded at me in encouragement.

"Our Jesus?" Dave asked.

I nodded, confirming.

Phoebe leaned forward. "What happened?"

"I think…" I paused, taking a deep breath. Then the words seemed to tumble out of me. "I think he wants to go home. And I need you guys to help me steal his remains."

CHAPTER THIRTY-FOUR

KEENE'S ELEVEN

There was a long moment of stunned silence.

Then Dave asked, "Are you insane?"

"No," I replied, suddenly feeling very foolish. "I mean, Mary experienced it, too."

"I felt something in the bookstore that day," she confirmed, "but I don't know what I think about the rest of this."

"Oh, I've no doubt you guys experienced something," Dave said. "I've had my own encounters with the paranormal over the years. And who knows? Maybe you did make brief contact with Jesus. It's possible."

I frowned. "Then why do you think I'm insane?"

"Because you're not talking about seeing his ghost. You're talking about stealing his corpse!"

"Ashes," I countered.

"Ashes, corpse—it still amounts to grave robbing, Brian!"

"And asking us to help," Phoebe chimed in.

"I'll do the stealing," I said. "I just need you guys to distract Jim."

Dave threw his hands up in the air. "Jim owns the store! If Jesus really wants to go home, why not just ask Jim to give you the remains?"

"I don't know," I admitted. "I mean, Jim got that nice memorial plaque made up. That wasn't cheap. And he went through a lot of work interring the urn in the wall. It would kind of be a dick move to ask him to tear the wall apart again."

Dave flailed his arms. "And it's not a dick move for us to tear his store apart and steal from him?"

"We're not stealing from Jim," I insisted. "We're just helping out Jesus. I think Jim would understand that."

Phoebe frowned. "Then why not ask him to give you the ashes?"

"I don't know," I repeated. "I just…I get the sense Jesus doesn't want me to."

"Then you have to at least tell Cathy," Mary said.

I shook my head. "We can't. Seriously. She's just now healing from it all—as much as anyone ever truly heals after losing their husband and best friend. I'm not going to fuck up her shit by telling her that I'm in touch with him, and that he wants to come home."

"So…" Dave paused. "What exactly is your plan?"

"Who said I have a plan?"

"You always have a plan," all three of them said in unison.

I shrugged. "Okay. You know I've got that jar of H.P. Lovecraft's grave dirt, right?"

At this point in our narrative, I should probably tell you about the dirt I dug up from H.P Lovecraft's grave many years ago. I visited the grave with Mary, Bev Vincent, Rio Youers, and a few other writer friends. While we were there, I scooped up a handful of dirt from the grave to serve as a memento. I kept it in a clear glass jar on my bookshelf. For the most part, it was just a knickknack, serving as a bookend between my complete collection of Lovecraft's Arkham House volumes and books by M. Stephen Lukac and Brian Lumley.

Occasionally, however, it had other uses.

One such usage was the fault of my friend Jason Parkin (who, in a bizarre bit of cruel synchronicity, as I told you in the beginning of this series, died of a sudden brain aneurysm two months before Jesus). A few years ago, Jason brought a stranger to my home. Now, usually, I trusted Jason's judgement, but this particular individual wanted to be a horror writer, and later that evening—after many drinks—he became obnoxious and aggressive, insisting that I help him achieve his dream.

Now, I've got a pretty good track record of helping people do just that in this business, but this guy...? This guy. I didn't like him. I didn't like the fact that he was using one of my oldest friends to get to me.

So, I got him drunker.

And then I pulled down H.P. Lovecraft's grave dirt.

And then I told him that there was a secret ritual—an initiation of sorts. I told him that every successful horror writer had done it. Stephen King, Robert Bloch, Dean Koontz, the Splatterpunks, Poppy Z. Brite, Richard Matheson, Clive Barker, Jack Ketchum, Tanith Lee, Richard Laymon. Even Bentley Little. All of us had snorted a line of H.P. Lovecraft's grave dirt, and that had led to our successes.

He was just drunk enough to believe me. I poured him a line of dirt, and cut it up fine with a butter knife. He declined my offer of a straw, hunkered down next to my coffee table, and proceeded to snort H.P. Lovecraft's grave dirt up his nose—half the line in one nostril, the second half in the other.

He started to scream and squirm pretty much instantaneously. His nose started to bleed after that.

Turned out I hadn't smashed up all the little pebbles in the dirt.

He left soon after, and as far as I know, he never took advantage of my friends again. He also never became a horror writer.

"My plan is simple," I told Mary, Dave, and Phoebe. "I'm going to swap out Jesus's ashes with H.P. Lovecraft's grave dirt. The girls will distract Jim up at the counter."

"How do we do that?" Phoebe asked.

"You have boobs," I said. "Jim likes boobs."

"I don't have boobs," Dave pointed out. "What am I going to do while they distract Jim?"

"You're going to stand in front of the horror section and be my lookout. If a customer comes toward it, you get rid of them."

"How do I do that?"

"Talk to them. That usually seems to work."

"No." Dave shook his head. "You need Lombardo."

"We're not bringing in Mike Lombardo," I said.

"Why not?" Dave countered. "He was as close to Jesus as we were. And distracting people is something he excels at."

"Lombardo's film career is just taking off. He's young. How's it going to look if we get busted? Getting arrested for grave robbing isn't going to look good on his IMDB profile."

"Point," Dave conceded.

"How are you going to get Jesus out of the wall?" Mary asked.

"I don't know yet," I admitted. "I guess I'll need a crowbar, and a cordless drill, and...shit, I don't know."

"Coop would know," Dave said. "You'll need Coop."

"No," I said. "Absolutely not. We are not bringing Coop into this either. No Lombardo. No Coop. Just us. This isn't fucking *Ocean's Eleven*!"

"But you need a construction expert," Phoebe said. "Somebody who knows how to get into the wall quietly and without making a giant hole. Who better than Geoff Cooper?"

"No." I pounded my fist on the table. The podcast microphones trembled.

"Why not?" Dave asked.

"I know why," Mary volunteered. "It's because other than me, Coop is the only person that can talk Brian out of doing something after his mind is made up. And his mind is made up."

"Yes," I confirmed, "it is. You're not talking me out of it, and Coop's not talking me out of it. I'm doing this. I'm getting our friend out of there, and I'm going to get him home. Back to his wife and daughter. I could use your guys' help, but if I have to, I'll do it alone."

"No, you won't," Mary said. "If you're set on this, Keene, then so am I."

Dave nodded, reluctantly. "Okay. Me, too. I'm in. But I still think you're insane."

I turned to Phoebe. "How about you?"

"Do you really believe this is what Jesus wants?"

I nodded.

She cocked her head. "And when Mary and I are distracting Jim—would I get to wear one of my Renaissance Faire dresses?"

"Sure." I shrugged. "That would probably add to the distraction factor."

"Then count me in."

Later that night...

Mary turned to me on the couch. "So, when are you thinking about doing this, Keene?"

"I'm not sure yet. Why?"

"Because I'll need time to save up bail money for you."

I smiled. "I've got to think about it a bit more. Plan everything. Figure out how to explain it to folks."

"What folks? You're not going to write about it, are you?"

I shrugged. "Sooner or later, I write about everything. You do, too. That's what we do. We bleed onto the page."

Mary nodded. "You're right."

"Maybe I'll put it in *End of the Road*. By the time I wrote about it for the column, the deed would already be done."

We turned back to the television, but my mind was elsewhere. Mentioning this column had reminded me—the road was still out there, waiting. I had a third and final leg of touring to do, and it was set to start the following Saturday.

CHAPTER THIRTY-FIVE

GO INDIE OR GO HOME

The third leg of the Farewell (But Not Really) Tour started off locally, at The Comic Store—an independently-owned comic book store in Lancaster, Pennsylvania (where I was joined by Mary). From there, it moved on to a pop-up signing in New Jersey, and then two independently-owned bookstores in Rhode Island (where scholar Jack Haringa led a Q&A), and Vermont (where I was joined by Asher Ellis), before eventually circling back home again for a signing at a corporate-owned Books-a-Million chain store in Harrisburg.

The Comic Store has been hosting signings with me for almost two decades. Situated directly across from the Amtrak station, the owner very wisely stocks books and magazines in addition to all the regular fare you'd find at any other comic book store. That's good for us, because he also happens to be a big fan of the horror genre (with Richard Laymon being his favorite). Every time Jesus and I had a new book come out, we'd sign there. So have other local genre folks such as Chet Williamson and Tim Truman. The store does a great job of promoting the events and hand-selling the books. More importantly, they keep the books in stock.

Books-On-The-Square in Providence hosted a wonderful, well-attended signing for me. They let fans linger and socialize after Jack Haringa finished his Q&A with me and I'd signed everyone's books. It was a very cool scene.

The Book Nook in Ludlow, Vermont, was equally professional and delightful. Author Asher Ellis, who calls Ludlow his hometown, set the signing up, and thanks to his efforts and the efforts of the store's management, it was a full house.

Now, all three of these are small, independently-owned shops. They don't have the space or parking for a big blowout, and yet all three events were well-attended. They don't have the financial resources to stock a hundred copies of *Pressure* or *The Complex* on hand for the signing, yet at each event, we sold out, or nearly sold out, what they had.

With those factors in mind—and also remembering that just a few weeks before, I'd moved thirty copies of *Pressure* at a Books-A-Million in the middle of nowhere West Virginia—you'd think a local signing at a Books-A-Million in Harrisburg would go well, right? I could probably move at least fifty copies there in three hours' time, correct?

Sadly, I never got to find out.

That's because Books-A-Million corporate decided to arbitrarily cancel the signing at the last minute.

I've known Jim, the manager of that Books-A-Million, for nearly twenty years. He hosted one of the very first signings I ever did for *The Rising*. Back then, he was managing a Waldenbooks. Then a Borders. Now a Books-A-Million. Jim is a fan of the horror genre. Early in their careers, he hosted one of the first book signings for

John Skipp and Craig Spector. When the signing was over, he had them sign the card table they'd been seated at. Years later, he had Jesus and I sign that same card table. But Jim is more than just a fan. He is the quintessential bookseller—knowledgeable, enthusiastic, and able to anticipate what his customers want and need. I've lost count of the times I've seen Jim hand-sell a book to a dubious customer. His love of books and reading are infectious. He transfers them to his staff and his customers.

Bottom line? Jim and I could have sold a lot of books during that three-hour signing had a vice president at Books-A-Million not decided on a whim to cancel the event with little to no notice.

Neither one of us ever got a reason for the cancellation. All Jim got was an email, saying, "Cancel it and return the books."

I didn't even get that.

Why would a vice president do something like this?

Because Books-A-Million and their biggest competitor, Barnes and Noble, are not run by people who love books, who are knowledgeable about books, who enjoy books, or—in some cases—even want to sell books. Understand, I'm not talking about the individual bookstore level. I'm not talking about the managers on the ground, or their staff, or even the regional managers. No, I'm talking about the people at the top—the people who are not booksellers, and yet are managing bookstores, and trying to sell books the same way one sells soft drinks or clothing or exercise equipment.

My circle of friends and acquaintances include many booksellers, both indie and corporate. I hear this repeatedly from the latter, in private. Over the last three years, I've featured several former Books-A-Million and Barnes and Noble employees on my podcast, or on my blog, who have said the same thing. I've also reported on the continued financial failings of both stores, as financial quarter after financial quarter after financial quarter, their profits continue a grim, slow slide. You know what Barnes and Noble blamed their most recent holiday season sales slump on? Adele. That's right, the singer, Adele. According to Barnes and Noble corporate, the reason they lost money during Christmas of 2016 was because Adele didn't release a new album. I'm not making this up. Google it if you don't believe me.

A retail expert recently told CNBC that with the expected upturn in the economy for 2017, lower unemployment, and higher consumer confidence readings, Barnes and Noble and Books-A-Million won't be able to blame the consumer for poor performance. Instead, they will have to look at how they perform as merchants and retailers. The best way for them to do that might be TO TRY SELLING BOOKS instead of toys, apparel, food, coasters, and all the other non-book related items that fill their stores. The Big Two claim that book sales are down, yet their biggest competitor—Amazon—and their other competitor—independently-owned bookstores—say otherwise. Book sales aren't down. People still buy books. They just don't buy them from Books-A-Million and Barnes and Noble. And why should they? Buying a book is an experience. Let's take a horror reader, for example. A horror reader wants to go to the store, find the horror section, and browse. They want to look through the books, see if there's a new Simon Clark available yet, pick up a book by an author they never heard of, grab that Sarah Pinborough novel they keep hearing about. Except they can't do any of this in Books-A-Million or Barnes and Noble because they don't have a horror section. The horror reader will have to go through general fiction, and science-fiction, and sometimes romance, and occasionally even metaphysical studies (no bullshit—I know of a Books-A-Million where the manager insisted on stocking all of Jonathan Maberry's backlist in the New Age/Metaphysical Studies section, for no reason at all other than the manager was a fucking idiot). And after the reader has gone through all that trouble—chances are eighty percent likely the store won't have the book they are looking for anyway. If they ask, a helpful employee will say, "We can order it online for you." And then the horror reader will politely decline and go home and order it online from Amazon, who still has a horror section, and who most likely has the book in stock.

So, what does any of that have to do with the reason for my cancelled signing? Because I highly suspect it was that type of corporate thinking that led to the cancellation. Some vice president looked at the event, saw that it was in August, saw that *Pressure* had come out in June, and decided that the store should no longer be stocking or selling the book, and should instead focus on whatever had just come out that week.

Throughout this tour, the vast majority of my signings took place at independently-owned bookstores. You can count on one hand the number of corporate chain bookstores I appeared at—Bradley's Books in DuBois, Pennsylvania; Barnes and Noble in Tucson, Arizona, and Orlando, Florida; Books-A-Million in Beckley, West Virginia; and what would have been Books-A-Million in Harrisburg, Pennsylvania. In each of those instances, it was because the staff and manager were booksellers who work around the systemic ineptness of their corporate overlords and know how to sell books.

When this column started, I told you I was going to examine the history of our genre over the last twenty years, and what has changed, and what remains the same. In bookselling. In publishing. In touring. In society. And in myself. For the last thirty-four weeks, I've done just that.

If I were to do this again in another decade, I could write about the death and disappearance of Books-A-Million and Barnes and Noble.

Because make no mistake, that's coming over the next ten years. Indie bookstores and Amazon are the way of the future. Independent stores will cater to those readers who love books, who love browsing through the shelves and seeing what they can find. Amazon will cater to the casual reader or to the folks who don't have access to an indie bookstore in their region.

Big box bookstores? They'll go the way of Circuit City and Woolworths, and that will absolutely suck for the good people who are employed by them.

But for the average reader?

The average reader won't even notice, because those big box bookstores are *already* gone from their minds.

Need a *Doctor Who* scarf or a set of bamboo coasters or a Moleskine journal or anything *other than a book*? Books-A-Million and Barnes and Noble have you covered—unless of course you decide to instead buy those things at Wal-Mart or Target or online.

Need a *book*? Get it indie, or get it at home.

CHAPTER THIRTY-SIX

THE BEGINNING OF THE END

"It's a fun job, but it's still a job. Save your money, man. A hit single don't last very long. There's gonna be another cat coming out, looking like me, sounding like me, next year. I know this." — Cypress Hill, "Rock Superstar"

"Right when you get good, they replace you. Best thing that ever happened to me." — Marc Maron

Time dragged on, and so did the third leg of the Farewell (But Not Really) Tour. By now, both my publishers and the general public had moved on to other, more immediate books. And who can blame them, really? That's just how things are these days. We are a civilization of immediacy. We want things now. We want things instantly. We have information, music, movies, books, sporting events, concerts, medical advice, legal advice, grocery shopping, and everything else in our lives available at the touch of a button. I know a woman who has not left her house to go shopping or consume any form of entertainment in over a year. Her groceries and other consumer products are all purchased from Amazon, via her couch. The media she consumes is purchased the same way. If it's not on Amazon Prime or Netflix, she's not watching it. If it's more than four months old, she's probably not watching it either.

Pressure and *The Complex* had been on sale for five months. They were now considered old. The publishers were focused on what was coming out next. The readers were focused on what was available now—not what was available five months before. If it wasn't a trending hashtag on Twitter, then it wasn't prominent in their minds.

What was prominent in their minds was the Presidential election. The deep partisan divide I'd noticed widening all summer long had pretty much split the country in half by September. A nation teetered on the brink of that dark, yawning chasm, yet most of them didn't seem to notice—caught up, as they were, with trying to push the other team into the crevice first, not realizing that in doing so, they'd drag themselves down, as well.

Most of my peers were talking about politics—telling their readers whom to vote for and why. I've never liked doing that. As a rule, I don't tell folks who to vote for, who to love, or what to worship. I believe equal rights for all people means just that, regardless of your race, your gender, your religious beliefs, your sexual orientation, or your political affiliation. Having this belief makes me a minority of one.

So, while all the other writers were arguing the benefits of Candidate Coke or Candidate Pepsi, I was still out there on the road and online, talking about *Pressure* and *The Complex*. You'd think, given the tenor of the nation, and given the fact that it seemed impossible to escape the political coverage, the public would have been receptive. You'd think I could have provided a distraction—an escape from it all. Instead, I got lost in the din. Nobody cared anymore. There were newer books and newer authors and newer hashtags. There was also an election to argue about. Who had time to read a book or go to a signing when—from the comfort of their home—they could belittle complete strangers who had committed the crime of having different values or beliefs than them? And thus, the public appearances, so well-attended in the months before, now had fewer and fewer people showing up. Sales, which had skyrocketed and remained steady throughout the summer, now started to slide down the chart.

And the worst part about it all?

The worst part was that I no longer cared. It wasn't just the road fatigue or the depression. I genuinely no longer cared. After twenty years in this business, I'd ridden this particular merry-go-round more than once. It doesn't matter what form of entertainer you are— writer, comic, musician, actor, artist. In the eyes of the public, you're only as good as your last release, and your last release better have been today, because if it wasn't, somebody else's will be. I was out here to say goodbye, and goodbye was what I intended it to be.

When the clock struck midnight on New Year's Eve, I intended to retire. Not from writing, but from the grind. Somewhere out there between Pennsylvania and California, between Florida and Rhode Island, between the big cities and the small towns, I'd decided to check out. No longer would I be a slave to social media, or self-promotion, or the constant demands of fandom. No longer would I be a slave to being a brand. A slave to being the horror genre's Batman. Life is too goddamned short to spend it doing that. I'd played that game for twenty years. Now it was someone else's turn. Or maybe multiple people's turns.

I thought about all the next-generation authors I'd seen this year, and I decided that the horror genre was in good hands. It faced an uncertain future. There were changes and upheaval to come. But there are always changes and upheaval to come. The horror genre is currently undergoing another radical paradigm shift, much like the one it was undergoing when I came on the scene twenty years ago, and there's a new generation ready to guide it and shepherd it and defend it just like I've taught them to.

I decided that no longer caring wasn't the worst part of all.

It was the best part.

At the end of September, I found myself in *Twilight Zone*-creator Rod Serling's hometown of Binghamton, New York—a beautiful little city that has both incredible wealth and incredible poverty. Author Kevin Lucia (who you seriously need to check out if you haven't yet—Lucia is this generation's answer to Charles L. Grant) had invited me to be a guest speaker at the high school where he teaches. I had a great time talking to several different classes about writing.

Brian and Kevin Lucia at RiverRead Books. (Photo copyright Brian Keene 2016)

Afterward, Kevin, myself, Dan Padavona, and perhaps a half dozen other authors (apologies for not being able to remember who all was in attendance) did a signing at RiverRead Books—the local independent bookstore. RiverRead is appropriately named, since it sits alongside the Susquehanna River—the longest river (at four hundred and sixty-four

EN9 OF THE ROAD ⬅

miles) on the American east coast to drain into the Atlantic Ocean, and a major waterway for the northeastern United States.

It also flows, literally, through my front yard.

I stood there, not far from the Susquehanna's origin point, and thought about home. How easy it would be to just jump in the water and float hundreds of miles downstream, until I arrived at my front door. The distance from my front door to the river's edge is exactly twenty-six steps. Less than that if I'm in the boathouse. How great would it be to dive into the water and leave it all behind—to be home with my sons and my girlfriend? To spend the days sitting by the river with them, and writing. To let the current wash everything else away.

It would be grand.

But I still had unfinished business to attend to.

I'd made up my mind regarding retirement, but the heist...?

I was still mulling that over as I drove south, passing through Syracuse and then Sleepy Hollow, and then New Jersey, and finally, Pennsylvania and home.

The river was there, waiting for me.

But so were the ghosts.

Racing the river home. (Photo copyright Brian Keene 2016)

CHAPTER THIRTY-SEVEN

THAT GUY

In early October, Mary and I climbed into the Jeep and drove from Pennsylvania to Louisville, Kentucky, where we were both guests at a fairly new convention called Imaginarium. The organizers put on an excellent event. It is geared primarily towards writers, and it encompasses all genres. I highly recommend investing the money and traveling to the next Imaginarium, particularly if you are a beginning author. There were some fantastic, informative panels, and some wonderful networking opportunities.

As we drove across the Appalachians, we debated taking a detour to see the Mothman Museum in West Virginia, or the Serpent Mound in Ohio, but ultimately, we decided to push ahead to the convention, and not stop until we reached Louisville. Mary was looking forward to signing and selling books, and doing some promotion for her latest novel, *Chills*. Me? As I told you last week, I'd had enough of signings and sales and promotion. I was looking forward to catching up with old friends in the area—authors Maurice Broaddus, Jerry Gordon, Mehitobel Wilson, and Deb Kuhn, publisher Jason

Sizemore of Apex, and many others. If I had not been given the gift of bourbon by my fans and readers during the tour (at this point in the narrative, I was up to ninety-eight bottles), I might have also been looking forward to taking a few distillery tours, and seeing if I could discover a bourbon I had yet to taste in life.

But mostly, I was looking forward to seeing all of the Hunter S. Thompson attractions Louisville has to offer.

Much has been written by others about the obvious literary influence authors such as Richard Laymon, Stephen King, Steve Gerber, and J.M. DeMatteis had on me, and all of that is very true. What often gets overlooked, however, is the impact Hunter S. Thompson had on me. Maybe it's because more people read my zombie novels than my political writing, but yeah, if there's a Mount Rushmore of "Writers That Influenced Brian Keene," then Hunter S. Thompson is the final face.

If Stephen King is our modern-day Charles Dickens (and I believe he is, say thankee), then Hunter S. Thompson is most certainly our modern-day Mark Twain. His work—both fiction and non-fiction— was simultaneously incendiary, profane, hilarious, and heartfelt. His insight into both politics and human nature are unequaled in our modern era's literary canon. He helped bring down Richard Nixon, introduced middle-America to the counterculture, and predicted an entire decade's worth of world events with eerie accuracy a day after 9/11. He was problematic. His alcohol and drug consumption were infamous, as was his abuse of editors, publishers, and other writers who crossed him. He was adored by both the Left and the Right, but skewered both with equal fervor. He could be abusive, and by all accounts was probably not the best husband or father. And yet, he inspired a fierce loyalty in those around him, winning over his detractors or crushing them beneath his typewriter keys. *Fear and*

Loathing in Las Vegas. Hell's Angels. The Rum Diary. Fear and Loathing on the Campaign Trail. The Kentucky Derby Is Decadent and Depraved. The Curse of Lono. And so many more.

Louisville, Kentucky, was where Hunter S. Thompson grew up. Of course, there would be memorials and attractions to this great American writer.

Except there weren't.

Well, okay. There are two murals, and they are both sort of neat to look at, but neither of these have any sort of official capacity. There's no HST Museum, no Information Center, or anything like that. Via Google, I found the address for Thompson's childhood home. It is currently a private residence. Surprisingly, it is not listed on any sort of historic register, and doesn't enjoy the benefit of any local, state, or federal historical significance. I get that people live there. I get that they don't want a sign in their yard saying, "HUNTER S. THOMPSON SLEPT HERE," or fans clomping through their kitchen, but you'd think such a site might be privy to the same protections as similar locations of historical and cultural importance. Morgantown, West Virginia, has a statue of their famous son, actor Don Knotts. You can't go twelve feet in Gettysburg, Pennsylvania, without finding a bronze plaque informing you of which Civil War General took a shit in that spot.

But Louisville has none of that. It's almost as if the city wants to disassociate iself from Hunter S. Thompson. Indeed, later that weekend, I signed books for a reader who had lived in Louisville all his life, and he confirmed for me that the majority of the city's elite are embarrassed by its connection to this great American writer, and don't understand the hoi polloi's continuing adoration of him.

Mary and I drove to his childhood home and parked on the street. It was early afternoon on a Thursday. I couldn't tell from outside if the people who live there now were home or not, but I still wanted to be respectful. I wasn't about to march up and knock on the door and demand to be shown inside the home or break a splinter of wood off the front porch to keep as a souvenir. I've had well-meaning fans show up at my door before, and I know how that feels. Indeed, it was one of the things that led to my last divorce. (The worst incident was right around the time *City of the Dead* came out. My wife-at-the-time and I were having a barbeque with about thirty friends in attendance. At one point in the afternoon, my wife wandered into the kitchen and found three teenagers sitting at our kitchen table. She asked them who they were, and they said they were fans of mine, and had seen the party going on, and snuck inside, hoping to meet me. When they asked her who she was, she informed them that she lived there, and then told them—as nicely as possible—to get the fuck out. The next day, I got a P.O. Box and began scrubbing my address from the Internet.)

But I digress.

Hunter S. Thompson's childhood home. (Photo copyright Mary SanGiovanni 2016)

So, yeah. I wanted to be mindful of that, and respectful of their privacy and boundaries…but I also wanted my picture taken in front of the house, because it was important to me, and because one thing this year on the road had taught me was that we may never come back to any of these places again.

I sat down on the porch steps, and Mary quickly snapped my photo, and then we left so as not to cause any discomfort or disturbance to whomever might be inside.

As we walked back to the Jeep, we passed a postal carrier, making her rounds.

"Excuse me." I pointed back to the house. "We're from out of town. I was wondering if the city does anything to recognize that landmark?"

She shrugged. "Well, I think that guy used to live there…?"

"Um…that guy?"

"Yeah," she answered. "That guy. I forget his name. If you're looking for landmarks, there's a whole bunch of Johnny Depp stuff downtown."

I stood there, blinking and sputtering. Mary ushered me back to the Jeep before anything else could happen.

That night, in bed in our hotel room at Imaginarium, Mary asked me what I was thinking about.

"That guy," I answered.

"Which guy? The one downstairs who hollered at you about the ending to *The Rising*?"

"No. The postal carrier. She said 'that guy.' She didn't even know who the fuck Hunter S. Thompson was, and she's delivering mail to his childhood fucking home! I mean, he hasn't even been dead—what? A decade?"

"Two-thousand five," Mary answered. "I remember, because you mourned for a month."

"So, a dozen years and change. Such a short amount of time, and his legacy has already been reduced to 'that guy.' One of the greatest writers in American history, and he's 'that fucking guy' even in his hometown."

"Well," Mary soothed, "he was a cult writer. Underground."

"So am I. So were Jesus and Pic. I was always sort of proud of that. It was cool, being a cult writer. It had a sort of dignity. But is this what we have to look forward to? We bust our fucking asses, always existing in borderline poverty, but we figure, hey, at least we gave the world *The Rising* or *Survivor* or *A Choir of Ill Children*. And then fucking cancer cuts us down and the next day we're just 'that guy'? Is that it? That's our legacy? What the hell is the point?"

"If Pic were here, he'd tell you the point is that this is what we are meant to do," Mary answered. "What was it he used to say?"

"That if he was stranded on a desert island, he would write stories in the sand with a stick. And that's how he knew he was meant to be a writer."

"And that applies to the rest of us, as well."

"Fuck that noise," I said. "I want a do-over. I want to learn computer programming or welding. I don't want to be 'that guy.'"

"You're not that guy to me," Mary replied. "Or to your sons. Or your friends."

She turned off the light and eventually fell asleep. I lay there for a long time, staring at the ceiling.

It was time, I decided, to rescue Jesus from his resting place. But it was also unfair of me to drag Mary and Dave and Phoebe into it.

This was something Jesus had tasked me and me alone with. One last caper, just me and him. No Coop. No Lombardo. No Swartwood. No other friends. If I got caught—and chances were about fifty-fifty that I would, in fact, get caught—then it should be me alone. I wasn't going to drag the others down with me.

It was Saturday night. Mary and I were due to drive home the next day. I figured I'd wait until mid-week, when the store was at its emptiest, and then I'd swap out Jesus's ashes with the dirt from H.P. Lovecraft's grave. That way, if someone ever did burrow through the wall to verify his remains were still there, it would look like they were.

He wasn't just that guy. He was my best friend.

And I had a promise to keep.

CHAPTER THIRTY-EIGHT

HOME MOVIES

Mary SanGiovanni and I have a ritual when we curl up on the couch at nine o'clock in the evening and watch television together. I always pick the first movie, and she always picks the second. We do this because I am always ready for bed by eleven at night, and Mary often stays up until one or two in the morning—and also because she likes to pick the worst horror movies you've ever seen. I'm talking films that make your average SyFy Channel schlocker look like Academy Award caliber movies. And it's not so much that she likes them, either. She doesn't. She just has a natural talent for picking bad films. The difference between us is she'll commit to watching the damn things, regardless of how terrible they are. I won't. If there's anything you've taken away from this series of columns (of which this is number thirty-eight) it's probably that life is too short. And if life is indeed too short, then it certainly shouldn't be spent watching shitty movies.

Especially if you are sleepy.

Tom Piccirilli watched some weird movies. I wouldn't call any of them shitty, but many of them were certainly bizarre. In my latest non-fiction collection, *Unsafe Spaces*, I write about how Tom and I used to call each other "big brother" and "little brother." He really was like a big brother to me, down to turning me on to cool movies that I would have otherwise never discovered—*El Topo* and *Holy Mountain* and *Riki-Oh: The Story of Ricky*. When Pic was still alive, and Mary and I had started dating, he and I had talked about us coming out to Colorado to visit for a week, and the four of us (Pic, his wife Michelle, Mary, and myself) could watch weird movies together.

Unfortunately, we never got the chance to do that. Pic got sick soon after, and the next time I got a chance to visit, it wasn't with Mary, but with authors Geoff Cooper, Mike Oliveri, John Urbancik, and Michael T. Huyck, Jr. instead. We'd gone to say "Get Well Soon" although it felt like we were saying "goodbye." And, as it turned out, we were indeed, mayhap a little early. But even then, we managed to watch a movie—*The Raid: Redemption*, which John, Mikey, and Coop hadn't seen yet, and Mike, Pic, and I didn't mind watching again.

But I digress.

Mary and I were home from Louisville, curled up on the couch and watching movies. Although I hadn't told Mary, I planned on pulling the heist the next day—by myself. (If you're a new reader to these columns, you should know that by this point in our narrative, I've become convinced that the spirit of J.F. "Jesus" Gonzalez wants me to steal his ashes from a bookstore where they are interred behind a wall. My plan is to replace said ashes with some dirt from H.P Lovecraft's grave, which I assume will look similar. Part of my inner circle also believes this is what Jesus wants. The other half of my inner circle believes it is all in my head, and that my brain has been irrevocably rattled after spending months crossing the United States of America in a bourbon-and-sleeplessness-fueled haze while on a book signing tour. Regular readers to this column are equally divided. Regardless of which camp you belong to, you should know that these things have already happened. I'm writing this in February 2017 and the events I'm describing took place in October 2016. You should also know that all of this is true. And you should also know that things are about to go terribly awry.)

Around 11:30 p.m., Mary found a terrible movie to watch on Shudder, and I kissed her good night and headed off to bed.

I dream often, but I rarely engage in lucid dreaming. I've done so, on occasion, but it takes my subconscious a little while to figure out that I am, in fact, dreaming, and even longer to figure out that, "Hey, you're aware you are dreaming and therefore, this is a lucid dream, and let's make shit happen."

That night, I began dreaming pretty much as soon as I fell asleep. Or, at least, it felt that way to me the next morning. And unlike other lucid dreams, I was aware of what was happening almost immediately.

I walked into a hotel lobby filled with hotel potted plants and hotel furniture. Music played overhead—the bland sort of music you hear in hotels and elevators, almost offensive in its inoffensiveness. Two women moved around behind the registration desk, but they were those faceless, almost formless sort of dream people that you've no doubt encountered in your own dreams. Even if they'd had features, I don't think I would have noticed. My attention was focused on Tom Piccirilli, who was sprawled out in one of the lobby chairs, grinning. Tom hadn't smiled much when he was alive, at least not in public. Neither of us had. But boy, when he grinned, it was fucking infectious. And it was that way now, in this lucid dream.

Returning the gesture, I sat down in the chair next to him. "Hey, Pic! This is great. I don't think I've had a dream about you yet."

His grin remained. He seemed so damned real, down to the fingerprint smudges on the lenses of his glasses. "Is that what this is? A dream?"

I nodded.

"What are dreams, really?" Pic leaned forward. "How are you doing, little bro?"

"I'm okay."

I started to say more, but was interrupted by a loud clamor from further down the hall. The corridor was hazy, and I couldn't see what was there, but it sounded like a bar. When I turned back to Pic, he nodded as if in confirmation.

"Well, now I know this is a dream," I said. "This is the afterlife I always joke about—a hotel convention bar, and you and Jesus and Dick Laymon and Rick Hautala and everybody else are all hanging out."

"Except you're not joking when you say it," Pic replied. "But yes, they're all here. Rick's having a cigar with Bob Booth, and waiting on Holly."

"So...that's a real thing? That's where we are right now?"

"Right now? Things don't happen in the order you experience them, little bro. This is happening now, but not for you. Not yet."

"I don't understand."

"This is now, but you won't get here until later. Time is a flat circle."

"You didn't write that."

"Neither did you, Brian."

"You've been reading my column."

There was another round of laughter from the unseen bar. Then Pic adjusted his posture and leaned forward.

"I have to tell you something important."

"What's that?"

"Listen to Mary, okay? She's one smart paisan. And I should know."

"Listen to her about what?"

"About the ashes."

"But I didn't steal the ashes yet, and I'm not taking her with me."

"After."

"This is all very confusing, Pic."

"It is now. It won't be later. Now, listen to me, little bro."

I leaned forward. "What's up?"

"Go home."

There were more dreams after that, but they weren't lucid, and I barely remembered them upon waking. Now, months later, I can't remember anything about them at all. Something about a sandwich, maybe?

I woke up at five in the morning. Mary snored softly (except she insists that women don't snore—they "snuffle"). I got up, made some coffee, read the news, looked at the Internet, drank the coffee, and then grabbed my kit bag. It was the same kit bag I'd carried with me on tour. The same kit bag I'd hauled around the country, except it no longer held my laptop or Kindle or Moleskine notebooks or pens or switchblade knife or bourbon flask. Instead, it held screwdrivers and a hammer and other assorted tools. The only thing from the tour still inside that bag was the ISIS psychic suicide bomb, and the only reason that was still in there was because Weston Ochse and Rain Graves had gotten the best of my superstitions, and I was afraid to touch the fucking thing.

I waited until the store was open, and then I carried the bag out to the Jeep. Mary was still sleeping (after a night spent watching terrible movies, she sleeps till eleven or noon).

When I got to the store, I was happy to learn that Jim was busy appraising a sizeable book collection a customer had brought in to sell. This was good. It meant he wouldn't wander into the back. We exchanged a few pleasantries, and then I headed to the horror section in the rear of the store. Nothing suspicious about that. No, sir. Not at all. And nothing suspicious about me stopping in front of the shelf behind which my best friend's remains were interred. And nothing suspicious about me kneeling down in front of that shelf. Had anyone walked by, it would have appeared that I was just perusing the book spines.

Nothing suspicious.

Until I began pulling the books off the shelf and placing them aside.

And then slid the shelf out of the way, coughing at intervals to mask the sound.

And then stood before the bare wall.

And then unzipped the kit bag.

And then realized that I'd forgotten H.P. Lovecraft's grave dirt.

I stood there, screwdriver in hand, looking at the wall. Jesus was there. I mean, I didn't feel him this time. There was no supernatural presence. No feeling. But he was there, physically. He was inches away, just behind that wall. All I had to do was pry it open. So what if I didn't have the grave dirt? Did it really matter? I could stick the ISIS psychic suicide bomb in there instead. I could still get Jesus out of there, still take him home. Wasn't that what he'd asked me to do?

Home, Jesus had said, when I'd last stood in this spot.

I thought about the previous night's dream. It had been a lucid dream. I had been in control. Why then had I not gotten up and walked down that hazy corridor? Why had I not gone to join the others in the bar? Would Jesus have been there if I had?

Go home, Pic had said.

But what had he meant?

I stood there a long time, debating.

And then I made a decision.

It was around two in the afternoon when I got home. Mary was awake, ensconced at the kitchen table, sipping tea and writing. She looked up from her laptop.

"Good morning, Keene."

"Afternoon, SanGiovanni. What are you working on?"

"That novel for Kensington." She glanced at the kit bag. "Have you been out having adventures?"

"I was at the Emporium."

"Oh." She nodded, then paused. Her eyes got wide. "Oh…"

"Is there coffee?"

"There's tea. And don't try to change the subject. Did you…?"

I raised my head and met her stare.

"Did I do it? You tell me."

Mary studied me for what felt like minutes. She raised her mug, took a sip, and placed it back on the table. Then she closed her laptop, and turned to face me again.

"You have always been the kind of person who was driven by impulse and impulsive ideas. When you were younger, you used to act on them."

I snorted. "And I don't anymore?"

"No, you don't. You might pretend that you do, for the public, but you don't, because you have more to consider now. To be honest, no, I don't think you stole Jesus's ashes, but I do think he is with you, and he communicates to you, even if you don't always recognize it for what it is. I don't think he's happy."

"Would you be disappointed in me if I didn't take them? Would you feel like I was betraying him?"

"No," Mary answered, "because it's not about where his body is, but where his mind is. He has always been fiercely loyal and protective—of his daughter, his wife, and you. He knows Cathy is tough, and can take care of herself. He knows she will take care of their daughter, and I think he knows that I'll take care of you. But he's not quite ready to let go yet—of any of you. He needs to be told he can go, that everything will be okay."

"Maybe so," I whispered. "But if that's the case, then what did he mean by 'Home'?"

Mary smiled. "I think you know, Keene. Think hard about it. You said you felt impressions of the words 'Home' and a sense of doom. But were they really?"

"It wasn't doom. It was more of a sense of things ending. A finale. Maybe change. I think I took that to be a bad thing, but now...I don't know. Maybe it's just time I focused more on this." I gestured around the house. "And less on what we do for a living. I mean, I guess I'd already decided that, in a way."

"You mean the plan to retire on January first?"

I nodded.

"They'll never let you retire completely," Mary said, "but I think you can get away with staying home for a good long while. And maybe be less involved in trying to remain the horror genre's Batman.

There's a new generation of writers that grew up reading you—not just your fiction, but the stuff you wrote about this business. Wile, Amber, Gabino, Asher, Kozeniewski...all the others."

I nodded again. "Too many to name."

"They were trained by you," Mary said. "You saw them out there at every stop on the tour, and every time you did, they told you that they've got this. It's time you stepped back a little bit and let them do just that."

I took my kit bag into my office and dumped it onto a chair. I didn't open it. Not then. Instead, I changed clothes, feeling guilty as I did so, because I'd done what Mary had accused me of doing when we'd started the conversation. I'd changed the subject. Not with coffee or tea, but with debating what Jesus had meant by "Home." If Mary ever realized that I never answered her question—did I take the ashes—she never mentioned it.

In the end, it didn't matter. What mattered was what was said when I'd gotten back home.

Dreamworld Pic was right. She's one smart paisan.

"Want to go out to eat?" she asked, after I'd changed my clothes and walked back into the kitchen.

I shook my head. "No. Let's stay home."

CHAPTER THIRTY-NINE

FULL CIRCLE

The second to last weekend of October, I made my way up north again, this time for the Merrimack Valley Halloween Book Festival in Haverhill, Massachusetts—a mass-signing event organized by Christopher Golden and involving about twenty or thirty horror authors. Podcast co-host Dave Thomas accompanied me for this part of the tour, and we stayed at the home of author James A. Moore.

Chris and I have both been doing this for twenty years now. Jim has been doing it a little longer than us. I consider the two of them to be among my closest friends in this industry. We have things in common. We are close to the same age, and share the same cultural touchstones. All three of us are prolific (as I write this, Chris just started his 107th novel, and in the time it takes you to read this paragraph, Jim will have banged out a dozen short stories). But that's not why I like them. I like them because they want the same things for this genre and this industry that I want. For the last twenty years, all three of us have stood up and went to bat for our fellow writers in issues of payment, rights, inclusion, diversity, and safety. We've done it in different ways. Chris is far more diplomatic than I am. I'm more blunt. And Jim cuts an imposing figure somewhere between us—quiet and thoughtful until it's time for him to act, and when he does, mountains scurry out of the way. Mary's theory is that I'm Batman, Chris is Superman, and Jim is Shazam. An editor whom I won't name here once put it another way, when she said, "Chris will patiently negotiate peace talks. Jim will stand there and intimidate you. Brian will burn your fucking house down."

Brian, Rio Youers, Christopher Golden, and Glenn Chadbourne get ready to sign. (Photo copyright Tony Tremblay 2016)

Twenty years I've known these guys—and everyone else from my generation of writers. All the folks who've made cameo appearances in this column over the last nine months. And one thing all of us have been doing over the last few years is mentoring the next generation of writers. You've met many of them in this series of columns throughout the last nine months, as well. There were others whom you didn't meet, but whom I've been following and reading and keeping tabs on. I call these up-and-comers kids, and some of them—like Wile E.

Young, Amber Fallon, Asher Ellis, Laura Lee Bahr, Gabino Iglesias, Adam Cesare, Josh Malerman, Shane McKenzie, and Stephen Kozeniewski, and many of the others who have appeared in this series of columns—are just that: kids in their twenties or early thirties. Others—like Bracken MacLeod, Errick Nunnally, Nick Cato, Jonathan Janz, and Dan Padavona—are my age, give or take a few years. It's not a question of when they were born. It's a marker of when they started writing, when they came into this. But I still think of them as the kids.

It struck me at the signing, watching Jim and Chris interact with this new generation of writers, just how far we've come, and just how much time has passed. Yes, time is a flat circle, but time is also a motherfucker, and you think crossing that circle will take twenty years, but it really happens in the blink of an eye. When we started out, we had guidance and help from Richard Laymon, Rick Hautala, Tom Monteleone, F. Paul Wilson, Charlie Grant, Ed Gorman, Edward Bryant, Ellen Datlow, Jack Ketchum, Chet Williamson, John Pelan, Ray Garton, Phil Nutman, Joe R. Lansdale, John Skipp, Simon Clark, Douglas Clegg, Gene O'Neill, David J. Schow, and so many more.

You look at that list, and half of them aren't with us anymore.

They helped authors like Jim and Chris and myself, and all the other writers that make up our "generation"—the writers that have appeared in this column, the old friends I saw out there on the road, and the ones I didn't get to see but who were never far from my mind: Tim Waggoner, Weston Ochse, John Urbancik, Jeff Strand, Tim Lebbon, Mary SanGiovanni, Wrath James White, Nick Mamatas, Bryan Smith, Maurice Broaddus, Jonathan Maberry, Kelli Owen, Paul Tremblay, Nicholas Kaufmann, Sarah Pinborough, Lee Thomas, Brian Freeman, Laird Barron, and again, so many more—including Jesus and Pic.

Especially Jesus and Pic. Because that's the point.

Yes, half of that first list above aren't with us anymore, but now that's starting to hit our generation, as well.

I started my career as the stereotypical "angry young man" and for years, I made that shit work for me. But I'm not a young man anymore, and it was this tour, and my coming to grips with Pic and Jesus's passing while I was out there on the road, that truly made me realize that. I'm no longer a young man. You can't be an angry young man when you're about to turn fifty. That shit doesn't work. And nobody wants to hear from an angry old man. If you doubt that, ask yourself how many people take Harlan Ellison seriously these days.

I never wanted to be Harlan Ellison. In fact, I remember a World Horror Convention in New York City many years ago, when a bunch of us stood aghast, watching Harlan Ellison do his shtick, and I turned to Steven L. Shrewsbury, and said, quote: "When we're his age, if I'm acting like that, I want you to knock the shit out of me." And Shrews promised he would. And so did Wrath James White and Michael T. Huyck, Jr. and Jack Haringa and Monica O'Rourke, and then a line started forming of fellow writers queuing up to punch me.

But I digress.

I never wanted to become Harlan Ellison. And that was what the whole "retirement" thing was about. It wasn't about retiring from writing or podcasting, or speaking up when my voice and platform and privilege could be put to good use to help out others in my field. It wasn't even about retiring from appearances, although there would never be another tour like this again. It was about retiring from being that guy, and about being home more.

And about being available more when I *was* home.

About not having to be Batman anymore.

Because there was a whole new generation in place and actively involved in doing the same thing—a generation who were perhaps too young to remember horror's mid-nineties crash (the crash that had birthed my generation) but who saw first-hand the collapse of the limited edition small press market and the Dorchester Wars, and who hadn't just read our books, but had followed our careers, and knew a good deal from a bad deal, and knew what was acceptable and what was not. An entire generation of new horror writers who are standing up and going to bat for their fellow writers in issues of payment, rights, inclusion, diversity, and safety. A Justice League, if you will. And just like we did, they're doing it in different ways. Some are diplomatic. Others will indeed burn your fucking house down.

And that makes me proud.

Watching Chris and Jim interact with this next generation—I got so proud of my friends and how far we've come that I had to excuse myself and go outside.

Brian reading at the KGB Bar in New York City. (Photo copyright Leza Cantoral 2016)

I saw it again a week later, when Mary and I read at the venerable KGB Bar in New York City. Neither of us are strangers to reading there, but this time, we were the veterans. The reading was organized by another young writer, Christoph Paul, and featured his generation—Leza Cantoral, Nick Cato, and Adam Cesare. Again, I was filled with pride listening to these kids read and watching them interact with their fans—readers of their generation and their age, some of whom merely viewed me as the token "old guy."

I witnessed it again in the middle of November when I went to BizarroCon in Portland, Oregon. Bizarro writers of my generation—authors like Carlton Mellick and Jeremy Robert Johnson and Kevin Donihe—advising and mentoring another entirely new generation of up-and-comers. And there was John Skipp, dispensing wisdom to them all the way he'd done for us over the years. You know that game, Six Degrees of Kevin Bacon? John Skipp is our Kevin Bacon. Think about it, and tell me I'm wrong.

Because I'm not.

I spent much of BizarroCon hunkered down with old friends. It was my second to last appearance on the tour, and rather than spending the time selling books, I wanted to spend it with friends. So, I did. I spent it in quiet corners of the bars and in my hotel room with fellow writers that I've known for twenty years—Michael T. Huyck and Nick Mamatas and Alan Clark, especially—and we reminisced, as people who have known each other that long are bound to do.

But mostly, we talked about the kids.

Michael T. Huyck and Brian enjoy some down time in Oregon as the end of the road nears. (Photo copyright Brian Keene 2016)

Nine months ago, when this series of columns started, I told you about the theory of Eternal Return—a concept in which the universe and all energy has been and will continue to recur an infinite number of times. This concept can be applied to the horror genre. It goes through the same cycle, over and over again—a cycle of birth, death, and rebirth. At least once in every decade since the First World War, the public has had a renewed interest in horror fiction. For the interests of our discussion, I have broken this era of modern horror down into six waves.

The first wave, spanning from 1900 to the mid-1920s begins, more or less, with the 1901 publication of M.P. Shiel's *The Purple Cloud*. It also gave us authors such as Lord Dunsany and William Hope Hodgson, and saw an increased public interest in ghost stories, particularly the work of M.R. James, Algernon Blackwood, and Edith Wharton. 1923 brought us the birth of *Weird Tales*, a magazine whose long and varied history is so entwined with modern horror that it's as difficult to imagine the genre without it as it is to imagine the genre without Stephen King.

The second wave, spanning the mid-1920s through the late-1940s, was an important period that gave us H.P. Lovecraft, Frank Belknap Long, Robert E. Howard, Clark Ashton Smith, Shirley Jackson, and Seabury Quinn, among others, and the early works of Fritz Leiber.

The third wave, spanning the 1950s and 1960s gave us more mature works from Fritz Leiber, as well as the work of Anthony Boucher, Theodore Sturgeon, John Farris, Ira Levin, and five writers who are as important, if not more important, to the genre than even the works of the esteemed Mr. King: Robert Bloch, Richard Matheson, Ray Bradbury, Rod Serling, and the early works of Ramsey Campbell. These five writers were among the first to truly begin centering horror fiction in contemporary settings, rather than crumbling New England waterfront towns or sprawling Victorian mansions. Their impact and themes still inform much of today's horror fiction.

During the first three waves, horror fiction was published as either mainstream fiction, science-fiction, or mystery fiction. There was no horror marketing category. That category wasn't invented until the rise of the fourth wave.

The beginning of the fourth wave, the Seventies and Eighties, brought us Stephen King, Dean Koontz, F. Paul Wilson, Thomas Monteleone, Karl Edward Wagner, Peter Straub, and others. When King became a bestseller in paperback, the marketing category of HORROR was invented. The genre waned briefly around 1979-1980 but then came back with a vengeance. The fourth wave also gave us Clive Barker, Charles L. Grant, James Herbert, T.E.D. Klein,

Robert R. McCammon, Joe R. Lansdale, Jack Ketchum, Richard Laymon, Rick Hautala, Ronald Kelly, the Splatterpunks, Brian Hodge, and Poppy Z. Brite.

This was where I came in, as a reader. Then, in the mid-1990s, the whole thing collapsed.

And that was where I came in as a writer.

Some say horror died in the '90s, but this is patently untrue. Horror as a marketing category to be stamped on the spine of a book certainly died, but the stories and books and readers were still there. From 1991 to 1995, the most prominent mass-market horror publishers were Zebra Books and the Dell Abyss line. With the fall of those two lines, other publishers began shying away from horror, as well. Unable to sell their work to mainstream publishers, horror authors turned to the small press. Likewise, readers who were unable to find horror novels in stores did the same. The '90s saw the rise of the small press, something which had always existed, way back in the first wave, but which really came to prominence in the '90s.

The '90s didn't kill horror. It was just a transition period. Horror fiction was still published, it just didn't reach as wide a readership. And it was also the birthing ground of the fifth wave.

That's my generation—the fifth wave. We rose to prominence in that last decade and in the first decade of this new century. We were the first generation to have the Internet. We bridged the gap between the fourth wave—authors who had to adapt to new technology—and your generation, the post-Internet generation. And our generation also lived through our own collapse, with the fall of Dorchester and the crumbling of the small press.

Now we see the rise to prominence of the sixth wave.

And once again, it is a great time to be a horror reader and a horror writer.

A lot of things have changed in twenty years—both for the genre that I love, and the industry that I work in, and myself. But the genre prevails.

Twenty years ago, the mainstream stuff was sold in mass-market paperback format, clearly labeled HORROR and available at any chain bookstore. The underground stuff was sold as pricey limited edition hardcovers from small presses. Today, the chain bookstores are vanishing, and there are only a handful of small presses still doing limited editions (Cemetery Dance, Subterranean Press, Thunderstorm Books, Centipede, PS Publishing, and a few others). Today, you can find horror at the bookstore, but it won't be at those vanishing chain stores—it will instead be at your local independent bookstore. And the underground stuff? It's still available, perhaps more than ever. But you're more likely to find it in a $3.99 Kindle edition than a $399 limited hardcover edition.

The delivery system may change, but the genre prevails.

People are born. Some of them grow up to become horror writers. Eventually, they die. There's no getting around it. But their work lives on—not only in the books they contributed to the genre, but in the example and spirit of those who remember them, and those who follow them.

The writers may change, but the genre prevails.

I have accomplished a lot in the last twenty years. I have been able to give back to a genre that has brought me incalculable joy throughout my life. I've written a lot of novels and short stories and comic books and other things. A few of them are described as "seminal" and "game-changing" and "had a noticeable impact on the genre" by people who are much smarter than me. I've got a bookshelf full of awards, including the 2014 World Horror Grandmaster Award, a 2001 Bram Stoker Award for Nonfiction, a 2003 Bram

Stoker Award for First Novel, a 2004 Shocker Award for Book of the Year, and Honors from United States Army International Security Assistance Force in Afghanistan and Whiteman A.F.B. (home of the B-2 Stealth Bomber) 509th Logistics Fuels Flight. My writing career has allowed me to (mostly) keep a roof over our heads and food in our bellies. I've had the opportunity to travel all over, signing books and delivering talks in bookstores, conventions, college campuses, theaters, and even three times inside the headquarters of the Central Intelligence Agency.

If I die tomorrow, I am proud of these things.

But the thing I am most proud of is this new generation of horror writers, and how this new generation of horror readers are supporting them.

You spend a year on the road, watching that unfold, and it makes the thought of leaving here much easier—because you know that the genre will prevail.

Time is a flat circle, and now I find myself not traveling its circumference, but standing still in the center, and touching all the sides at once.

Thank you. Just in case I don't get to say it later, thank you for allowing me in your homes and your study halls and your commute and your breakrooms and your beds. Thank you for allowing me to earn a living doing something I would have done for free if I had to. Thank you for allowing me to give back. Thank you for not kicking me out the times I was an asshole. Thanks for being there. Thanks for everything.

Ad capere tenebris. Seize the twilight.

We have now come to the end of the road.

EPILOGUE ONE

November 16, 2016

Between a signing in Maine and a signing in Oregon, Brian and his oldest son have spent a week in Seattle. His oldest son, now twenty-five, is a social worker by day and a budding rock guitarist by night. He is a fan of Alice In Chains, Nirvana, Foo Fighters, Mother Love Bone, and the rest of the grunge-era music (which is now considered classic rock—something that makes Brian feel that full weight of fifty that he knows will be drawing down on him next year). Given this, Seattle makes sense for what will be their first father and son vacation since the now-young-man was ten years old.

This is the first time Brian's oldest son has ever been to Seattle. It is Brian's fifth time. The streets are haunted here, but in a good way. Every corner and alley and landmark summons the ghosts of memories for Brian—book signings past and conventions of yore. He remembers road-tripping here with Ann Laymon (wife of the departed Richard Laymon) and the artist Gak—because even twenty years ago, there was always someone else along on the journey. The first book Brian ever wrote, a long out-of-print (and deservedly so) collection called *No Rest for the Wicked*, made its debut right here in the city. Geoff Cooper used to live here, in a house with Edward Lee and John Pelan. When he and his son walk past Coop's old home, Brian grins, remembering a night when he and John Urbancik had to fake snoring on Coop's enormous sectional couch while two other horror writers made love on the floor behind it—just inches away from where Brian and John were supposedly sleeping.

During their time in the city, Brian and his oldest son have seen the Space Needle and the iconic Pike's Place Fish Market and the condominium complex where Layne Staley, lead singer of Alice In Chains, died. They have visited the EMP Museum and marveled over its collection of horror and rock memorabilia— Kurt Cobain's guitars, Dave Grohl's drum kit, a sentinel from the first *Phantasm* movie, the Greedo mask from the original *Star Wars* film. They make a pilgrimage to Jimi Hendrix's grave, and spend a day hiking deep into the forests of Mount Rainier, looking for Bigfoot and just enjoying nature.

The one thing they don't do, is sign books.

Brian had considered doing a pop-up signing while in town. His oldest son has assured him it will be okay if he wants to. But Brian refrains. He has spent the entire year traveling around the country for other people. He wants to enjoy this moment for himself.

The road will still be there waiting when he's done.

December 31, 2016 – January 1, 2017

The clock is ticking and the countdown to the New Year looms, but the small group in Brian and Mary's hotel suite barely notice. The convention is being held at a Holiday Inn Conference Center in Allentown, Pennsylvania. The Farewell (But Not Really) Tour may have started with a roar, but this—the last official appearance—has been decidedly anticlimactic. The convention attendees consist of approximately fifty cosplay fans, and perhaps another dozen gamers. Brian and Mary are still unsure why they are Guests of Honor, but the convention organizers have been wonderful, and the attendees—while not buying books—are pleasant to interact with.

Still, it's not a total write-off. Brian and Mary ring in the New Year with dear friends like Sixth Wave authors Stephen Kozeniewski and Mary Fan (who have also been signing at the convention) and the handful of non-cosplayer, non-gamer, actual Brian Keene or Mary SanGiovanni fans who attended for the weekend. One of these fans is Augie, a guy Brian has been signing books for since the publication of *The Rising* back in 2003. The four writers and the half-dozen readers sit in Brian and Mary's hotel suite, listening to music and talking and partying until the calendar switches over to 2017.

The next day—January 1st—the convention attendees have dwindled down to a dozen. Brian finds Mary SanGiovanni sitting in a deserted conference room, dispensing Fifth Wave wisdom and advice to Sixth Wave Stephen Kozeniewski and Mary Fan. Joining them is loyal reader Steve (whose last name Brian can't remember as he writes this—my apologies, Steve).

Soon, both Marys will head back to New Jersey. Kozeniewski and Brian will head towards the central part of Pennsylvania. Brian's not sure where Steve the fan will go. He assumes Steve is local. As they are all driving separately, Brian doesn't have to wait for his girlfriend or his protégé. He peeks into the conference room, pauses a moment to listen to Mary, and smiles with pride. Then he clears his throat.

"You heading out?" Kozeniewski asks.

"Yep," Brian replies. "I'm done."

And he is.

"No worries," Kozeniewski says. "I've got this."

And he does, as well.

Brian walks out of the convention, hops in the Jeep, and the road is there, waiting.

January 31, 2017

One month into the new year, and Brian is dealing with the financial fallout of the previous year spent on tour. Yes, the Farewell (But Not Really) Tour was a success, and yes, he sold a lot of copies of *Pressure* and *The Complex*, but he won't get paid for those copies of the former until this summer, and the royalties for the latter (paid monthly, same as his other Deadite Press-published titles) have gone toward the rent and utility bills. There is still food and gas and other things to be purchased, and Brian's bank account is currently empty. Plus, taxes are coming due. Brian knows that in addition to next month's check from Deadite Press, he'll get advances from Thunderstorm Books and Apex Book Company for a forthcoming novel, *Return to the Lost Level*. But between now and then, his youngest son needs to eat and go to school, so Brian sells a few boxes of books for money.

He takes them in to The York Emporium, just as he did months earlier in this column. Jim goes through the books and offers Brian a fair price, and Brian takes the cash. Then Jim tells Brian that the bookstore's landlord is making some changes to the building. The back-end of the store, which is currently occupied by the Horror section, is going to be turned into a spa and yoga studio.

Jim informs Brian that he's going to have to move the Horror section—and J.F. Gonzalez's ashes.

Brian nods at this. He asks Jim when this move will take place. Jim tells him not until spring. Brian nods again. Then he bids Jim farewell and thanks him again for the cash, and walks outside.

He climbs into the Jeep, pulls out onto the busy road, and looks at his reflection in the rearview mirror. Then he ponders what Jim just told him, and realizes he's going to have to plan a reverse-heist.

"Shit…"

February 18, 2017

If this is global warming, Brian thinks, *then let's have more of it, please.*

He and his youngest son and his youngest son's mother (Brian's ex-wife) are out for a walk. All three are dressed for summer, and why not? The late-winter temperatures feel more like a spring day.

The tour has faded to memory now, and promotion for *Pressure* and *The Complex* are nonexistent. There are new books being written and released, and promotion will soon switch to those. In the genre, there have been a few crises, and a few more controversies, and a few more predators, but Brian has only publicly waded into one of these situations. The others…? He let the Justice League handle those. On a bigger scale, Trump's still in power and although the world hasn't ended yet, it is beginning to look like the start of a Bizarro novel. But right now, Brian isn't thinking about any of these things.

Right now, he's telling his son about the ghost of a Civil War soldier who is said to haunt this particular stretch of railroad tracks the three of them are currently walking down. In the past month, during Brian's retirement from the road, his youngest son has decided that he wants to be a cryptozoologist and ghost hunter when he grows up. Today, they are doing both—walking a stretch of unused, weed-choked, and supposedly haunted train tracks near Chickies Rock, which legend names as the home of Central Pennsylvania's Bigfoot population (called Albatwitches by the locals). His youngest son gets to indulge his newfound passion for paranormal investigation. Brian and the boy's mother get to indulge in some exercise. Everybody wins.

When the walk is over, and they emerge from the river bottoms and railroad tracks and back into town, trees and undergrowth give way to concrete and a chain link fence. The Jeep, which has crossed much of the country the previous year and still runs fine, sits parked beneath an overpass. Brian's youngest son points at the road.

"Where's that road go, Dad?"

"I don't know," Brian answers. "Let's find out."

Starting down another road. (Photo copyright Cassandra Burnham 2016)

EPILOGUE TWO

Twenty Years Ago
  Now
Tomorrow
Twenty Years From Now
Whenever it happens, eventually, the road leads you here.

Some get here before you, and some get here after you've been here awhile.

Some departed before you but will arrive after you.

Some departed after you but get here before you arrive.

Some come to this place right away. Others go elsewhere, having other things to do first. Some hang around this place. Others only pop in for a quick hello before moving on with others not connected to this group.

Regardless, everyone is here at the same time, because this place is outside the circle.

When you arrive, the first thing you notice are a series of circular patio tables arranged outside the door. Several people you know are seated there, puffing cigars, because even in this place, there is no smoking inside. Several other people you know are standing over them, laughing, drinks in hand.

You talk awhile. When it's time to go inside, one of them stays seated, watching the road, waiting for someone. You offer to sit and wait with him, but he tells you that he's okay, and reminds you there is no time here, and besides, there's a table reserved inside for you, and others are there, waiting. She's there waiting, too. You tell him that's impossible, because you left long before she did. He chuckles, and explains once again how time works outside the circle. Smiling, you squeeze his shoulder and follow the others into the hotel.

Inside, someone shouts "Keene!" across the room the way he always does whenever your paths cross. You smile and wave, thinking not for the first time how much he looks like his father, and it's a wonder that pseudonym worked for as long as it did, but before you can go over to him, someone else sweeps you off your feet in a great big bear hug. There is no time outside the circle, but there is also no pain, and it doesn't hurt when he does this, nor does it hurt when someone else who used to be a World Class kickboxer and mixed martial arts trainer turned writer squeezes your hand, or when the guy from Texas who invented his own martial art slaps you on the back.

You make your way through the crowd, and everyone is glad to see you. Everyone is in their own groups, seated at their own tables. Some gather in large, loud parties. Others huddle in small, quiet corners. A few prefer to sit alone. But everyone is together, regardless of their seating arrangements, and everyone is smiling.

Time is a flat circle. Outside the circle, everything is smiles, and the only sound is laughter.

At the back of the room is your table, and she's sitting there, along with your best friends, who you've been waiting to see again. Their smiles can power solar systems.

It is an excellent evening. Occasionally, you visit the other tables, or the folks from the other tables visit yours. A few people use their phones to check on those still in the other place. At one point, a friend best known for writing comedic horror and another friend who doesn't like pickles and a third friend who everyone always assumed was a girl because of his first name all team up to harangue you about ripping off the afterlife from the season finale of *Lost*, and how this place is all your fault, but they say it with smiles and laughter and love.

Eventually, everyone has to leave. Maybe it's last call, or maybe it's time for a panel or a signing, or maybe there is other business to take care of.

But you cannot stay here.

Some depart together. Others leave on their own. Regardless, you all leave together.

You say goodbye to everyone as you all file out.

One by one, folks step out onto the road. There's a light shining on the horizon. They walk toward it.

You stand there with your friends, holding the hand of the woman you love—your soulmate. You stand there with your cabal. With your collective. Your posse. And then, they too begin to walk down the road toward that light.

"Forest rangers this time?" one of them asks.

"Not me," says another. "I want to be a kung-fu master this time around."

"You always want to be a kung-fu fighter," another replies.

"What about you, Brian?" asks another.

You shrug, staring at that light.

"I don't care," you answer. "We can be cows standing in a field. We can be drops of rain. It doesn't matter to me what we are, as long as we can all find each other again."

And we will. We will find each other over and over again.

And each time, when we've reached the end, we will always meet up in a place like this. Maybe it won't be a convention bar and maybe we won't be writers, but we will be composed of the same energy and the same atoms, and that attraction—that magnetic force—runs deep. The universe and all existence and energy have been recurring, and will continue to recur, in a self-similar form an infinite number of times across infinite time and space.

She and I are the last to go. We walk down the road, hand-in-hand.

I promise her I'll find her again, and see her in a little while, and she tells me not to take so long this time.

The light gets closer. Soon, it surrounds us.

Then we reach the end of one road and start down a new one.

→ ←

BRIAN KEENE writes novels, comic books, short fiction, and occasional journalism for money. He is the author of over fifty books, mostly in the horror, crime, and dark fantasy genres. His 2003 novel, *The Rising*, is often credited (along with Robert Kirkman's *The Walking Dead* comic and Danny Boyle's *28 Days Later* film) with inspiring pop culture's current interest in zombies. Keene's novels have been translated into German, Spanish, Polish, Italian, French, Taiwanese, and many more. In addition to his own original work, Keene has written for media properties such as *Doctor Who*, *The X-Files*, *Hellboy*, *Masters of the Universe*, and *Aliens*.

Several of Keene's novels have been developed for film, including *Ghoul*, *The Ties That Bind*, and *Fast Zombies Suck*. Keene's work has been praised in such diverse places as *The New York Times*, *The History Channel*, *The Howard Stern Show*, *CNN.com*, *Publisher's Weekly*, *Media Bistro*, *Fangoria Magazine*, and *Rue Morgue Magazine*.

He has won numerous awards and honors, including the 2014 World Horror Grandmaster Award, 2016 Imadjinn Award for Best Fantasy Novel, 2001 Bram Stoker Award for Nonfiction, 2003 Bram Stoker Award for First Novel, 2004 Shocker Award for Book of the Year, and Honors from United States Army International Security Assistance Force in Afghanistan and Whiteman A.F.B. (home of the B-2 Stealth Bomber) 509th Logistics Fuels Flight.

A prolific public speaker, Keene has delivered talks at conventions, college campuses, theaters, and inside Central Intelligence Agency headquarters in Langley, VA.

The father of two sons, Keene lives in rural Pennsylvania.

Printed in Great Britain
by Amazon

49783087R10203